Chapter 1
A Patient Demise

"The sky is falling," Michael whispered to the nurse as she handed him a medicine cup full of pills. He stared at them for a moment, mesmerized by their different shapes and colors.

As he watched, they began to move – snailing around each other before blurring into a uniform purple blob. Shrugging, he brought the cup to his lips, threw his head back, and gulped them down.

The nurse offered him water, which he refused. He opened his mouth and stuck out his tongue so she could see he'd swallowed all of his meds, and then he repeated his statement.

"It really is, you know." She looked up at the ceiling and he followed her gaze to the obviously stable structure. Not what he meant, but he couldn't explain it further.

He paced the unit as he usually did after the morning vitals and med pass, from one locked door to another...to another...to another.

Past his fellow comrades, who were pacing as he was. Locked in as he was. Lost as he was. Their expressions were different and yet exactly the same. Sick. Stuck. Scared. Saneless.

Many were sprawled on the couches in front of the television, attached to the wall within its transparent shatterproof box. A talk show was on, primarily for background noise: lots of unhappy women griping about their privileged lives. Try this one on for size, Michael thought to himself, and then guffawed loudly at his own joke.

The patient passing him at that moment jumped, startled by his outburst. Just admitted that morning, she was young and fresh-faced. Probably a trust-fund college kid who'd threatened to slit her wrists when she didn't get what she wanted from her obnoxiously rich parents.

Michael gazed at her sympathetically. It happened all the time. Kids said the darnedest things. Didn't know what they were getting themselves into. Played with matches and got burned real bad. Now here she was, stuck in the loony bin with real live crazy people. I didn't mean it. I was just trying to get attention. Get even. I don't belong here. I'm not crazy. I'm not like *them*.

Too late, girlie. You did the crime, now you'll do the time. Seventy-two hours. She was on hour three. Tick tock, little sorority girl. Sucks to be you. Michael nodded at her genially and continued his pacing.

He felt funny today – not funny, ha ha; funny peculiar. Like his feet were on the end of utility poles. He looked down at them, surprised to see they weren't a mile away. He began to think that these were in fact someone else's feet. Someone who was playing a trick on him. Someone who had put his old scuffed brown shoes on their own feet and then placed them next to his legs. Yes, of course – he was being messed with, bigtime.

He spun around, determined to catch the asshole in the act, but no one was behind him except Miss Collegiate USA, now cowering against the wall and staring at him as if he had grown two heads. He didn't have time to offer a kind word or even a benign smile to put her mind at ease. He had to find his real feet.

In spite of his best efforts, by the time he'd reached the double-tempered full-length window at the end of the hall he'd forgotten about this particular predicament. His mind had tangented its way to a wide variety of new concerns regarding the funny feeling that had persisted since he'd awoken that morning.

The sensation that the sky was pressing down around him had returned, and he found himself gasping for air. He sat on the floor by the window and leaned against the wall behind him until the heaviness lessened, which, mercifully, it did within minutes.

Now as he gazed out the window at the enclosed courtyard where the patients took their smoke breaks he let his mind wander to his daughter, Sarah. He would get to visit with her next weekend in the presence of his case worker. He wished he could spend time with her alone, but at least he had something. He'd been estranged from her mother since well before Sarah was born, and he knew he was lucky to get to see her at all.

Lots of the guys at his group home had kids they'd never even met, kept away from them by paranoid mothers and a system that criminalizes mental illness. How could anyone think they'd hurt their own children? They were sick, not delinquents. He'd never done one illegal thing in his life.

Not like the resident cheerleader over there. She probably drank like a fish every weekend even though she couldn't yet be twenty-one. He threw her an infuriated glare and she bolted for the nurse's station. Tattletale. He hated that bitch. He stood to follow her, determined to give her a piece of his mind, but she'd disappeared.

Disheartened, he realized what he really wanted was to lie down, but the patient rooms were locked for the majority of the day to force them to participate in the activities on the unit.

He snorted at that: going to group to listen to everyone tell you how sick you are, or recreation therapy where you could make bracelets out of yarn and beads, or patient education where you learned about all the horrible things your meds could do to you. No, thank you. He didn't need any of it.

But if he asked for a sick day to be allowed into his room he'd lose his cigarette breaks, and that would be a complete downer. He muttered to himself about the injustices of the world as he passed the darkened group room, one wall windowed so that the techs could do their fifteen-minute rounds without opening the door and interrupting the proceedings. A gigantic white board covered the front wall, windows to another courtyard comprised the far wall, and bookcases filled with self-help materials, leisurely reading, and resources for staff to use during their patient sessions lined the back.

Michael tried the knob but the door was locked, as it always was when there was no group in progress. Far too many ways to hurt oneself in there. He frowned vehemently at the empty room and kept walking.

At the end of the hallway was another floor-to-ceiling window, but this one faced a busy street. He stopped there for a long while, watching the passing cars with yearning. What was it like to be in one of those cars? To be able to drive like the wind to nowhere and everywhere all at once? How free that must feel. He wouldn't know. He didn't drive. Didn't even have a license. Took the bus sometimes, but mostly walked.

He looked down at his shoes again. There they were, closer than it felt like they should be. He wiggled his toes and was startled to see them move between the torn soles and the worn leather. He struggled to understand how that could be, his mind whirling around itself in a frenzy of disjointed thoughts.

A sudden rush of pain pierced his chest and he clutched at his heart. It had to be the guy with his shoes. Standing close behind him again in an effort to replace his feet. Except this time the son-of-a-bitch had stabbed him in the back. Yes, that had to be it.

Michael lurched around, intent on socking the jerk, but no one was there. The guy was obviously too fast for him, but he'd sure as shootin' catch him next time. He'd be damned if he'd let the sneak jack with him like this.

Then the nurse from earlier was approaching him, her pretty pouty lips moving and her dark eyes concerned, but he couldn't hear her voice over the buzzing in his ears. Suddenly, she was running. Shouting. And she had unexpectedly grown three feet taller as she reached him...but no, that wasn't right. He had actually fallen to his knees, his legs giving out of their own accord.

Then her hand was at his neck, and when she pulled it away it was covered in his blood. He could vaguely hear her calling to someone over her shoulder as she knelt beside him, laying him gently on the floor. He gazed at her, attempting to recall her name. So pretty. He tried to reach up to push her hair away from her face, but he couldn't move his arm. Riley. That was it. Strange name for such a beautiful girl.

And there it was again. The sky. Just above his face now. Crushing him. He struggled with its weight...trying to remember something. Oh that's right – he'd have to be sure to tell Riley about the extra pills Doc Tacee'd given him during their last session. She'd need to chart them in that computer the nurses were always staring at so she wouldn't get in trouble. He sure didn't want her to get in trouble. She was always so nice to him.

He smiled serenely at her as she began pumping his chest. She smelled like wildflowers and lemons. He was glad of the scent since he could barely see her anymore through the red haze that was slowly filling his field of vision.

And then as abruptly as it had begun, the buzzing in his ears stopped. That was nice. So quiet and peaceful. He wished he could thank her for stopping that God awful noise...

"Shit! We've lost him!" Riley shouted, panicked. They were the last words he'd ever hear.

Chapter 2
Aftershocks

Riley slid into the booth across from her best friend at their favorite hangout, the Bleu Goose, and fisted her hands into her hair in frustration. Needing no further prompting, Eva signaled for their server and ordered a shot of Rumplemintz, chilled. Riley nodded to her gratefully as she began to tremble from head to toe.

After giving her a chance to drain her libation and gather her wits, Eva leaned forward. "Tell me."

"We lost Michael today."

Eva sat back against the booth with a shocked huff. "How'd he do it?" she finally asked, but Riley shook her head, setting her dark bob swinging around her shoulders.

"It wasn't suicide." Eva's mouth fell open. She was too stunned to hold herself to her usual poised mannerisms. "It was...I don't know what the hell it was. Awful," Riley continued.

Eva closed her perfectly penciled lips and ran a graceful, manicured hand through her platinum blonde hair, miraculously leaving every smooth strand from the well-maintained roots to the precisely clipped ends in place. She was so flawless Riley sometimes had trouble believing she was real, but now her friend's face had become drawn, and lacking in its usual serenity.

Eva was Michael's therapist, and had been seeing him since she went into private practice ten years ago. She had a soft spot for him, as she did for most of her patients with schizophrenia. She was utterly floored.

"Explain," she admonished. Riley often had great difficulty getting to the point.

"He was down the hall, by the Eighth Avenue window, and he just...started jerking. Then he dropped to the floor, and blood came gushing out of his mouth. He wasn't...screaming or anything. Just...just staring at me like he wanted to say something."

"Did he? Say anything?" Eva prompted.

"No. No, nothing. And then he was gone..."

"He'll have an autopsy, of course..."

Riley nodded, and then shuddered, remembering. "God, Eva, it was like his heart was pushing all the blood in his body out of him...out through every place it could."

"Is that even possible?"

"In conditions like congestive heart failure the heart pumps so hard it pushes blood out of the vessels and into the lungs and then the patient coughs it up."

"Gross."

"Yeah, well..."

"So maybe he had that?"

"No, it was more acute than that. More...sudden," Riley chewed her lip as she stared blankly at a spot somewhere over Eva's head.

"What is it?"

Riley hesitated. "It's strange, but my gut tells me there's something more to this. Something, I don't know...sinister. But I can't figure out what..."

Eva nodded, pensive. Riley shook her head, clearing it. "Every time I compressed his chest more blood spilled from his mouth. And I couldn't stop. It took forever for the paramedics to get there, and I just had to keep going. I knew he was gone. It was no use. But I couldn't stop," she ended on a nearly hysterical sob, and Eva raised two fingers in the air. Two more shots down and Riley finally stopped shaking.

"So," she said on a shuddering breath. "How was your day?"

Eva put her hand on Riley's in comfort and graciously allowed the subject change. "Oh, you know...the usual," she quipped.

The two had met when Riley had responded to a safety code in Eva's family session in the psychiatric intensive care unit of the freestanding mental health facility, the Psychiatric Institute of North America, or PINA as it was known, where Riley worked.

The husband of Eva's patient had become irate when the woman had told him she needed some time apart to work on her recovery, and he had put his hands around her neck, intent on choking her into changing her mind. Eva had pressed the panic button, and within seconds the code team, with Riley in the lead, had responded.

They had been friends ever since, and often joked about the absolute lack of normalcy that existed in their careers. Their routine vent sessions at the Bleu Goose provided sanity for both of them – especially Riley, whose attorney husband couldn't begin to understand what she dealt with on a daily basis.

Because Eva was affiliated with PINA, seeing many of its clients in her practice on an outpatient basis, she was considered a 'covered entity' in terms of confidentiality. This meant Riley could talk to her about most anything, or anyone, without committing a dreaded HIPAA violation. As a result, they had been able to talk each other 'off the ledge' many times, and both were grateful for each other's support.

Riley glanced at Eva's hand still covering hers and marveled for the hundredth time at the difference between them. Eva's were soft as velvet and smooth as satin, while her own were neither. Slightly reddened, yes. Well-used. Strong. Capable. Nurse's hands.

"How's the baby-making coming?" Eva asked, finally withdrawing her hand and interrupting Riley's thoughts.

"No luck yet, but we don't mind trying..." Riley knew better than to ask the same. Eva believed her ship had sailed even though she wasn't yet forty.

Besides, it was becoming difficult to hear over the noise as the hotspot began to get crowded. It was the destination of choice for many of the nearby businesses' employees, either leaving work for the day or returning downtown to blow off steam.

Sometimes Riley envied them their mundane careers. She couldn't imagine they were fulfilled, but they probably didn't have her level of life-or-death stress, either. Eva would call her biased and maybe even egocentric for her thoughts. She allowed herself a small, self-deprecating smile – Eva was probably right.

As if on cue, the local retro band the owner, Mark, had hired for the night started playing an old jam that brought back fond memories, and the two women squealed with delight. Eva catapulted herself out of the booth and grabbed Riley's arm to drag her onto the dance floor. Tipsy as hell, Riley complied and the pair lost themselves to the music for several songs. It was just what they'd needed – they returned to their table in much better spirits.

"What do you have going on tomorrow?" Riley asked as she picked at the nachos Eva had ordered for her when she'd first arrived. It hadn't gone unnoticed that Eva hadn't even touched them, as usual.

"My first client has OCD. Lost her job for recurrent tardiness. She can't leave the house without straightening the fringes of each of her rugs. We've been working on getting rid of them one by one so she has fewer to deal with."

"How's that going?"

"Well, she started with ten..."

"And now?"

"Down to five."

"That's fantastic!" Riley knew the goal in treating people with obsessive-compulsive disorder was not to eliminate the object of their compulsions altogether, but to gradually decrease the time spent with their rituals so that they were able to lead a more productive life.

"My next client was diagnosed with borderline personality disorder."

Riley almost chuckled at Eva's poorly disguised antipathy. Patients with this condition were particularly difficult to deal with on any level because they were often petulant, manipulative, and passive-aggressive. It was a draining combination, and Riley knew her friend couldn't be looking forward to that session.

"What are you working on with her?"

"Him."

"Far worse –"

"– and I've just introduced DBT." Dialectical behavior therapy is a cornerstone treatment for patients with a personality disorder, as they're taught to reframe their pattern of pathological thinking and reacting. It can be quite effective if the client is willing to put forth the effort.

"Is it working?"

"No...he's quite resistant to change."

"Aren't we all?"

Eva demurred, raising her club soda in a toast and draining her glass. Though Riley felt she could use another drink, she refrained out of deference to her friend.

"My last appointment is with Craig," Eva mentioned, summoning their server for the check. Riley had been stifling yawns for the past ten minutes, and Eva was nothing if not observant.

Craig was what they called a 'frequent flyer', in that he returned to the Institute time and time again, unable to maintain his illness outside of the hospital. Like Michael, he had paranoid schizophrenia, and when he stopped taking his medication he became psychotic.

"How's he doing?"

"I'm not sure," Eva shook her head, a frown creasing her otherwise porcelain smooth brow. "He missed his last appointment and his mother scheduled this one. I have a bad feeling he's off his meds again."

"It's been a while since he's been hospitalized. He's probably due." The cynical statement was not an insult; it was born from intimate experience with the 'revolving door' that symbolizes mental health care in this country.

"Next time," Eva said, declining her friend's attempt to pay their tab.

"Like always," Riley laughed. On their way to the front of the restaurant they waved to Mark, who had chivalrously intervened many times in the past when a client got too overbearing with them on the dance floor, or even at their dinner table.

Then they were out the door and saying their goodbyes.

***

At his table near the back of the restaurant, Pauley watched the two friends with interest. It was no secret he loved women in all their shapes and forms...that he delighted in beautiful things.

He glanced briefly past the bar at the guy they'd waved to, noting his obvious distraction with whatever was happening in the kitchen nearby. Pauley would have had no such draw on his attention from beauties like them. He returned his gaze to the door they'd just exited, watching them hug and separate through the heavy plated glass.

"Ahem?" He was startled out of his reverie by his date, who wasn't nearly as adept at holding him rapt. In fact he was quite bored with her already. What was her name again? Dina? Dana? Didn't matter. She was in the past.

He let his gaze drift around the bar until he settled on a piece of eye candy moving seductively on the dance floor. She'd been staring at him all night from under the longest lashes he'd ever seen. Fake. All of it. Fake eyelashes, fake hair extensions, fake tits. He liked.

Across the table, Danielle watched him in frustration. She really liked this guy. Okay maybe lust was a more appropriate term – she barely knew him. They'd been out together only a handful of times but he had charmed the pants off her – literally – and she was smitten.

The quintessential tall, dark, and handsome, he had the bearing of a movie star – and a bank account to match, if his designer clothes and showroom convertible were any indication. He was smooth, alright – she'd never seen him coming. And now it appeared he was leaving just as quickly, his eyes returning to her with disdain in response to the impatient tapping of her fingernails on the table.

Little did she know her fizzling relationship would be the least of her concerns once she discovered her brother's death. They had been extremely close growing up, and she was still Michael's biggest champion.

In fact, she had been instrumental in getting him visitation with her niece, encouraging him to fight Sarah's mother for custody, helping him pay for a decent lawyer, and vouching for his stabilized mental health regimen.

He'd been able to keep himself out of the hospital during that crucial time thanks to Danielle. She'd made sure he took his meds when he was supposed to, that he was sleeping eight straight every night, that he was eating three hots a day. It was exhausting, but well worth it when the court rewarded his progress with supervised visits.

Once that happened and Danielle had gone back to focusing on her own life, Michael had returned to his usual poor habits, including frequent hospitalizations. But at least Sarah was in his life, and that's all that really mattered.

Danielle's focus was abruptly brought back to Pauley as he raised his hand for the check. She wasn't even finished with her wine. Pauley noted her exasperation and shrugged his shoulders.

"I've got an early morning," he said by way of an excuse. Bull shit. She'd be shocked if he got his pampered ass out of bed before noon. She didn't know where his money came from, but she'd bet her left tit it wasn't from a nine-to-five kind of gig.

Danielle guzzled the remaining contents of her glass like a dime store wino and stood, throwing her elegant cape over her shoulders. She had taken forever to get ready for Pauley tonight, but she needn't have bothered. He had already checked out and she was suddenly desperate.

As they walked toward the door she ran her fingers up his back but he deftly sidestepped her touch. She slipped her hand into his and he briefly squeezed her fingertips but quickly released them, putting his hand in his coat pocket to avoid further contact. Once they'd settled into his car she turned to him, schooling her features so they didn't appear fraught.

"You coming in for a nightcap?" He shook his head. "How about a lively fuck, then?"

"Maybe another time," he mumbled without even turning his head in her direction. So this is how it's going to go down. Danielle was pissed. They'd spent nearly every waking moment together over the past week and now he thought he was just going to abandon her?

"Fucking bastard." He had the nerve to smile. Not an apologetic or even embarrassed smile. A genuine, heartfelt smile. In that moment she would have gladly shot his face off if she'd had a gun.

He was chuckling by the time he pulled to a stop in front of her brownstone, and she couldn't get out of the car fast enough. She slammed the door as hard as she could, hoping to shatter the window. No such luck – stupid well-made foreign automobile.

As she flounced up the steps, she heard him gun the engine and speed away. He was down the street and around the corner before she could get her key in the security door, and she was left alone on the darkened porch in the quiet neighborhood.

Her eyes blurred with tears, and she struggled to fit the key into the lock. She breathed a sigh of relief as she entered the vestibule, and burst into tears once safely ensconced in her main floor apartment. Asshole! She threw her keys at the counter and sank onto the couch, heaving huge sobs that shook her sizable frame.

How could he do this to her? The sex was mind blowing. They shared a dark sense of humor. They enjoyed the same television shows. They had everything in common...

She pulled her cell phone out of her bag, praying he'd had a change of heart and tried to call her. Her heart soared when she saw the light blinking on the screen, then crashed when she discovered the missed call was from the Institute. Michael, of course – calling to say hello.

She dropped the offending device on the floor and slumped against the couch cushions. It rang again and she lunged for it, almost screaming in frustration as the hospital's number appeared on the screen. She ignored it – she wasn't in any state to talk to her brother now.

After the call had gone to voicemail, she tried Pauley's number to no avail. Becoming more and more agitated she called him several more times with no luck. Her final call went straight to voicemail.

She lurched to the bathroom, dropping to her knees in front of the commode and vomiting violently. When she was finished, she huddled on the tiled floor, hugging her knees to her chest. How was she going to live without him? Why was he doing this to her? To them? She lay there keening, an inhuman sound she couldn't control.

Somewhere deep inside she recognized that she was being irrational. That these feelings of loss should not be associated with the termination of such a short relationship. She should be disappointed, yes. And maybe angry because of the way the coward had ended things, sure. But this abject misery? This desperation? A sickness.

But knowing this, subconsciously or otherwise, did not change what was. She felt like her life had ended – she would never meet anyone else like Pauley. Pauley, with his cocky smile, his seductive swagger, his easy style. He was nothing short of perfection.

And the way he'd treated her in the beginning; the lust in his eyes...he hadn't been able to stay away from her, keep his hands off her. It had been paradise. She had never felt so wanted, so needed, in her entire life. No, there was no one like Pauley, and she couldn't – she wouldn't – live without him.

She heaved herself off the floor and drew a glass of water from the tap. She took a sip, staring at herself in the mirror above the sink. She was big, blonde, and beautiful - that's what Pauley called her. His "Trip B.".

She released another whimper and opened the medicine cabinet. The pill bottle was half full...that was enough. Had to be enough. She downed the Ativan with the remainder of the water, laid on her bed still fully clothed, and sobbed until the pills had taken her away.

***

Once Pauley turned the corner of Danielle's street he settled back in his seat and breathed a sigh of relief. Free! He ran a finger under the crew neck of his sweater. Man, he hated feeling restrained.

As much as he loved the huge tits and ass on that one, she'd started getting that dreamy look in her eye much sooner than usual, and he'd immediately began plotting his escape. It had been much easier than he'd thought, though the broad probably hadn't even realized she'd never see him again. Dumb blonde.

It wasn't his fault chicks dug him. Threw themselves at him. Anywhere...anytime. It was just who he was. This one had been no different. He'd met her at her job of all places, and she hadn't taken her eyes off him the entire time. When he'd left she'd slipped him her card with her phone number scrawled through a lipsticked pout on the back. So cliché.

But he hadn't wasted any time calling her. He'd never been with a big girl, and he was intrigued. Not to mention she was a knockout. Even her business suit was unable to hide her many assets, and he couldn't wait to fraternize.

Thankfully she wasn't a prude, and other than a couple of token refusals he slid into home base the first night he'd taken her out. She'd been eager and intense, and the night had ended in a satisfyingly exertive manner.

At first he couldn't get enough of her – he didn't have to worry about hurting her with his exuberance, and many of their endeavors in the sack could have qualified as a competitive gymnastics routine. But once the shine wore off there wasn't much left.

He was adept at pretending to listen, laughing at all the right times, and agreeing with her assessment of whatever happened to be on TV without really hearing her. Tonight, though, he'd found himself weary of even that little bit of attentiveness.

The end was no longer worth the means – a clear sign that it was time to move on. His only sign, really. He was in it for as long as it was easy and fun. When it ceased to be either, he was out of there.

Surprisingly, he didn't lack insight. He knew exactly what he was doing, and didn't sugarcoat his behavior for the sake of his own conscience. But all parties were consenting adults, he never made promises he had no intention of keeping, and he didn't pretend he was something he wasn't. As far as he was concerned, he was the most upstanding and honest of men. If more of his kind were like him, there'd be a lot more happy women in the world.

He smiled to himself as he dialed his phone through the car's dashboard controls. Her voice filled the cabin of the vehicle with a sultry grumble when she finally answered.

"Are the kids in bed?"

"How do you know I'm alone?"

"I just left the restaurant. Your man was knee deep in guacamole and queso. He won't be home any time soon."

"Yes, they're in bed."

"On my way," he disconnected and turned up the sound system, bobbing his head rhythmically to the beat of the music.

Ironically the relationship he had with a married woman, as on and off as it had been, was the longest he'd ever had. Maybe because he didn't have to worry about commitment issues, or coming on too strong, or how often he should call to avoid an argument.

Things with Tiffany were easy. He phoned only when he wanted to screw, and she didn't call at all. He knew she wanted him – she devoured him with her eyes whenever they saw each other – but she had her own life she didn't need him messing up for her.

Her husband had a decent job, they had two small children her mother-in-law watched anytime they wanted, and they'd just bought a nice new house with a 30-year mortgage. She couldn't afford to make trouble for Pauley, and that's exactly the way he liked it.

They'd been at it for two years now, and he couldn't see that changing. Why should it? They fulfilled a physical need for each other and weren't hurting anybody in the process.

Pauley started humming as he ran a hand through his hair and checked his perfectly straight, professionally whitened teeth in the rearview mirror. After ignoring several phone calls from Doreen's – Diana's? – number, he turned off his phone and slid it into his jacket pocket.

Most of the female contacts in his cell were labeled by first initial only, simply because he figured it was a waste of time to enter their entire name. He was rarely with anyone long enough to justify it. Even Tiffany had never been elevated from a 'T' in his address book.

That didn't make him a jerk did it? No, of course it didn't. He was just a realist, that's all. If he'd learned anything from his pragmatic father it was that feelings and emotions had no place in one's pursuit of success, whether in business or otherwise.

And James was nothing if not successful. He'd just opened his sixth luxury car dealership in a tristate area, and money was pouring in. Not that Pauley saw much of it, he thought bitterly.

He'd been pressing James for an increase in his sizable monthly allowance fruitlessly; his father acted as if he were a bum on the street looking for handouts. He was his own son, for fuck's sake! Pauley slapped his palm on the steering wheel in anger and impotent frustration. He hated that feeling, and hated his father for making him feel it.

Pauley had accelerated unintentionally while he was distracted by his thoughts and groaned at the red and white lights flashing behind him. Goddammit! Fucking pigs!

He took several breaths and pulled to the shoulder of the road. "Evening, officer!" he smiled brightly, placing his hands on the steering wheel where they could easily be seen. His tone was sincere. Engaging.

"Do you know how fast you were going, sir?"

"No, I don't, Officer. I'm so sorry – I usually keep an eye on the speedometer but today's my little girl's birthday and I was so excited to get home to spend a little time with her before she goes to bed. It was careless of me."

The man appraised him for a moment, but Pauley exuded nothing but genuineness and sincerity. The cop finally nodded and motioned him on his way.

"Be more careful from here on out."

Pauley nodded enthusiastically. "Yes sir, absolutely. Thank you, sir!" He pulled away from the curb, driving slowly the rest of the way to Tiffany's. He should be grateful – not even a warning – but instead he beleaguered the stop. Waste of his precious time, asshole pig.

Wasn't there somebody being attacked in this city? Robbed? Raped? Killed? Why were resources being spent on harassing white guys in the nice part of town? He had a mind to write his senator over this nuisance.

He parked his car on a side street near a playground and jogged several yards up the walking trail until he reached Tiffany's backyard. Glancing around for prying eyes, he darted into the bushes that bordered the lawn and crossed the moonlit expanse to the sliding glass door on the patio. He tapped gently and was immediately admitted into the darkened house.

Once he was safely inside, Tiffany turned on the lamp next to the couch. "What took you so damn long?" she demanded in a loud whisper, her hands on her hips, her amber eyes flashing gloriously. A petite brunette with a spiky pixie cut, she wasn't beautiful by any means, but Pauley found her feistiness refreshing.

"It's nice to see you too, Tiff," he summoned his best charmingly apologetic grin and she melted. A little. But it was enough for him to step in for a kiss, backing her onto the leather couch.

He deftly divested her of her silk nightie, then straightened to remove his own clothes. Her eyes had become molten as she watched him standing above her, all bronzed muscle and masculinity. Yes, this is the life, he thought, as he sank into her awaiting body.

Chapter 3
Lost Ones

"Dude, did you screw my wife or not? It's not a difficult fucking question!" Mark bellowed. Dennis wiped his hands on his apron and glanced at the half-closed door through which he could see customers glancing up from their food, curious about the source of the commotion.

"Could we maybe do this after the bar closes?"

"Why should you care? It's not your place – or were you planning on getting your stinking hands on my restaurant, too?" Dennis cringed and put his hands up, palms facing outward as if to ward off his irate boss.

He was well aware he needed to appease Mark; he'd just been promoted to kitchen manager at the Bleu Goose and couldn't afford to lose his job. He knew he probably should've thought of that before he'd banged the boss's wife, but she'd come on so strong he couldn't say no.

Not that he'd tried very hard, he had to admit. A man just couldn't ignore a woman like Lilah for long, he mused as he thought of her curtain of fiery red curls, emerald cat eyes and sultry laugh. Even her husky voice was an invitation, and her body was reminiscent of a sixties pinup model. He gave himself a mental shake, thankful his betraying dick was hidden behind his apron.

"She came in while I was doing the pantry order. No one else was around. She said you guys had separated. That you hated her. Didn't want anything to do with her." He pushed the words out through tight lips, hoping to say something that would get him out of hot water. His wife would kill him if he lost this job.

"Whether that's the case or not, you don't stick it in somebody else's wife, you fucking dirtbag."

"Man, I'm sorry. She cried on my shoulder. Told me you ignored her – that I'd be doing you a favor getting her out of your hair." Mark almost felt sorry for the guy. He knew Lilah well...knew her flighty nature and girlish charms. She was nearly impossible to resist when she wanted to be.

But he needed to save face with his staff. He wouldn't fire the man; he was a good manager, which was worth its weight in gold in this business. But he'd sure as hell make his life miserable for a while. Let him question his job security.

He'd already pulled Dennis's employee file for his wife's cell number and had texted her about the affair. It had been a petty thing to do, but he couldn't care less at this point.

"I can't stand looking at you. Get your ass back to the kitchen until I decide what to do with you."

"Thanks, Mark – I'm seriously sorry, man. Anything I can do to –"

"Out!" Dennis ducked out of the office, closing the door quietly behind him. After he'd gone, Mark dropped into the swivel chair behind his desk. He couldn't believe that bitch had chosen one of his employees to seduce, and then threw it in his face this afternoon after he'd refused to increase the credit limit on her Macy's card.

He hadn't believed it at first, assuming she was just trying to get under his skin as she often did when she didn't get what she wanted. But she'd described the walk-in freezer in such detail that he was forced to acknowledge she'd spent time inside it – and not with him.

Their love life had taken a beating over the past three years since she'd caught his eye when she first began frequenting the restaurant. Back then he'd been young, naive, and fully enamored with this colorful creature. He had fallen for her instantly, and had married her within six weeks.

It was a decision he'd regretted almost immediately. Once he'd gently placed the stunning four-caret diamond on her finger the fun-loving sex kitten he'd adored was replaced by a childish, selfish gold digger who had no intention of being an equal partner in their marriage.

Intent only on spending his money and flaunting her leisurely life in the lap of luxury, she'd splurged on Brazilian waxes and tanning sessions, mani-pedis and blowouts, designer shoes and mounds of lingerie. She'd wasted no time accustoming herself to a life of privilege.

Now that it was obvious those negligees hadn't been for his eyes only, he wondered how many of her late nights had been spent with other men. He seriously doubted Dennis was the first; she'd seemed too comfortable in her taunts for that to be the case. When he'd left the condo this afternoon, she'd still been raging at him for his selfishness with 'their' money, and had seemed to relish in spewing ridiculing insults regarding Dennis's sexual prowess.

Mark had been at a loss for words and had left without comment, which only seemed to goad her more. Now, however, he was more than ready for a confrontation. He'd gotten confirmation of their affair from Dennis, had been in touch with his accountant about securing his assets from his wife's purview, and had surprisingly quickly come to the decision to end his marriage.

After bolstering himself with a drink from the bar, he snuck out the back door and drove home, oblivious to the amazing view of the city lights from the top of the bluff that usually awed him. For a small town country boy who'd made good, he was humble of his wealth and success, and remained thankful for all he had that many didn't.

Perhaps the thing that annoyed him most about Lilah was the person she'd turned into as a result of her unprivileged childhood. She had become arrogant and entitled, and it had turned her beauty into pure ugliness as far as he was concerned.

It was obvious that most men refused to see that side of his wife, and he was more than willing to let them have her. It would be good riddance, and by the time he pulled into the parking garage of his building, he was anxious to be done with her.

He tapped his foot impatiently as he rode the elevator to the fourteenth floor, taking long strides down the hallway before pausing in front of his door.

He'd purchased this place after the Bleu Goose had passed the dreaded two-year mark that claimed many new businesses, and had spent all his spare time producing just the right ambiance – a balance of blacks and grays interspersed with warm woods and travertine tile. All clean lines and comfort with a decent balance of masculine simplicity and a touch of color in the accents he'd chosen.

The result was exactly him, and he was proud of it. He was also grateful Lilah hadn't taken an interest in redecorating it to incorporate her tastes, though he'd given her carte blanche to do so. Maybe that should have been his first red flag: her lack of desire to imprint herself on his home, or his life, for that matter.

He unlocked the door and stalked into the room, his gaze resting on his wife lounging on the chaise by the balcony doors as if she hadn't a care in the world. She didn't even glance up from her magazine when he slammed the door behind him.

Her filmy negligee struck him as too little too late, assuming she'd even donned it for him in the first place. He stopped in front of her and stared down at the top of her head for several moments; he had truly believed he'd spend the rest of his life with this woman. Dumb hick.

"You have one week to leave my home," he finally said. "If you're still here after that, I'll call the police to have you removed." He turned on his heel and walked toward the bedroom.

"Don't you think you're being a little dramatic?" she asked, never taking her eyes from the page. He studiously ignored her, continuing into the soothingly appointed master suite to pack his duffel bag. When he was finished, he re-entered the living room and headed for the door.

"Where are you going?" He stopped without turning around, his back the only thing he was willing to give her.

"I've checked into a hotel. I'll be back when you're gone. I don't ever want to see you again."

"Mark, wait..." but he was already out the door, and by the time she'd covered her near nakedness and raced out to the hall, he was gone.

***

"Oh my God, it hurts," Eva panted.

"Just a little further, sweetheart," Josh crooned, readjusting her shapely leg over his shoulder and continuing to push forward.

Moisture beaded on her brow and above her lips, which were currently stretched over her teeth into a grimace. Her eyes squeezed shut, she tossed her head from side to side as if attempting to rebuff the discomfort.

She was sexy as hell, Josh thought to himself as he pushed himself even further over her body. Just then her eyes snapped open and her hands shot to his broad shoulders.

"Okay, I'm done. You can torture me some more tomorrow." With a great deal of reluctance, he gently shifted her leg back to the floor mat.

"Fine, sissy. Five minutes on the elliptical and make sure to stretch before you hit the shower."

"What do you call what we were just doing?" she muttered, leaping lithely to her feet, her long ponytail swinging behind her. "Besides, I'm the least sissified member here," she looked around the nearly empty gym while draining her bottle of water. There were only a few diehards there this early, and none of them had even broken a sweat.

"Don't get all cocky on me now," Josh warned playfully, flicking his towel at her firm backside.

"Never," she danced away from the assault and tossed him a wink before heading to the aerobic machines. Josh watched her for a minute before returning to the front desk. Damn, she was fine. He wished for the millionth time that she was single, or at least unfaithful. But alas, she was neither, and all he could do was fantasize.

After attacking the elliptical machine fervently for twenty minutes – "Five my fat ass," she hissed to herself – she stretched at the bar and then slipped into the showers. Forty-five minutes later she breezed through the gym toward the front door looking like she'd just left the beauty salon. Josh whistled appreciatively as she passed the desk and she blew him a kiss.

It was still dark outside – she'd gotten an earlier than normal start that morning so she could swing by her sister's place before work.

She steered her Jeep into the complex parking lot and found a space in front of Marin's building. She knocked on the door and waited several minutes before opening it with her key. It was pitch black inside the apartment, and she assumed Marin was still sleeping.

She flicked on the lights inside the door, intending to pass through the living room to the bedroom – but she stopped short when she spotted her sister sitting at the dining room table staring into space.

Her hesitant "Marin?" yielded no response, and as she approached her sister she was overwhelmed by the smell of urine and feces. Eva knelt next to the chair and stared at her identical twin – although at the moment they barely looked related, let alone like mirror images.

"It's okay, sis. I'm going to get you some help." She gently took her sister's hand and held it above the table. When she let it go, it remained raised of its own accord. Waxy flexibility was the psychiatric term. Eva closed her eyes with grief.

Marin was catatonic, and there was no telling how long she'd been like this. It could have been a few hours, or even since Eva had last checked in on her a couple of days ago. She was probably dehydrated, sleep deprived, and physically exhausted, but she wouldn't be able to resume purposeful activity without medical intervention.

Eva guided her sister's arm back to her lap, dug her cell phone out of her purse, and dialed 9-1-1. When the ambulance arrived a few minutes later she gave the paramedics the information they needed and then followed them to the emergency room.

There they would start an IV to hydrate her, give her dextrose to bolster her nutritional status, draw blood to check her electrolytes, and then send her to PINA to treat the catatonia.

Eva returned to Marin's bedside after she'd given the registration desk her pertinent information and sat on the chair next to the bed to slip her hand through the side rail. She interlaced her fingers with her sister's, tears sliding down her face as she stared at her. So broken inside.

The products of blatant abuse during most of their childhoods, Eva's psyche had revolted, making her strong and independent – at least that's the image she portrayed. But Marin's had been all but destroyed, leaving her incredibly fragile and fractured. She was like a little girl still – easy to please, easier to hurt.

Eva cursed their parents – drug addicts who'd exposed the girls to their wild parties and copious orgies at a tender age, and then used them as sex toys for the highest bidders. Their reward was usually more drugs.

By eleven, the twins were addicts themselves, and by twelve they'd had multiple episodes of nonconsensual intercourse with adults old enough to know better but too drunk, too stoned, or too high to care.

At sixteen Marin got pregnant, and rather than risking exposure, their parents had hired some back-alley quack to perform an abortion in their kitchen, one of their near constant parties raging in the next room. She'd nearly bled to death as a result of the procedure, but still they'd refused to take her to the hospital. She eventually recovered from the physical trauma, but she would never be able to carry a child.

Furious for her sister, Eva had vowed she would take her away from their life as soon as she could manage it. The day they graduated from high school Eva stole their mother's beater of a car and drove them as far as she could before the vehicle broke down. She left it at the side of the road, thumbed for rides to the nearest big city, and checked into the local YWCA.

A motherly caseworker helped her find a steady job, enroll in evening classes at the community college, and rent a cheap studio apartment in a relatively safe neighborhood. Though there wasn't much money and even less leisure time, Eva thrived under her own steam.

She earned a full scholarship to the local university to finish her bachelor's degree, then immediately started on her master's degree in psychology. Her caseworker had inspired her to explore drug and alcohol counseling, and she'd realized she loved all types of therapy.

She completed her studies with honors, and was finally able to set Marin up in her own apartment while she rented a unit for herself in the same building. She wanted to help her sister stand on her own two feet, and to leave the ordeal of her childhood behind her as fully as Eva had done. But Marin seemed stuck in that tragic place, and, try as she might, Eva couldn't drag her mind out of it like she had her body.

Eva jumped when the doctor pulled the curtain. "We're ready to transfer your sister to PINA now."

She nodded, dazed from her memories, and squeezed Marin's limp hand. "I'll meet her there."

The sky was just beginning to lighten when she drove out of the parking garage. The new car smell arousing her senses, she mused about the way her life had turned around. She was married to a sweet, sexy man, and she could afford the better things in life. Even taking care of Marin was no longer a huge strain on her finances.

She had diligently become the person she wanted the world to see. Outside. Inside, she was scared. Anxious. In constant fear of succumbing to the eating disorder that had claimed her after she'd left her childhood behind. Or the substance addictions that had ruled her before that. When Marin was sick, she was a blatant reminder of their past. And she had never been sicker than she was now.

Wiping her tears and checking her makeup in the visor, Eva took several deep breaths before heading into the lobby of the Institute. She'd texted Riley before she'd left the ER, and she was waiting for her inside. The two hugged, and Riley assured her she would take good care of her sister, as always.

"She's really bad this time, Riley..."

"It's nothing we can't handle. She's in the right place." Eva nodded, fighting a new onslaught of tears. "Other people need you, Eva. I'll text you if anything changes."

Riley watched the older woman leave – it was the first time she'd seen her look beaten, and she found herself worrying far more about Eva than her sister.

***

Her memories were vivid flashes of still shots – the earliest in the womb. Intertwined with another exactly like her, yet never jockeying for space. Fighting only against a hostile environment; in utero receiving shot after shot of whatever drug their host had refused to abstain from even after her pregnancy became apparent. There were few nutrients, but a constant flow of helplessness and fear.

She had never told anyone about these memories; not even her sister – Eva thought she was crazy enough as it was. Logically, she knew it wasn't possible that she remembered being a fetus. But then again, she did.

She cycled through her images as though part of a photo album. Her parents never took photographs, and certainly didn't keep scrapbooks – but her mind, as fallible as it could be, recorded each and every moment of her life.

She could pull the pictures from her memory at will, and sometimes, when she was really sick, they would shift over and over as if on eternal replay. This time she felt so lost inside the still frames she wasn't sure she would ever come out.

Though she was petrified, she couldn't concentrate on producing sound. She couldn't move. Couldn't scream. All she could do was watch the pictures go by.

Her favorite were of her mother caring for her when she was a baby; feeding her, carrying her, and a few – a very few – of kissing her. In those she could see her mother's face close up; every line and pock mark that marred her once beautiful features. And oh, she loved her.

She knew Eva didn't have these memories. Could only remember the bad times. When they were older and the abuse had gone from mere neglect and inattention to something so much worse.

But Marin remembered, and loved her mother for it – wanted nothing more than her love in return. She knew she was capable of it; after all, she'd experienced it before.

But it never came again. And that had been what had shattered Marin's mind in the end. Had she never known her mother's love her transgressions against her could have been tolerated, at least to some small degree. But the betrayal was so great that she couldn't process it. It couldn't exist within the same context as her memories of the loving parent.

And so her reality shifted so significantly that she often didn't know what was real and what wasn't. Depersonalization-derealization disorder is what they called it. It affected everything about her, from the way she thought to the way she moved.

She drifted through her days ghost-like as if being blown by a meandering breeze, seemingly directionless – when she could move at all. Sometimes her depressed states rendered her immobile for large spans of time – in bed like an invalid for days on end, the strips of film in her head clicking from one scene to another in a relentless silent horror movie.

Eva would come then – her beautiful, neurotic doppelganger – and take her to the hospital. She hated it there. The lights were too bright, the sounds too loud. She was allowed the sanctity of her room only for a few days – once the medication kicked in she would be required to interact with the staff and, much worse, the other patients.

All with their own Pandora's Box just waiting for the lid to be removed so they could go well and truly crazy. They scared her, with their needless clinging, their incessant banter.

Sometimes there would be a safety code announced over the loudspeaker that would bring the security guards and nurses and techs from elsewhere in the hospital converging onto the unit, as if propelled by a vulgar need to punish and control.

The hapless patient at the center of the commotion would be surrounded, swarmed like bees around a nest of honey. Consumed in the crowd of responders and taken away to a white room consisting of nothing but a steel bed bolted to the floor. He would be secured to the heavy frame with leather straps, their metal buckles locked with a key all staff carried like a badge. One strap for each wrist, each ankle, and across the chest – a five-point restraint.

He would then be locked in the room alone, screaming the most vile curse words he could think of. The nurses would watch him on the monitors, occasionally making notes in his chart. His screams would go on and on, muted but still maddeningly intrusive.

The other patients would whisper among each other. Why? It was easy to forget the transgressions leading to his seclusion after witnessing his undignified displacement. Now they were all the same. Locked in. At the mercy of others. Today, him. Tomorrow, maybe one of them.

Their panic rising, their conversations growing in volume so as to nearly overwhelm his waning screams. Many doses of Haldol later, not only for the restrained but for most of the rest of the patient population as well, all becomes quiet again. But the trauma remains; the fear and paranoia not nearly as easily dissipated as the noise.

When the transgressor finally rejoins them, later that day or the next or maybe even the next, he would be sheepish. Or belligerent. Perhaps slowed by the meds they'd put him on to keep him quiet and subservient. But surely never the same.

Yes, there was much to fear about the hospital. The funny farm that was in fact neither. In her strange mind Marin sometimes saw animals like cows and chickens doing hilarious things when Eva mentioned the Institute. But it was no laughing matter, this place of terror and loathing. She was sure one day she would be locked in and never let out again.

This was not a baseless fear – it was definitely true of the old days before the ACLU started campaigning against the unfair treatment of the mentally ill. When the state hospitals that housed them were death traps from which most would never escape. When horrendous experiments involving insulin, frigid water, and even electricity were performed with complete disregard for their rights.

Marin had heard Eva preach about how much things had changed for the better. But what could be worse than being imprisoned for an illness as opposed to a crime? And yet here she was.

Her mind registered the fact that she was in the intake room of the dreaded Institute even if her physical being did not. The sounds of hushed voices and brisk movements and jangling keys were unmistakably connected with places such as this. They were its theme song, as recognizable to those familiar with this environment as a childhood lullaby.

The face of her sister's friend swam into focus in front of her, interrupting her reverie. "Marin, it's Riley. You're back at PINA. You're safe." Marin's eyes wouldn't focus on the nurse, so she remained a nonperson. A disembodied head floating in a nebula.

Though Marin didn't – couldn't – react in any way, Riley continued as though she had. "I'm going to take good care of you," she placed her hand on Marin's, limp on her lap where it had been positioned by the admissions nurse. Riley's hand felt odd on her own. Neither warm nor cool, neither soft nor hard. It could have been any object, living or non.

"We're going to need to give you an injection. It'll make you feel a lot better. We're going to stand you up now. You understand?" It was a rhetorical question to which Riley knew she would receive no response.

She nodded to the other nurse and they gently lifted Marin from the chair. Riley tugged down the waistband of her yoga pants and stabbed her buttock with the long needle. Though Marin felt the pinch of the shot and the sting of the medication being injected into her muscle, she was unable to do anything other than remain outwardly stoic.

Riley took her to her room in a wheelchair, and then she and some other blurry anybody positioned her in the bed. She assured her she would be back often to check on her and then she left the room, leaving a sitter outside her door.

Immobile and alone, Marin stared at the ceiling blindly. The still frames whirled through her mind faster and faster. Men, and sometimes women, on top of her – squeezing her breasts, plundering her flesh – never looking into her eyes.

Fetid breath, sweaty palms, rutting like animals in heat. Taking. Destroying. Leaving nothing behind.

Her cherished twin on the other bed, crying, clawing, screaming. Too much trouble.

Alone now, finally. Sobs from one side of the room, silence from the other. Nothing left.

***

Tentatively, like a drunk waking to the unforgiving spotlight of the morning sun, Danielle opened her eyes to the light streaming through the partially closed curtains of her bedroom. Crap. She was alive. She very clearly couldn't do anything right.

An enormous furry head butted her shoulder – Saint Cecelia. What had she been thinking? She hadn't even left enough food in the cat's bowl to last a few days until her body was discovered, peaceful and lovely under her artfully arranged duvet. And Michael in the hospital; he needed her too.

No, she hadn't thought through her plan at all. She heaved her–almost–wasn't–self out of bed to forage for food – cold pizza for her and dry cat food for Cece, who expressed a significant degree of disdain over the meager offering.

"Ungrateful feline," Danielle muttered to the retreating animal as she checked her voice mail. Seconds later she was on the phone with the unit secretary at the hospital, her heart beginning to race. "This is Danielle Gregory. I just got your messages – is it my brother, Michael? Is he alright?" Can't say. Must talk in person. How soon can you come?

Breaking an equal number of records and laws, she arrived at the foreboding building breathless and panicked, and was immediately ushered into the office of the medical director. Dr. Emil Barry was a little bald man who looked neither compassionate nor particularly sorry.

There she was told her kid brother was dead. Gone forever. Hyperventilating, she stared at Dr. Barry's peculiarly shiny dome. "You're telling me my brother died here in this hospital, under your watch, and you have no idea why?" Her voice grew louder with each syllable until it was very nearly a hysterical scream.

He had the grace to look chagrined as he averted his eyes from her glare. "There'll be an autopsy, of course –"

"You bet your ass there'll be an autopsy!"

"– and we're prepared to pay restitution to the family depending on the findings."

"Like bringing my brother back? You got some kind of Frankenstein machine down in the crypt of this creepy building, Doc? Cause otherwise your restitution doesn't mean shit!" she sat back in the uncomfortable guest chair, crossing her arms over her ample chest.

He winced at her language, or her tone, or both, and folded his hands primly on his desk. He wished he didn't have to deal with this brash woman, but it was his job, and he was paid a great deal of money to do it.

"I assume you'll want to see him."

"Of course. Is he in his room?"

"Uh, no...he's been transferred to the morgue."

Danielle slapped the desk with both palms, causing the diminutive physician to jump as if he'd been goosed by a jackhammer. "Why the hell is he at the damn morgue?!"

He hadn't thought it was possible for her to get any louder. He couldn't be more wrong. "Please, Miss Gregory. Understand we've been unable to reach you and had to take action in a timely manner." With that, predominantly because he'd made a valid point, she lunged out of her chair and swept from the office, the heels of her thigh-high boots echoing abrasively on the bare floor.

Dr. Barry watched her go, his eyes narrowed and his fingers steepled under his chin. He glanced out the window at the gathering storm clouds. There would be an investigation, he ruminated, and his mood darkened until it matched the roiling sky.

A few blocks away Danielle stood in the empty viewing room of the morgue staring down at Michael's innocent face. His complexion was ruddy and his tongue protruded slightly from his mouth, but otherwise he was the same old Michael.

They would be doing the autopsy soon, and she would never again see him intact. She ran her hands gently over his face, his head, his chest. She held his hands and kissed his eyelids. Finally she leaned over him, covering his body with hers.

Anguished cries escaped her as she gripped his shoulders, her ear pressed against his chest. She was sure if she stayed that way long enough she would hear his heartbeat. The movement of air through his lungs. He couldn't be dead. He couldn't be.

But he was. The inside of him was as quiet as a vacated dream, his skin as cold as regret. She didn't move until a tech came and guided her to the elevators. They were starting the autopsy. Wasn't there someone she should call?

From across an ocean her mother's voice sounded far closer than it should. Guilt washed over her. She was supposed to take care of him. Forever and ever.

"Mom..." The ocean became her tears and choked off her ability to answer her mother's alarmed questions. She whispered what she could and moaned the rest, pressing the phone hard against her ear as if its substance could give her strength.

They would leave Germany as soon as they could. It might be a couple of days. "You know how the military is, remember, darling? Be a dear and make the funeral arrangements, won't you, sweetheart? Bye for now."

"Sure, I remember. Bye," Danielle murmured to an already disconnected line. Michael would get a kick out of that one. He always did.

For all her efforts, Michael's funeral was little more than a family affair. Extended relations had long since drifted away, and the family's frequent moves during his childhood had prevented the formation of any lasting friendships.

Danielle sat at the front of the church, sandwiched by her parents. Sarah sat across the aisle next to her caseworker, her eyes wide and scared. The poor child had never met any of them – had only seen her father a handful of times, and during most of those visits he had likely been disorganized and seemed extremely odd to her.

Danielle felt sorry for the little girl and could have kicked her parents for not even attempting to speak to her. Didn't they want to hold onto something of his? Didn't they want to nurture a grandchild?

She'd answered the question before it had been fully formed. Of course they didn't. They didn't want to nurture their own children; why would they open their arms to their granddaughter?

Danielle had been Michael's nurturer. His parents. His siblings. All the friends he'd never had. She was his end all and be all, and now he was gone and she was nothing. A loud sob escaped her before she could smother it, and her mother glanced at her in surprise. Don't mind me, Mom. Just mourning the loss of your son.

From the pew behind her, one of Michael's nurses put her hand on Danielle's shoulder and she turned to smile at her with gratitude. How was it that a stranger could provide more comfort in such a personal moment than one's own mother?

As she glanced behind her she saw several of Michael's staff from both the hospital and his group home, as well as his psychiatrist, Dr. Tacee. Danielle nodded to her briefly and then turned her attention back to the coffin at the front of the church.

Maybe Michael's life had touched others more than she'd realized. The thought lifted her spirits a bit, and she was able to accept the guests' condolences and words of comfort without losing her shit. But by the end of the service she was exhausted, and welcomed the cold drizzle that sent everyone scurrying for their cars.

Finally, she dropped her parents off at their hotel, where they said their goodbyes. They would be returning to their full life overseas early the following morning, and were obviously not planning on spending any more of their precious time with their only living child. Apparently they believed their role in their children's lives was over.

They had offered to take Michael with them when they were first stationed overseas but Danielle had pleaded with them to allow him to stay. Though not adequate by a long shot, mental health services in the states were superior to those in Europe, she'd be able to look after him here, and this was the most stable environment he'd ever known. They'd relented, and now he was dead.

They were suddenly and fully absolved of any responsibility over their adult offspring. She wondered if they had even shed a tear for their son. They certainly hadn't for her. And in that moment, she found herself hating them. It was their fault Michael was gone. Their fault she was alone. Their fault. And Pauley's.

Chapter 4
Lies

Trying to settle into the day's routine at the office following the upheaval of the early morning, Eva poured herself a cup of coffee – black – and took a fortifying sip. She'd much rather be at the hospital with Marin, but there was nothing she could do except stare at her sister in frustration.

It disturbed her greatly that Marin seemed to be decompensating to such an extreme degree, and wondered if she'd been taking her meds like she'd assured Eva she was. She made a mental note to stop by the apartment after her appointments to check Marin's pill bottles.

Her phone buzzed, interrupting her thoughts and indicating her first client had arrived. Let the games begin. She opened her door to admit Julie, who approached timidly, as though they hadn't been working together for the past two years.

"How's it going, Julie?"

"Okay, I guess. The thoughts have been really horrible lately."

Eva settled into her chair behind her desk, crossing her legs and directing her gaze toward the large comfortable chair where her client was sitting, wringing her hands and biting her lip.

Julie was looking everywhere except directly at her therapist, and Eva followed her flitting gaze around the huge office, viewing it from her perspective.

Decorated in neutral shades and light tones, it was warm and welcoming, with plenty of natural light filtering through the drawn shades over towering windows. Eva's practice had grown to be quite successful, and she was proud of her accomplishment.

"You seem more anxious than usual. Tell me what's been going on," Eva invited cordially, attempting to put the woman at ease.

After several moments of silence that Eva refused to fill with chatter despite the growing discomfort in the room, Julie spoke, her voice so quiet Eva had to strain to hear it.

"I'm up for a promotion at work."

Refraining from the automatic response she was inclined to give – That's great! Congratulations! You should be thrilled! – Eva instead commented, "That's a big responsibility."

Julie breathed, pushing air out of her body in relief – Eva understood if nobody else did. "Yes! I don't know if I can do it."

"It seems to me it's not a matter of 'can'. I doubt you would've been offered the promotion had there been any question that you're the best person for the job."

Julie peered at her from behind a protective veil of hair. "Go on...," she prompted.

"It appears to be a question of readiness."

Julie nodded. "Am I ready to take on this new job..."

"...and let go of a bit of control over your life."

"Maybe. If I can keep my rugs," Julie said after a brief hesitation.

"Of course. We can delay reducing how many you have until you feel more comfortable in your new position."

"Yes," Julie nodded emphatically, her mood obviously much improved. "I can do this."

"I believe you can," Eva responded in validation, rising from her desk to walk the woman to the door.

"Thank you. I feel so much better."

"I'm glad. I'll see you next week."

After she'd left Eva returned to her desk to write her notes about their session. Julie had come to her after being released from the hospital following a suicide attempt. Her obsessive-compulsive disorder had become so restrictive she could barely leave the house or see to her own needs.

In OCD, the client has recurring unpleasant thoughts that cause a great deal of anxiety. In order to deal with the unbearable angst, the sufferer is compelled to perform rituals, or repetitive actions, which act as a buffer for the anxiety that the obsessive thoughts produce.

In Julie's case, the obsessions, or unwanted thoughts, involved children being flogged in public until their bodies bled, and her compulsions, or repetitive ritualistic actions she used to thwart those thoughts, was straightening the fringes of the rugs in her apartment. The ritual was exact, requiring her to use a ruler to ensure each fringe was perfectly straight and equidistant from the rest.

By having her placed on antianxiety medication, introducing conscious coping strategies, and gradually reducing the number of fringed rugs she owned, Eva had been able to help her lead a more full and rewarding life, though there was still quite a way to go.

While Julie's case was severe, Eva had seen worse. She'd had a patient with the disorder who was obsessed with germs, ritualistically washing her hands so often they chafed and bled. She became septic when opportunistic bacteria, which are naturally found on the skin, entered the bloodstream through the open sores in her palms. She eventually died once the massive infection overwhelmed her body.

Eva shook her head sadly at the memory as her phone buzzed again. Taking several deep breaths to clear her mind and prepare herself for her next client, she stood and strode to the door. Before she'd fully opened it Bill bounded past her and settled himself in the chair behind her desk.

Giving herself a mental shake Eva closed the door and motioned to the two chairs arranged around the fireplace on the other side of her desk. Rolling his eyes, he moved to the client chair Julie had just vacated and flopped onto it.

"Where's your sense of humor, lady?" he asked snidely.

"At home, where it belongs. Now, tell me how your self-affirmations have been coming along."

"Stupid. Pointless."

"It's not a futile exercise, Bill. The point is to reprogram the negative messages in your brain – the ones that inform all your destructive behaviors – to positive ones."

"Can't I just take meds instead of doing this bullshit?"

"We can give you things for your anxiety and for depression resulting from the way you've lived your life as a result of those negative messages, but the reformatting of your brain has to be accomplished through your dedication and hard work."

Bill had been diagnosed with borderline personality disorder, which is a fairly common condition in which one's true personality is pushed aside or minimized in favor of one that is perceived to be more acceptable.

When this occurs during childhood on a frequent basis, a healthy personality is never adequately developed, and the child grows into an adult who doesn't know who he really is. Subsequently, he goes through life having difficulty relating to others, being lonely, anxious, and depressed, and having no sense of appropriate boundaries.

Eva felt these were by far the most difficult clients to treat because they could be quite manipulative and intrusive of others. Bill was no exception, and she found herself praying for patience every moment she was with him.

"Did you complete the worksheets I gave you?"

He waved his hand dismissively. "I threw those worthless things in the trashcan by the receptionist's desk before I left last week."

Eva barely refrained from exploding – this guy was killing her. She ran her hand over her smooth bun to buy some time; she didn't trust herself to respond until she'd counted to ten.

"Bill, I can't help you if you won't help yourself. There's nothing more I can do for you at this point except dismiss you from my practice. Perhaps another therapist would be more cathartic for you."

"Your loss, doll," he trilled flippantly as he hopped up from the chair and headed for the door. Before he had the chance to open it, the receptionist poked her head into the office with an exasperated look.

"I'm so sorry to interrupt, Eva – but we have a situation out here..."

Bill eased past her with a wink. "You deal with your crazies. I'm outta this circus."

Eva followed him into the reception area but stopped short when she saw her next client huddled behind a chair. He stared askance at Bill, cowering as the man passed him and exited the suite. He then swung his wide-eyed gaze to the two women standing at the door to Eva's office.

"They're coming to get me," he whispered tremulously, his entire body shaking with fright.

"Who is, Craig?" Eva asked, crouching before him, but remaining out of arm's reach – he could be labile as well as psychotic.

"The FBI...they want to do terrible scientific experiments on my brain!"

"Then we'd best get you to the hospital where you'll be safe." Jesus, she thought to herself...this had been one hell of a day.

***

Mark finished up his books in his small office, thrilled that his finances were finally reflecting the wild success of the Bleu Goose. Although his bank account would take a hit from his week-long hiatus at the hotel, he would more than make up for it now that he was no longer footing Lilah's numerous expenses.

With that in mind, he made his way through the restaurant, stopping to schmooze with the patrons he recognized, and taking some time to greet those he didn't. He put out a couple of fires behind the bar and in the kitchen, then headed to the hotel to gather his things.

It wasn't a luxurious room – he hadn't wanted to splurge on this temporary self-imposed move, and had taken the least expensive accommodations he could find. He'd used the space to sleep and shower, and otherwise spent all of his time at the restaurant.

He'd considered asking his parents if he could stay with them at the family farm less than an hour away, but didn't want to hear their 'I-told-you-so's' just yet. There'd be plenty of time for them to throw the failure of his marriage to "that little tramp" in his face once everything had been settled.

He quickly showered off the stink of the day, changed into fresh Dockers and a button-down denim oxford, and ran a brush through his thick blond hair. With his fair good looks and perpetually tanned skin from years on the farm, he would look more at home on a California beach than behind a bar.

He flashed the mirror a devastating grin, his dimples belying the darkness that had begun to gather within him at the thought of dealing with Lilah again.

Though he had given her the week to remove herself and her belongings from his place, he had serious doubts that she had complied. He anticipated another confrontation and possibly having to forcefully remove her from the premises. His attorney had assured him he would be within his rights to do so, but he didn't relish the act.

Maybe she would be reasonable and save him the trouble; after all, stranger things have happened. He snorted at the thought as he gathered his suitcase and travel bag and checked out of the hotel.

The perky desk clerk nearly oozed with desire as she processed his bill, her gaze lingering pointedly at his bare ring finger. "Will you be staying with us again, Mr. Donahue?" she asked, barely concealing the hope in her voice.

"Probably not...but the service has been impeccable," he said smoothly, adding a wink for her troubles. A pretty blush spread over her cheeks and he commended himself for remembering his charm. It had been a long time since he'd bothered to use it, and he'd expected it to be rusty with neglect. Instead it seemed to be the opposite, and the parting smile he offered the clerk was genuine. Bemused, she absently touched her cheek as she lifted her hand in a half-completed wave.

He sauntered to his car, whistling as he tossed his luggage in the trunk. He felt he was on the verge of a new beginning – out with the old, in with the new. He hadn't realized how much Lilah had been weighing him down, but now he felt as light as a feather and looked forward to the life ahead of him.

He found he was in no hurry to meet someone new, but when he was ready he would take it slow this time. He would make sure they had the same values, and that their marriage would be a healthy union between two adults who had no interest in hurting each other with petty games.

Maybe they would get a dog. And one day they would have children and she would be the best mother in the world. They would have a boy and a girl. The perfect little family.

He didn't see Lilah's flashy little red sports car as he rounded the parking garage, easing into an empty space near the elevators. He felt a glimmer of hope – so far so good. Hopefully she hadn't trashed the place.

His buoyant feeling was replaced with trepidation as he approached the door to his condo and found it ajar. What the hell? Swinging the door open and taking a step into the entry, he nearly tripped over his wife lying prone in the wide doorway of the living room.

Dropping his bags he knelt beside her, touching her forehead in shock. She was warm, and her eyelids fluttered at his touch. She turned her head toward him weakly, trying to open her eyes further.

"Mark..." she whispered, her throat dry and raspy.

"What happened?" he urged, looking around for signs of a struggle. She opened her hand, which had been fisted around a bottle of Xanax. He grabbed the bottle and shook it, but it was empty. Peering at the date, he noted that it had just been filled.

"Jesus!" he exclaimed, fumbling for his phone to call an ambulance.

"Mark...don't leave me..."

"I'm right here." Where was the fucking ambulance?! "Just hang on. Help is coming."

Lilah shook her head slightly. "All I need is you. Just say you won't leave me." The wail of sirens grew closer, and Mark squeezed her hand. "Promise me, Mark," her voice became insistent and he shushed her gently.

"I'm here now. That's what matters, right?"

A knock on the door and then he was barraged with questions as paramedics surrounded Lilah. He found he couldn't provide much information, and realized he really didn't know all that much about his wife. She'd never been forthcoming with him, only telling him that she'd never known her father and that her mother had worked menial jobs to take care of the two of them. She'd said the woman had died relatively young from a hemorrhagic stroke as a result of her stressful life.

After a brief assessment Lilah was loaded onto a stretcher and taken by squad to the ER, where they pumped her stomach and ran an IV to rehydrate her. She was then taken to PINA and placed on suicide watch. Mark signed her admission paperwork as her next-of-kin and was then sent home – she wouldn't be allowed visitors for the first twenty-four hours.

A list of items she wanted from home was thrust at him as he was seen out of the locked unit, and he glanced at it on the way to his car. Curling iron, make-up bag, a few of her designer fitness outfits, her satin loungewear...really?

She was in a psych ward for attempted suicide, for God's sake. Why would she need all this stuff? Granted, he'd never seen her without make-up, or dressed to kill for that matter, but shouldn't that be the least of her concerns at this point? Sighing, he rubbed his temples – he felt the beginnings of a crushing headache.

Back at the empty condo he sunk onto the couch and listened to the silence surrounding him. Instead of being comforted by it, though, it seemed ominous. He thought about Lilah and how low she must have felt to do something so drastic. And the way she'd pleaded with him not to abandon her...he should have reassured her.

She obviously regretted what she'd done to him, and now the guilt was overwhelming her, overriding the normal quest for survival common to all animals, humans notwithstanding. Maybe this would be the impetus for her to turn over a new leaf...to become a better wife. An active member of their marriage.

Mark meandered into the kitchen, pulling a beer from the fridge and tossing the twist cap into the trashcan by the counter. They would build a stronger marriage together. She would want children now, would no longer find the need to indulge in her spending sprees. They would trade in her car for a family-friendly SUV. Or even a minivan.

He took another swig of beer and pulled his wedding ring out of his pants pocket. Turning it over, he read the inscription: Forever in love. Yes, he'd made a vow to this woman, and he would not abandon her to her pain. As he turned it back over to slip onto his finger, it fell from his grasp, clattered onto the counter and rolled into the trashcan.

"Goddammit!" he exclaimed, reaching for it – but it had already made its way through the shifting garbage. Sighing loudly, he began removing discarded cans, bottles, and yogurt containers until the receptacle was nearly empty. At the bottom of the bin next to his wedding ring was a baggie containing twenty-seven Xanax.

***

Riley squinted at the window on the stick, willing the line to appear. When it did it was so faint she could barely see it. Maybe she was imagining it. She rubbed her eyes and moved into better light near the bathroom window – now it was unmistakable.

She gave an undignified whoop and threw open the door. She flew down the stairs and into the living room, where her husband was watching the news. Throwing herself onto his lap, she covered his face with kisses. He laughed, putting his arms around her and accepting her display of affection.

"We're pregnant!" she squealed, giddy.

"Finally! Let's celebrate...where to?"

"Bleu Goose!"

"Of course," he laughed again, indulgent now.

She bounded off his lap and raced back upstairs to change – the tank top and boy-cut underwear she'd been lounging in would hardly be appropriate for a night out. She giggled to herself at the thought. She was so excited she felt like she would float away, and she wrapped her arms around herself, attempting to calm down.

It seemed like it had taken forever to get pregnant, and she found herself fluctuating between disbelief and exhilaration. She rechecked the pregnancy test several times while she was getting dressed, and consequently it took her much longer than usual.

"Are we going today? Or next month?" Steve called up the stairs impatiently. She rolled her eyes at his sarcastic tone, but nothing could spoil her mood.

"Coming!" she sang as she waltzed down the stairs. She'd paired black pencil pants with a thin black sweater and red heels. The ensemble looked sophisticated with her sleek shoulder-length bob, and she'd done a smoky palette on her lids to showcase her thick dark lashes and startlingly deep blue eyes.

She looked the way the wife of a successful attorney should, and Steve winked at her in appreciation when she reached the bottom step. "Are you finally ready, Mrs. Wood?"

"Wasn't I worth the wait?"

"Always."

She entwined her arm through the one he'd offered, and he patted the hand resting in the crook of his elbow. As she often was, she was struck by how paternalistic he was toward her. She marveled to herself for the millionth time that she'd chosen a father figure to marry almost immediately after her own father had died of a heart attack. There was most likely a pathology to that, but she preferred not to dwell on it.

Steve was a good man; a provider and companion if not an equal partner – the decisions that affected the household were his alone, and brooked no argument. Everything from where they lived to where they bought their groceries was his choice, but that was fine. After all, he was the one with the analytical mind and an eye for their future. It only made sense that he be the one to plan every aspect of their lives.

In the beginning, she'd welcomed his dictates – she had been lost and he had found her. She'd been more than happy to follow his lead. Now she was used to it and didn't see the good in arguing such insignificant points. Who cared where they went on vacation as long as they were together?

She gazed out the car window at the lights of the city below them – a city that was not her own, but one that had become familiar to her over the years. She'd come here at Steve's insistence when he'd wanted to leave his law firm and strike out on his own. This was the place to do it, he'd said, and, though they weren't yet married, she'd consented.

He had arrived first, and by the time he'd sent for her he had already bought the house they lived in and hired the interior designer who'd done his offices to decorate and furnish it. It was like walking into someone else's life – even the bath towels and bed sheets were already in place from the moment she'd been shown through the door.

Steve said they had an image to uphold if he were to be taken seriously in the legal community, and though she tried to be gracious, she couldn't help feeling like a pawn in his much bigger end game. But she'd kept her mouth shut and they'd enjoyed a relatively peaceful life together.

She glanced at his profile in the dim light from the dashboard and he squeezed her hand in response. They truly had it all. His law firm had grown exponentially, and he'd added two junior partners to his roster; they had plenty of money in their 401K; and now they were going to have a baby. What more could they possibly need? Riley returned her gaze to the passing scenery, her hand rubbing her flat belly protectively.

Once they'd reached the lively joint and been seated, Steve waved away the menus and ordered for them both, asking for a sparkling water with lemon for Riley instead of her usual vodka tonic. She appreciated his display of concern, but she was a big girl. She could make appropriate decisions for her baby without his input.

She shook her head – why was she being so touchy? The pregnancy hormones couldn't be kicking in already, could they?

"Something?" he asked, noticing her gesture.

"Nothing," she said with a smile, taking a sip of water to collect herself. It wouldn't do to start searching for discontentment in her marriage now. She had someone else to think of besides herself. She would pick her battles, as always.

When she'd first told Steve of her plans to go to nursing school, as her mother and grandmother had before her, he had rebuked her. "Nursing is beneath us. Medical school is the way to go. Why settle?"

She had bristled at that – she had always admired her mother's work...had watched her get ready for her shifts at the hospital with rapt attention. "I'm going to nursing school. I can always go to medical school after that." It was a rare show of independence, and he had conceded begrudgingly.

When she'd graduated, he had refused to come. "I'll be there with bells on when you graduate from med school," he'd told her. But her mother and her aunt had come, tears in their eyes during the candle lighting ceremony and recital of the Nightingale Pledge. Riley's heart had soared when she spoke those words, and she knew she was where she was supposed to be.

To Steve's utter disgust, she would not go on to med school – would, in fact, add insult to injury by choosing the least acceptable nursing field of all.

"You got a job where?!" he'd nearly screeched.

"Psychiatric Institute of North America," she'd repeated slowly, in case he'd gone daft. "It's one of the best mental health facilities around, and –"

"Are you insane?!"

"I'd sure like to help the insane...that's kind of the point," she'd quipped.

That had been the first time he'd raised his hand to her. He hadn't hit her, but she had cringed as though he had, and things had never been the same. She no longer felt comfortable enough to tease him or even to let go and really be herself.

It wasn't the last time he'd used his power, size, or strength to intimidate her, and she'd never told another soul. She was ashamed. Embarrassed. And when she dealt with victims of domestic violence at work she felt like a hypocrite encouraging them to leave their abusive environments. But it was different when it was you.

Throughout dinner she'd been inside her own head, making appropriate comments at the right times. It was disconcerting that he couldn't tell the difference between her being present in the moment and not, but she was grateful for his ignorance this evening.

"Dessert?" he asked, and she shook her head.

Melancholy was threatening to set in as a result of the dark direction of her thoughts. She suddenly missed her family so much it hurt. Her nurturing mother; her strong, silent father; her awkward brother who had never fit in, but had the biggest heart she'd ever encountered. And the tragedy that tore them apart. Her parents had sent Abel away to college in hopes he would be accepted for who he was in a way he never could be at home. Instead he had withdrawn into himself and finally took his own life.

The entire family had been devastated, and their father had never really recovered. He'd aged decades in a few short years and succumbed to his own death as a mere shell of the man he once was. Her shattered mother had taken refuge with her sister in Florida, and Riley was left with nothing but memories of the people she'd loved most in the world.

She'd been vulnerable, empty, and directionless when she met Steve. He had been interning at an estate law firm and she had been barely out of high school. She was perfect for his plans for the future – she was moldable, had no family to get in the way, and was beautiful in a wholesome, nonthreatening way. What wasn't to love about that?

Yes, he had gotten exactly what he'd wanted thus far, Riley mused as she readied herself for bed that night; but now she had exactly what she'd wanted. Her life was complete, and nothing else mattered.

Chapter 5
The Institute

Craig awoke to a shadowed figure sneaking stealthily into his room to stand over his bed. He squeezed his eyes shut and then opened them again. Still there. A hallucination? He couldn't tell...

Suddenly a beam of light appeared out of the shadow, aimed at his chest. He assumed he was going to be shot, but just as quickly the light was extinguished and the figure withdrew, closing the door behind him. Her. It?

Craig sat up in bed and patted himself, thankful that he appeared to be intact. He peered around the room to get his bearings, but the surroundings were unfamiliar, and the only light came from under the door through which the mystical being had just exited.

This was it then: the FBI test site. They'd gotten to him after all. No...that couldn't be right – that was a delusion he'd had. Now he remembered. He was at the Institute. His angel, Eva, had brought him here. Things were going to be okay. He promptly fell back to sleep.

He dreamed of rainbows and unicorns – black ones with golden horns and manes spun with stars. It was a good dream. A happy dream. Unlike the malicious nightmares he'd been having before his hospitalization. He was not at all thrilled to be startled out of sleep by the brusque knock on his door signaling the beginning of the day.

"Vitals!" an outrageously cheerful voice called. There was nothing vital about being yanked so obtusely from such a fascinating dream, he thought, grumbling to himself.

He yanked the covers over the recently abandoned bed in a half-hearted attempt to make it. Should be good enough to pass the morning inspection, at least. Couldn't understand why he had to make his bed every morning when he'd just be sleeping in it again every night.

The staff would say it was all about discipline; learning how to go about one's day in a positive and consistent manner. They talked about ADLs, or activities of daily living, as if they were the magic formula for a successful life. Make your bed...brush your teeth...comb your hair. A broken record. Who needed it?

It was far less time consuming to simply never change out of the clothes you'd worn for the day. That way when you got out of bed in the morning you were already dressed and ready to go. He could teach these people a thing or two about energy conservation.

But that would have to wait for another time. Right now he'd better stand in line and drink the Kool-Aid so he could get out of here sooner. He could really use a beer or six.

Satisfied with the bed, he turned to gather his clothes in the white plastic hamper each patient was provided upon admission. Yet another ADL. What kind of hospital makes you do your own laundry? He snorted as a knock sounded at the door, a timid head poking into the room.

"Just doing rounds," the head murmured, its nervous voice barely audible. A new psych tech. Not the flashlight-wielding staff member from last night...change of shift would have already occurred, and the rounds board handed off to this baby. She would be responsible for noting each patient's whereabouts every fifteen minutes over the course of her shift.

A relatively easy job, especially when everyone was in the same place, like during a group session. But at other times he'd entertain himself by hiding from the rounds tech, darting about the unit to make it difficult to nail down his location.

An inexperienced staffer might panic, raising the alarm with the charge nurse. Craig Phipps is missing. He must've eloped. Send out the guard. In the meantime he would position himself in plain sight, watching with amusement while the nurse pointed directly at him. "You're saying you can't find *that* patient, Newbie McNewbster?" What a hoot! It made his whole day.

Aloud he said, "Hey, can you let me into the laundry room?" He held up his hamper and stared at the youngster expectantly.

"Uh...sure..." They really should vette these kids before hiring them. This one was obviously petrified. He followed her down the hall and into the small laundry room, staring after her as she skittered away. And *he* was the crazy one.

Next he stood in line outside the exam room to get his vital signs taken. The nurses did it every morning and every evening as a routine, but he still became nervous as his turn approached. He hated the way the blood pressure cuff tightened around his arm. It felt like a massive hand grabbing him as if it were an angry monster that didn't ever plan on letting go.

By the time he sat down next to the Dynamap, he was sweating, flushed, and panicky. His wide, wild eyes flew around the room as if searching for the target of his distress. He wanted to lash out at it to rid himself of these uncomfortable feelings.

His gaze finally settled on the nurse taking vitals this morning. He relaxed slightly when he recognized her; she'd been his nurse for the past couple of days.

"Hi, Craig; I'm Riley, remember? I'm your nurse again today," she said as she snapped open the blood pressure cuff attached to the machine.

He jumped, his eyes growing even wider as he stared at the Dynamap in terror. After a brief pause, Riley returned the cuff to the basket attached to the machine's rolling stand and pushed it into a corner of the room. From a drawer, she removed a manual blood pressure kit. "I'll tell you what. We'll do this the old-fashioned way, okay?"

Craig nodded, his stare drifting from the Dynamap now standing ferociously in the corner as if being punished to the gadgets Riley had placed on the counter. They looked benign enough: a thermometer, a stethoscope, and a blood pressure cuff that was attached to a small gauge instead of the horrendous banished machine. He glanced at it again to be sure it hadn't moved.

"I'm just going to put the cuff around your arm, and I'll even let you use this ball to pump it up for me." She handed him a small black pump that looked like a thick rubber balloon and showed him how to expand the cuff by squeezing the ball over and over again.

Once he'd inflated the cuff so that it was as tight as he could stand it, Riley took over, listening to the brachial pulse in the crook of his arm through the stethoscope while watching the gauge as she slowly released the air from the cuff. As the constriction lessened, so did his anxiety. It was all over in no time, and he left the exam room with one last look at the monster in the corner.

Time for his morning medication, and he wouldn't miss it for the world; he recognized that he was being paranoid, and had enough meds in him to acknowledge they were helping him. After his experience in the exam room, he would happily take anything they gave him if it would make the terrifying delusions go away.

When he reached the front of the line at the medication room he was glad to see the nurse had left his meds in their sealed packages. Some of the less experienced ones took them out and put them in a med cup. No way would he take them that way – who knew what they'd put in them? They might be trying to poison him for all he knew.

After he'd opened all the packages and swallowed the pills, he stuck out his tongue to let her see he hadn't cheeked any before turning to the hallway leading to the dayroom. Maybe he'd catch a show. He didn't care which; he just enjoyed the sounds – they distracted him from his cluttered mind.

He stopped short when he saw Eva at the end of the med line. She was a wreck, and for a moment all he could do was stare. Her hair hung down her back limply, her clothes hung loose around her slight frame, and when she eventually met his gaze her eyes held a vacancy that was unsettling.

"What are you doing here?" he blurted, unaware of the many social norms he might be breaking.

"Same as you," she muttered, shuffling forward in the line. Even her voice sounded defeated. Beaten. Surrendered.

What had happened to her in such a short time that had ruined her so completely? His blood began to boil as he thought of the suffering his sweet savior must have experienced at the hands of some lunatic. His face reddened, his fists clenched. Whoever it was, he would make them pay.

***

"Five minutes," the tech announced to the room in general, glancing at her watch and then returning to her magazine. Lilah glared at her as she calculated how much longer it would take her to get ready for the day.

It was beyond ridiculous that she only had access to her makeup bag and flat iron for half an hour each morning. She couldn't even hope to complete her extensive beauty ritual in that amount of time.

"Can't I just have a little more time?" she pleaded.

"Them's the rules," the tech replied, not even bothering to look up from her magazine this time.

"Bitch," Lilah muttered, but was staunchly ignored. Sighing, she focused on finishing her makeup – she'd just have to pile her hair on top of her head again today. She grimaced at her reflection; definitely not her best work, she thought, as she stuck her tongue out at the offending mirror. In her periphery she saw the tech grin. Tedious curmudgeon.

It was bad enough that she didn't have free access to her things; she had to be watched at all times when she did. Just yesterday she'd had to beg for her razor to shave her legs and pits, only to discover that staff had to be within arm's distance until she'd relinquished the sharp object. How blatantly inhumane was that?

As much as she hated it here, she wouldn't be allowed to leave until she'd convinced the doctor that she was no longer suicidal. She was sure that old hag was keeping her here to teach her a lesson – how many more million times did she have to say she could contract for safety before she could go home?

"That's it. Grooming time's over." The tech stood, jangling her keys impatiently. Lilah gave herself a final once over, admiring her perky, all-natural boobs and tiny waist in the tight t-shirt and faded jeans she'd chosen for the day. Not bad, considering the hostile conditions.

"Group!" yelled a disembodied voice from across the lounge. God – how boring. But her room was locked and the TV and phones were turned off during 'programming', so unless she wanted to sit around staring at nothing, not to mention be reported to her doctor, she had no choice but to attend.

As she entered the group room, the therapist was handing out paper and colored pencils. Oh goodie. Coloring time. She released a long suffering sigh.

"Today we're going to do something a little different. I want you to draw a picture consisting of the following things: a house, a tree, flowers, a path, the sun, water, and a snake. You can include anything else you want in the picture – after all, it's yours. But you have to include at least the things I mentioned."

He had to repeat his instructions several times before the entire group seemed to be on the right track, and then everything was silent except for the scratching of pencils on paper.

After thirty minutes he asked them to put down their pencils and turn their attention to the white board on which he'd drawn his own picture.

"Before we continue let me assure you there is no right or wrong way to draw the elements I asked for. These things are thought to be unconscious components of the mind."

Lilah looked around the room and saw that each picture was as different from the others as the patients themselves. Well, she wasn't crazy like them, so of course hers would reflect that. But then again, hers didn't look anything like the one on the board either.

"First, I want you to examine your house. What's its size in relation to everything else? Does it have doors and windows? Are they open or closed?"

Lilah glanced at the house she'd drawn. It took up much of the page, but she'd forgotten to add windows or a door. What did that mean?

"The house represents you. How important are you to your own life? Big house, very important. Small house, not so much." That's right. I'm the shit. "Are your windows open? You're loving and accepting. No doors? Closed off and inaccessible to others." Huh.

"How about the sun?" Where did I put that th– oh, there it is. Way over there. Behind the hill.

"That's your father." Out of sight. Figures.

"The tree is your mother." Sickly. Dying. Crouching in the shadow of the enormous house. That was about right.

"The snake represents sexuality. Is it a big or small part of your life? Is it creeping through the grass like a thief in the night? If so, you may need to work on your sexual identity."

Lilah glanced at her snake and nearly laughed. The large cobra was coiled and ready to strike – and she had drawn the reptile *inside* the house. No issues there, she thought, smirking.

"How about the water element? Did you draw a stream meandering alongside your house? A waterfall? A pond? An ocean surrounding your house on its own island? The water represents your emotions. How integrated are they? How isolated?"

Lilah examined her picture, realizing she'd accidentally left out the water. Where would she have put it had she remembered? She couldn't tell – there wasn't really room for water. Oh well, not important.

Shrugging, she moved on to the next element before he did. Please tell me I drew a path...yep, there it is. Going from the top of the hill to somewhere outside of the picture, on the opposite side of the page as her house. Obviously she wasn't some antisocial freak.

"The path represents your relationship with other people. Does your path lead to your house? You welcome friendships. Does it avoid your house? You may not be the friendly sort." Fuck you, buddy. I'm friendly as hell. Just ask all my friends.

"Finally, we have the flowers. Did you draw many?" No, I drew one big beautiful aromatic doozy of a flower, you asswipe.

"A picture with many flowers of all shapes and sizes means you value diverse friendships from multiple sources. Did you include just a couple of flowers? You have a few close friends with whom you share everything. If you left off the flowers altogether – and no, that's not a symbol of manliness," he paused, drawing a chuckle from the group, "you may be an introvert, preferring to spend time with a good book than a bunch of noisy friends."

Another chuckle. Working the crowd. Ain't he slick?

"What if I drew just one flower?" asked a petulant voice from the back of the room.

"Well, one big flower would be indicative of feeling above the need for friends. That flower represents you, devoid of any friendships, including with yourself." He raised a warning hand as the voice began a loud grumbling at his response. "Please remember this exercise isn't about judgment..." Oh yeah? What's it about then? "...it's about exploring your psyche and perhaps starting a conversation about things you may need to change to be more successful in your recovery."

Lilah rolled her eyes – she had no intention of conversing with anybody about this bullshit analysis. Draw a picture of a house, my ass. Stupid group. Were these people actually paid to do this worthless crap all day?

So what if she didn't have friends. It wasn't like she hadn't tried. Other women were too jealous of her to befriend her, and the only thing men wanted from her was sex. She hadn't asked to be born with a perfect body and a face to match.

And it wasn't always a good thing, either. She'd had to ward off her fair share of unwanted advances. More than her share...she was sure the average woman didn't attract attention like she did. Hell, most of the time she didn't even dress that provocatively. She was just that irresistible – she could barely refrain from staring at her own reflection excessively; how could she expect others to do so?

No, her lot in life was not without its own set of hurdles, and she found it incredibly unfair that her sensibilities were being trampled on for the sake of some silly art project. As group ended she felt like stomping her foot and slamming a door, but knew that would get her nowhere in her bid to leave this place.

Instead, she went off in search of the owner of the other single flower. She'd show these bastards who could win friends and influence people.

***

This is Eliza, giving shift report for the 7pm to 7am shift for Unit A. I was charge tonight, and we currently have twenty-eight patients. We are closed to admissions and transfers as we are full.

Reporting on my assigned patients: Marin Jonas is a thirty-eight-year-old female admitted for catatonia secondary to psychosis. She is a previous long-term substance abuser related to childhood trauma. She was placed on Abilify in addition to her Seroquel and Depakote, which has been effective in relieving her catatonic state. She is now attending to her own ADLs, but continues to need prompting to take her medication. Her discharge plan is to remain on the acute inpatient unit for medication management until she clears further. She was admitted under emergency police custody, but has now signed in voluntarily. She was a long time patient of Dr. Underwood, but switched to Dr. Hobson when he retired. Eva Jonas, one of our on-call therapists, is listed as her next-of-kin.

William Bellows, who goes by 'Bill', is a twenty-eight-year-old male newly admitted following a suicide attempt: he hung himself from a pipe in the basement of his apartment building, and was apparently knocked unconscious when the pipe broke and he fell to the floor. A maintenance worker found him after hearing the commotion, and he was taken to the ER and placed on twenty-four hour observation for a moderate concussion before being released to us. He signed in voluntarily under Dr. Epstein's service, and seems to like being here. Be careful of your interactions with him; he has a diagnosis of borderline personality disorder and can be quite gamey. He was fired by his therapist and has refused to follow-up with anyone else, so he does have a social work consult that needs to happen before he leaves. He denies having any next-of-kin for the record.

Craig Phipps is a thirty-five-year-old male admitted under Dr. Tacee's service for acute psychosis as a result of his paranoid schizophrenia. Craig is here often due to medication noncompliance. He drinks alcohol and uses street drugs occasionally, though he maintains contact with his AA sponsor, Gabe Sampson. He's now back on his monthly Invega injection and q 4 hour Ativan, and seems to be clearing well. Eva Jonas is also his outpatient therapist, and hopes to set up a family meeting with his parents before discharge. His affect is typically flat and he is anhedonic, although he seems

*pretty taken with Marin Jonas, so we'll need to watch their
interactions closely. Craig's legal next-of-kin are his parents.*

*Last but not least by ANY stretch of the imagination is Lilah
Donahue, twenty-seven-year-old female admitted for an alleged
suicide attempt. She supposedly took a full bottle of Xanax to stop
her husband from leaving her, but he later found the pills hidden in
the trash. He's since terminated his spousal obligation and filed for
legal separation, and she has no other relatives. She's anxious to
leave because she's sure she can fix things with her husband, Mark,
who owns the Bleu Goose down the street. She refuses to sign herself
in, so she remains on a Board of Mental Health hold filed by the
hospital psychiatrist. She continuously insists she is no longer
suicidal, but hasn't even begun to be willing to address the
underlying issues that brought her here, so she probably won't be
allowed to leave anytime soon. Good luck with this one – she has
been nothing but triangulating and manipulative with staff and
overtly provocative with a couple of the other patients. Last night
her little entourage stayed up making popcorn and watching movies
out in the lounge until I sent them to their rooms for being too loud
and disruptive. Now I'm the bad guy. You're welcome!*

That concludes my report...have a great shift!

Riley pushed the button to disconnect the automated
recording system and looked around the room. She was charge
today, and was determined to make things as smooth as possible.
She was off for the next several days and was eager for a disaster-
free last day.

Sitting around the table in the report room were the rest of
the staff assigned to the unit for the shift; five other nurses, three
psych techs, and one sitter who was assigned to Thea, a suicidal
patient who couldn't contract for safety and was actively self-
harming.

The sitter would stay within arm's length of Thea at all times
to keep her from doing anything to hurt herself – an exhausting job
that needed to be rotated to prevent burnout. Riley smiled at her and
offered a thumbs-up. The girl laughed; she knew she was in for a

grueling day, but she was a trooper who rarely complained. God love her.

Riley glanced at the techs, all of them seasoned and reliable. Tony Rankin, the most dependable by far, flashed his signature lopsided grin and she nearly swooned.

He was all man with his arrogant nose, warm brown eyes, and sensual lips surrounded by a rakish goatee. Six-foot-two-inches of olive skin, toned muscle, and a haphazard wave of black hair that often found its way over his eye. She really should just reach up and – whoa girl, what are you thinking?! She gave herself a mental shake to refocus on her job as opposed to her handsome tech.

She took a moment to consider if there were any potential problems with staffing, determining that there was only one loose cannon she might have to deal with as she looked across the table at the nurse in question. She could be a snarky bitch and Riley prayed for patience, or maybe for a hex to appear and render the woman mute for the day. Riley smiled sweetly at her and received a blank stare for her trouble. Just great. What's up your ass today, sunshine?

Aloud she embarked on her standard pep talk, adjourned report, and opened the door to allow everyone to file from the room. As Tony passed her he winked playfully and she swatted his arm with her report sheet. He was too alluring for his own good. Or at least for hers.

Thankfully the morning passed quickly, and she glanced around the quiet unit appreciatively as she sat down with Lilah for their one-to-one. She glanced at the mood scale Lilah had filled out before breakfast and wasn't surprised she'd rated everything a zero on a scale of zero to five – zero signified no symptoms and five represented the most severe. She obviously wasn't about to admit to her feelings.

"Wow, so no anger, no depression, no anxiety, no suicidal or homicidal thoughts," Riley prodded anyway, unable to help herself in spite of the uselessness of the attempt.

"Nope! Everything's great!" Lilah chirped, her wide smile never quite making its way to her eyes. She really was outlandishly gorgeous, Riley realized as she stared at the younger woman, trying to get a bead on something real within her.

"So even though your marriage is over –"

"My marriage is fine. Mark just needs time to come to his senses," she argued with such conviction that Riley had no choice but to believe her.

"And if something else goes wrong? Another fight? Another separation?"

Lilah shrugged noncommittally, her arms crossed over her chest. "We always work it out. He can't live without me."

Riley had to bite her tongue to imprison her snide laugh. Lilah was the one in the hospital on suicide watch and Mark's the one who couldn't live without her? She must be delusional.

"Be that as it may, it's not healthy to be so dependent on another person that their absence would cause you to take your own life – even if it's your spouse."

"I didn't t–" she slipped, biting her lip. She had never admitted that she'd faked her suicide attempt, even when shown the baggie Mark had found. Riley was quick to address it.

"Threatening suicide to keep someone from leaving you is codependent, Lilah. It's a form of addiction, and we need to work hard to get it under control or you'll never be happy inside yourself. Is that the life you want to live?"

"What is it with you people? You think your life is so much better than mine? You're sadly mistaken. No one in their right mind would trade being me for being any of you." Her lip curled in derision.

Riley refused to take offense. Lilah was sick, and her job was to help her. "That's not the point..."

"I'm done here," she interrupted as she jumped from her chair and stormed off to find Bill, probably for moral support in the face of such heinous accusations.

Returning to the nurse's station, Riley began charting their conversation, using words like 'histrionic' and 'narcissistic' as opposed to 'raging lunatic' and 'conceited bitch'. Keeping it professional.

Her fingers itched to type a subjective soliloquy on the insufferable diva. But she reminded herself, as she so often did in these situations: What Would Nightingale Do? Riley heaved a sigh and continued with her tempered documentation of the abbreviated interview.

She glanced at the nurse sitting next to her at the desk overlooking the lounge – her problem child – and saw her eyes narrow on Lilah as she approached them. Riley looked to Lilah expectantly – maybe she had something to add to their conversation.

"I'm going to need my razor so I can shave my legs sometime today," she demanded haughtily.

Though she was addressing Riley, it was Miss Pissy Pants who answered her. "Why? So you can wrap your smooth legs around someone else's husband?"

Lilah's mouth opened and closed like a fish out of water, while Riley spun around in shock. "Tiffany!"

The nurse didn't acknowledge Riley at all, but continued to glare at Lilah. At a loss for once, Lilah burst into tears, and Riley signaled to Tony to intervene.

She finally turned to Tiffany after he'd guided Lilah away from the desk. "You need to come with me," she demanded, leading the other woman to the empty physician's dictating room behind the nurse's station and closing the door. "What was that about?" she asked, struggling to modulate her tone. She felt like shouting.

"That slut fucked my husband!" Tiffany had no such qualms, her voice shooting from her tense body like a bullet.

"How do you know that?"

"Mark told me. And when I heard report this morning, I put two and two together." No wonder she'd been grouchier than usual during report.

"Then you should've asked to be reassigned to a different unit."

"How's that fair to me? I have to work with old people who stink or kids on a unit I'm not familiar with because of that bitch? Hasn't she screwed me over enough already?"

Riley didn't know what to say. She'd made a valid point, but they were nurses – it wasn't about them as individuals. It was about the patients, and the team.

"I'm sorry, Tiffany. I really am. But you can't be here as long as she's with us. You decide which unit you'd prefer, and then send me your replacement. If you have a problem with that you're going to have to take it up with the DON." Riley touched her arm and then left the room.

Tiffany slammed out of the unit – she was pissed at Riley, but understood her decision. Lilah, on the other hand, she could kill with her bare hands. It wasn't just that the whore had been intimate with her man – as much as she hated Dennis, she could care less about that part. They barely even spoke anymore and their marriage had degraded to a level beyond irreconcilable. But it infuriated her that she'd been made a fool of.

Nevertheless, with two young children, a mountain of student loan debt, and no close family, she felt she had no choice but to remain captive in her crappy marriage. It was now undeniable that they had reached a stalemate and were intent on making each other as miserable as humanly possible.

Chapter 6
Changes

"Where's the damn Ambley file?" Steve barked at his harried legal assistant, who scrambled away to find it. "Idiot," he muttered under his breath as he ticked through his extensive to-do list in his head.

The Ambley case was a doozy with a lot of family money – old money – on the line. He represented the husband, who was trying to keep the family fortune away from his soon-to-be ex-wife, who was just as determined to get it.

He would win, of course – he always did – but not without a lot of sleepless nights for everyone involved. That's the way of nasty divorces, and he was the best divorce lawyer in town.

But he had no intention of doing this forever. Once he gained enough support and positive momentum he would propel himself into the world of politics, first vying for a seat in the senate, and after that the presidency.

He was no slouch; he'd graduated at the top of his class, hailed from a prestigious family of trial attorneys, and boasted all-American good looks reminiscent of JFK. All of that, combined with his pretty working-class wife and a couple of well-behaved children, would make him a shoo-in. Just a few more years with his nose to the grindstone and he'd be ready to enter the stratosphere.

Sure, there'd been bumps in the road when Riley had insisted on going to nursing school and then confided in him the family secret of her brother's suicide. But after taking some time to process the situation, he'd decided it could work to his benefit.

The sympathy vote could be substantial, and he would be more relatable to other working stiffs. And who didn't love nurses? Nobody, that's who. In fact, he had so fully come to accept his wife's career decision that he often forgot it was not he who had orchestrated it.

The only downside was that she'd chosen to be a psychiatric nurse. There was such a stigma attached to mental health in the lay community, and certainly in politics, that any advantage her career added to his cause would be negated by the type of nurse she was.

He had plenty of time to fix this problem, though. He would demand that she transfer to one of the big trauma hospitals in town – maybe to the ICU, or the ER, or even surgery. Then she'd be a real nurse, saving lives every day. Real lives. Worthy lives. Lives of his constituents.

He locked his hands behind his head and leaned back in his chair, swiveling toward the windows that lined two walls of his huge corner office. He gazed at the cloudless sky and indulged in a daydream about his lofty future.

His other obstacle – having children; a must for anyone with political aspirations – had finally been overcome now that Riley was pregnant. They were going shopping for the nursery after work, and though he'd wanted to hire the same designer who did the house to decorate the nursery, Riley's excitement over doing it herself had become infectious.

The only issue left was her increasing propensity to oppose his decisions. While he had granted her wish to see to the nursery on her own, it hadn't escaped him that she had blatantly argued with him about it until he had given in. It was a bad precedent to set, and he would need to squelch her growing independence before it became a problem.

He wasn't accustomed to people not jumping to do his bidding. His parents were prominent citizens of the town where he grew up, and he'd been the most popular kid in school, commanding the respect of the other students and teachers alike.

He was the jock with the cheerleader girlfriend, restored vintage muscle car, and access to all the things money could buy. There was never a question that he would attend an Ivy League school and become a lawyer. The only decisions were which one and what kind.

Life was his for the taking, and when he left work that afternoon he was in high spirits. He let the top down on his Mercedes, relaxing into its rich leather surroundings and enjoying the light breeze through his hair. It was an unseasonably warm day, and he felt nothing could dampen his mood as the luxury car glided smoothly over the road.

He whistled a jaunty tune and smiled at his distinguished visage in the rearview mirror. It was the kind of day made for people like him – modern day cowboys who wrangled their chattel into order; disciplined and well-heeled...requiring little effort to maintain.

He loosened his tie and adjusted his shades as he pulled into the driveway of his impressive home. The beautiful manor sat on a lush lawn in a tree-lined neighborhood known for its gentrified residents – young corporate America, at your service.

All classic red brick and white trim with black shutters and matching window boxes filled with seasonal greenery – the epitome of sophistication with a touch of humility. He looked up and down the street with pride. Yes, life was good. At least it was until he entered the bedroom that had been designated as the nursery.

"Hi, honey!" Riley called from the top of the ladder on the opposite side of the room. Roller in hand, she was finishing the last wall with the most atrocious color Steve had ever seen – a brilliant Easter egg yellow in a house dominated by muted golds and burgundies; a house that was understated and elegant. What was she thinking?

"We'll do white furniture with accents in green and yellow so that it works for either a boy or a girl." She attacked the wall with vigor, covering the sophisticated beige with an irate yellow 'W' that was so hostile to his senses he had to turn away.

He was suddenly quite grateful that she hadn't been involved in the color scheme for the rest of the house – he shuddered to think of the poor choices she would have made if she had. She was lucky he'd found her, and had curtailed her waywardness. Well most of it, anyway, he thought, as his glance returned to the obnoxious room.

That evening they meandered through the furniture store, she holding his hand and swinging it between them playfully. He noticed she frequently touched her stomach with her palm, as if not wanting to miss the moment it lost its concave shape.

She pointed out many modern furniture sets, all sleek white plastic. He shook his head emphatically. She could have her yellow room and white furniture, but he insisted on a traditional style at the very least.

He stopped at a display with a heavy sleigh crib and matching dresser with changing table. He asked a nearby salesperson if the set came in white, and was rewarded with a nod. It was obvious Riley didn't love it, but she was happy he'd found something they could both live with.

That night they grilled steak on the flagstone patio in the backyard, enjoying it with a green salad, baked potatoes and warm French bread. After the filling meal Steve relaxed with a beer after bringing Riley a club soda with lime. He could sense her hesitation as he handed her the glass and knew she would have preferred to join him in a beer, but this was not in the baby's best interest.

Being the responsible adult in the relationship meant he had to make the best decisions for all of them, just like his father did for his family, and his grandfather before him, and his great-grandfather before that. It was their lot as men.

Women needed to be taken care of, and directed, and corrected if they ventured down the wrong path. They were incapable of independence – just look at all the prostitutes and druggies out there who tried to live without a man, whether their father or their husband.

Even the divorcees who hired him were not above scorn. He would certainly take their money, but his personal belief was that they were shirking their duties in their marriage and had become arrogant enough to believe they could live productive lives without a man. They would discover sooner or later that they were sadly mistaken, he had no doubt.

After they'd finished their beverages Steve led his wife to the bedroom to partake in their usual standard run-of-the-mill sex. He did not appreciate wacky hijinks in bed, or anywhere else for that matter.

Riley had tried to 'mix it up' a little a couple of times in the early days, but he had made it clear that this was not acceptable. Missionary relations and the occasional blowjob, thank you very much. He drew the line at cunninglingus and felt dirty even talking about anal sex. He knew lots of guys enjoyed such endeavors, but not him. He was not a pervert.

After he had made love to Riley she turned on her side and spooned into him. He relished the feel of her flat, firm belly and knew it wouldn't be long before they would have to curb this closeness. He wasn't about to screw a fat cow.

***

"Okay, time's up, ladies." The tech stood, preparing to lock up the grooming room. Lilah took a last glance in the mirror, impressed with how quickly she'd done her hair and makeup this morning.

Today she'd been determined to wear her hair down, and it fell in heavy waves over her shoulders and down her back. Not that she had skimped on her face – her makeup application was just as precise as usual, and she was rewarded with the vision of perfection that stared back at her.

This was a special day – she would see Tony again. She hadn't seen him since he'd been so warm and charming to her after that horrendous nurse had been so mean. Thankfully, she hadn't seen her again either. She should've insisted she be fired.

But her distress had been overshadowed by Tony, who'd taken her to a sitting alcove off the main lounge and apologized for the nurse's behavior. He'd said something about 'professionalism' and 'reprimanded' but by then she wasn't listening. She'd been mesmerized by his closeness.

He'd been leaning forward so that he could speak to her quietly, their knees almost touching, his breath lightly fanning her face. He'd smelled clean and masculine and woodsy, a touch of peppermint drifting through the air when he spoke. She'd had the urge to slide to the edge of her chair and press her lips against his to see if they really were as soft and full as they appeared.

But before she'd had the chance to act on the desire he patted her shoulder and stood up. Apparently he'd ended the conversation without her awareness, and she felt bereft without his heat so near. She stood too, barely reaching his broad shoulders. He grinned and turned to walk away, leaving her staring after him and daydreaming of running her hands over the taut muscles evident under the thin material of his cream sweater.

Several times throughout the day he had approached her to ask how she was doing, his gaze delving into hers intently, as if looking into her soul. Then he'd smile, his beautiful lips baring his straight, white teeth and sending shivers down her spine. She could just imagine what those teeth could do to her, which led her to imagine what her teeth could do to him, and she'd been thinking about him nonstop ever since.

Now she couldn't wait to see him again, and looked around eagerly when she arrived at the lounge. She'd asked a tech from the previous shift if he was scheduled for the day and had been assured he was, so she was beyond disappointed when she didn't see him.

It wasn't like she wanted to start a lasting relationship with him; he was just a psych tech. He couldn't possibly provide her with the type of lifestyle she'd grown accustomed to. But a dalliance was certainly in order, and she couldn't recall ever having been so attracted to someone. Men were a means to an end for her, and she was sure the end with Tony would be extremely pleasurable for both of them.

There he was! Her breath quickened and her heart started beating erratically as she watched him leaning against the counter of the nurse's station while his patient put her empty breakfast tray in the food cart. Her heart stuttered to a stop as she realized he must be a sitter today.

Dejected, she picked at her own breakfast, her effusive mood dwindling by the minute. He wouldn't be accessible to her if he was shackled to another patient. This was not what she wanted at all.

As his gaze roamed around the lounge, his eyes arrived to hers, his eyebrows shooting upward in appreciation. She smiled at him, tossing her hair over her shoulder flirtatiously. Realizing he was staring, he looked away quickly, but she'd seen all she needed to. He was not immune to her, and she planned to use that knowledge to her advantage, regardless of his responsibilities today.

She pretended to pace around the unit, like many of the patients did, making it a point to meander past him every time she entered his patient's hallway. Each time she would pause next to him and make a witty comment or touch his shoulder briefly. They were subtle maneuvers to remind him of her presence, and they seemed to be working.

The last couple of times she'd passed him he'd begun the conversation, saying something about getting exercise and then mentioning that there was a treadmill she could use next to the lounge. He was obviously quite attentive to her, and she was emboldened to ask if he had a girlfriend during her next pass.

"Uh, no..." he'd replied, as if taken off guard.

She wondered if he was playing with her or if he really was so dense that he didn't know she was coming on to him. It probably didn't take much intelligence to do his job, but he didn't come across as stupid by any means. Maybe she just needed to be more obvious. Some men liked that kind of thing.

The next time she passed by he seemed intent on something in his patient's room – the woman was gathering her laundry and placing it in a basket under his watchful eye. Lilah quickly found another tech to unlock her room so she could do her laundry as well. She yanked the clothes she'd just washed the previous day from the drawer to fill her own basket – more work for her, but she'd be damned if she'd let this opportunity slip away.

She approached the laundry room just as Tony unlocked the door. "Isabelle's got dibs," he told her as he held the door open for his patient.

"That's cool. Can I just put my basket in there so I don't have to haul it back to my room?" she batted her lashes at him when he hesitated.

Finally he grinned at her. "Sure."

She brushed past him, inhaling deeply. What a guy. While Isabelle was busy with the washing machine, Lilah turned and pressed against Tony, molding her body to his. She'd snaked her arms around his waist before he'd regained his senses and firmly set her away from him. He stepped into the hall, still holding the door open.

"You need to leave this room," he said through gritted teeth, the usual twinkle in his eyes replaced by something far less playful.

Lilah was astonished. "But I thought –"

"Now." She jerked as if slapped, though he hadn't lifted a finger or even raised his voice. She stomped away furiously, not stopping until she'd reached the alcove the two of them had so recently inhabited. Fucking asshole! How dare he treat her like that! Like he could ever hope to have the attentions of a woman like her.

She remained ensconced in the little area, glaring at patients who dared come in to use it, until it was time for lunch. Eventually she calmed down and forced herself to think rationally about the situation. Maybe she had simply taken him by surprise and he hadn't reacted like he normally would. After all, he couldn't have expected that someone so obviously out of his league would be interested in him. Or maybe he was just used to making the first move.

Either way, now that he knew she was available he'd have no qualms accepting her advances. Even though it had been awkward to be sure, her actions were probably just the impetus their fledgling interactions needed to progress. In fact, he'd probably been looking for her to apologize for his reaction and beg her to resume their flirtations.

Bolstered by her pep talk, she ran her fingers through her hair to tousle it becomingly and headed for the hallway that housed his patient's room. She was surprised to see another tech there and asked for Tony's whereabouts. He shrugged and directed her to the nurse's station.

How odd, she thought – maybe he'd gone to lunch. Not so, she was advised by the charge nurse. He had requested to be transferred to a different unit for the duration of her hospitalization.

Game over, Lilah – you lost your King.

***

"Good morning, one and all, and welcome to this open meeting of the PINA group of Alcoholics Anonymous. My name is Gabe, and I'm an alcoholic. We'll open the meeting with a moment of silence to do with as you wish, followed by the Serenity Prayer."

Hushed stillness, spanning time and space.

"God, grant me the serenity to accept the things I cannot change, courage to change the things I can, and wisdom to know the difference.

The AA Preamble is as follows: Alcoholics Anonymous is a fellowship of men and women who share their experience, strength and hope with each other that they may solve their common problem and help others to recover from alcoholism. The only requirement is a desire to stop drinking.

Who would like to read the AA Twelve Steps to Recovery?"

"Craig, alcoholic."

"Hi, Craig."

"From the Big Book: We admitted we were powerless over alcohol, and that our lives had become unmanageable. We came to believe that a Power greater than ourselves could restore us to sanity. We made a decision to turn our will and our lives over to the care of God as we understood Him.

We made a searching and fearless inventory of ourselves. We admitted to God, to ourselves, and to another human being the exact nature of our wrongs. We were entirely ready to have God remove these defects of character. We humbly asked Him to remove our shortcomings. We made a list of all persons we had harmed, and became willing to make amends to them all. We made direct amends to such people wherever possible, except when to do so would injure them or others.

We continued to take personal inventory and when we were wrong promptly admitted it. We sought through prayer and meditation to improve our conscious contact with God as we understood Him, praying only for knowledge of His will for us and the power to carry that out. And having had a spiritual awakening as the result of these steps, we tried to carry this message to alcoholics, and to practice these principles in all our affairs."

"Thank you, Craig. Does anyone have anything they want to share?"

"Hi, I'm Don. I'm an alcoholic."

"Hi, Don."

"Before I came to the Institute I got drunk and gambled away my family's emergency fund. Now my wife is divorcing me, my teenagers won't talk to me, and I've hit rock bottom. I don't know how I'm ever gonna dig myself out of this hole."

"Thank you for sharing your story, Don. I know life seems hopeless right now, but you have to remember it's not in your hands. It's in God's hands, and He is capable of enacting miraculous changes in your life if you let Him. Drinking got you into this situation; it won't get you out of it."

"So where do I start?"

"First things first: maintain your sobriety after you leave the hospital by attending twelve meetings in twelve days, stay in contact with your sponsor, and HALT yourself from becoming too hungry, too angry, too lonely, or too tired. These are friends of the drink, and enemies to our sobriety." There were many murmurs of agreement. "Does anyone else have something to share?"

A timid voice spoke up. "My name's Reggie. I'm an alcoholic."

"Hi, Reggie."

"I'll have twelve years of sobriety next month." Clapping. Murmurs of approval. "I used to drink because my voices told me to. I learned that alcohol muted them, but they came back worse than before when I wasn't drinking.

I was finally put on meds that worked for me, but the voices still come back sometimes, and that's when the cravings are the worst. When that happens I call my sponsor, even if it's three in the morning. I double up on my meetings. And I remind myself that one drink is too much and a thousand's not enough. It's on my fridge at home in case I forget.

You just have to get through one day at a time. Not one week, one month, or twelve years. Just one day."

"Thank you for sharing your story, Reggie, and for those powerful suggestions. Would anyone else like to share with the group?"

"Hi, Gabe," called a voice from the back. He nodded in acknowledgement and gestured for her to continue. "I'm Marin. Alcoholic and meth addict."

"Hi, Marin."

"I haven't used in almost twenty years. My mind can't keep track of exactly how long," she raised a frail hand to her temple as if for emphasis, though it was an absent gesture. Gabe nodded to her in encouragement, while a smattering of applause filled the group room.

It was obvious the others didn't quite know how to react to her disclosure – what addict didn't know the exact date...the exact moment...of her sobriety? It was the most important day in their lives, even more so than their weddings and job promotions, the birth of their children and deaths of their loved ones. Wasn't it? But they didn't know Marin's decrepit and wondrous mind. Not like Gabe did.

"It's okay, Marin. Go on," he reassured her.

"Back then, I was just a kid. And those bad things used me just as much as I used them. I could escape inside a bottle and it would take me over. I wasn't me anymore. And that was a really good thing. The meth. The alcohol. They were my friends. I loved them more than anything else in the whole entire world. And even now, after all this time, I still miss their friendship so much it hurts inside."

This time the applause was deafening. Every single person in the room could relate. Her pain was theirs, and they were united in their suffering. Gabe caught her gaze and held it, nodding approvingly. He had never seen her so insightful, and he was proud – but also inexorably sad for reasons he couldn't decipher.

"Thank you for sharing your story, Marin. Would you do us the honor of leading us in the Lord's Prayer?" Nodding, she stood, her quiet voice growing louder and stronger until it was nearly indistinguishable from her sister's.

"Our Father, who art in Heaven, hallowed be Thy name, in Kingdom come, Thy will be done on Earth as it is in Heaven. Give us this day our daily bread, and forgive us our trespasses; as we forgive those who trespass against us. Lead us not into temptation, but deliver us from evil. For Thine is the Kingdom, and the Power, and the Glory forever and ever. Amen."

"Amen."

Affected far more than he could understand, Gabe's head remained bowed after he'd adjourned the meeting. After the last patient had filed out of the room he wiped the tears from his eyes and took several deep breaths. "Lord, help us all," he muttered as he gathered his things and locked the door behind him.

He tried to shake off his feelings of gloom as he drove away from the Institute, but they had taken hold like an adventitious weed in a flower garden that threatened the beauty all around it with its methodically creeping tentacles shooting sprouts of poison in every direction, stealing nutrients from the soil that supported it and choking off life indiscriminately.

He had to pull himself out of this funk. It was a trigger for him, and he wasn't about to ruin fifteen years of sobriety over an unsettling day. He wondered if he was getting too old for this, though at forty he wasn't exactly elderly. He had few wrinkles, a trim waist, and a strong heart.

But maybe the constant emotional roller coaster of his sponsorships and speaking circuit was getting to him. Though discipleship and active involvement in the organization were cornerstones of AA, he took on much more than that, and maybe it was time to slow down. He made more than enough money from his books to maintain his lifestyle, enjoyed a rock solid marriage, and wanted to start a family eventually.

Maybe eventually had arrived. He wasn't getting any younger, and there would always be excuses to delay having kids until one day it would be too late. Life would have passed him by, and as much good as he'd done in the world, the lack of children would be one regret he would never recover from.

He parked his motorcycle in front of his townhouse and took off his helmet, running his hand through his salt-and-pepper crew cut that was still more pepper than salt. His eyes roved over the façade of his home as if seeing it for the first time. One of many attached brownstones along this well-maintained avenue, it had clean lines and well-crafted trim – he'd fallen in love with it immediately, and it had suited him well.

But as happy as he'd been here maybe it was time to move on to a house with a yard...a school across the street...a minivan in the garage. He patted the hard dome of the helmet as he secured it to his bike and smiled at it wistfully. Just maybe.

***

It didn't take Tony long to refamiliarize himself with the Child and Adolescent Inpatient Psychiatric unit – his new home for the remainder of Lilah Donahue's stay at the Institute. He'd done his time there when he'd first started at PINA three years ago, and though he was very good with the kids, he'd been happy to make the change to working with adults.

There was something extremely disconcerting about a four-year-old who'd been hospitalized for trying to burn his house down – along with everyone in it. By the end of his year-long stint there he had developed an unhealthy, morose kind of hopelessness that invaded every aspect of his life. If children could be so warped and broken, what hope was there for the rest of humanity?

Thankfully, after much time away from its pervasive effects, Tony had returned to his usual positive mindset, to the relief of those who knew him. It was distressing to see someone so bright dimming relentlessly day after day until it seemed likely his very essence would be extinguished.

But unbeknownst to most, it was not the darkest period in his life. Not by a long shot. Losing his parents stole that show.

He'd been in his first year of med school when he got the call – the one that had effectively ended his life for many years. They had both been physicians, devoting the latter part of their lives to missionary work. Travelling extensively to underdeveloped areas, they would spend months training the local population in the provision of health care; gifting their time, money, and hearts fearlessly and endlessly.

They died in a plane crash, sending Tony off the deep end. He dropped out of med school and headed blindly to Europe, nothing but a backpack for company. He mindlessly trekked through country after country, experiencing nothing but his pain and loneliness. He'd refused to cut his hair, didn't shave, and rarely bathed, successfully isolating himself as his stench and disheveled appearance thwarted any meaningful contact with those around him.

He'd lived inside his memories; the frequent family game nights where his quirky parents would make up rules as they played, the free clinic they ran for the homeless while Tony was still in school...

His allowance had been contingent on him volunteering his time at the clinic on the weekends, and he'd never told them he would've done it for free. He'd come to love the pro bono philosophy, and saw a huge need for mental health care in the homeless population. He always knew he'd be a physician, but now he had a calling of his very own...he'd become a psychiatrist.

He had continued to volunteer at the clinic during his undergraduate program, but stopped at his parents' behest once he'd started med school. They wanted him to focus on his studies instead of the problems of the real world.

He'd complied, though he could easily have done both. But he wasn't a contrary person, and truly never felt the need to rebel. He was given plenty of freedom, heaping doses of reality, and enough love to fill all the oceans on earth. He was a lucky kid, and he knew it.

It took him five years after his parents' death to slow down enough for his aunt's letter to reach him. She wanted him to come home – he'd been away long enough...it was time to reconnect with the only family he had left. He didn't return right away – her letter had provided the impetus to want to take care of himself again, but not quite enough to come back home.

He definitely reconnected with life, though. He was charismatic. He was charming. He was hot as hell. And he was alive. His parents wouldn't have wanted him to check out as thoroughly as he had. So he'd spent a great deal of time with his long lost friend Hedonism – they'd had a lot to catch up on.

Soon enough, though, he'd become bored with the bars and the women and the parties. His waters ran far too deep to be satisfied with those things for long. So he came back home, enrolled in the prerequisite courses he'd have to complete to reapply to medical school, and got a job at PINA.

He figured if he was going to be a psychiatrist, he'd better learn all he could about the real side of mental health care before med school taught him what it deemed more important. He'd also moved in with his aunt at her request – her house was more than big enough for the two of them and she claimed she was lonely without his mother.

An unlikely excuse – the sisters had barely been on speaking terms since his mother and father had married. Aunt Ollie had believed his father unworthy, and thought it far more likely that he would run through Regina's inheritance than make her a good husband. She'd been dead wrong, of course.

Luke Rankin had made Regina happy, had given her an heir to her family's fortune, and had made his own savvy investments that had eventually mirrored his wife's wealth. When they died they were quite affluent, and Tony could easily live the life of a jetsetter without working a day in his life if he were so inclined. But he wasn't, and would've given it up without batting an eye if it would bring his parents back.

Instead he was left with a demanding, dictatorial old woman twenty years his mother's senior to remember her by. Yet he couldn't leave her in that mausoleum she called a home all by herself. True, she was cynical and bitter, but she had no one, and she was all he had left of his mother. He'd leave some day, but for now the arrangement suited him fine.

"You're like, totally mackalicious." A titter erupted amongst the group of girls sitting around his table.

"Yeah. Totally!" the others chimed in, eager to be included in the conversation.

"Are you chewing gum?" he demanded of the first speaker, without reacting to her comment in any way. She reddened and swallowed it immediately. He glanced around at the rest of the patients, relieved that they suddenly found their homework more interesting than his looks, or whatever mackalicious was.

He was nearly old enough to be their father and yet they swooned as if he was a teenaged heartthrob. Another reason he'd been glad of the change to the adult unit. Adolescent females could be a raunchy lot, talking up one side and down the other before you could get a word in edgewise.

Add a pathology on top of that, and they could be the most dangerous creatures in the world. He raised an eyebrow in challenge to one girl who had refused to be kowtowed, anticipating a confrontation. Thankfully she nodded and returned to her own homework. Friend or foe he wasn't sure, but he'd keep an eye on her just in case.

Left alone again for now, Tony chided himself for his earlier reverie. This environment was too labile, too volatile, to allow your mind to wander, even for a few moments. He recalled many situations in which a lack of attentiveness proved to be detrimental.

One time a female physician had preceded a client into the exam room to complete the admission H & P, or history and physical. The patient followed, closing the locked door on the tech, who was supposed to be accompanying them for safety purposes – he'd been distracted and hadn't reacted quickly enough when he'd realized what was happening. He called a code and was able to get into the room with security's assistance, but not before the patient had nearly choked the doctor to death.

Another time a patient had been given the phone by a nurse who stood nearby for the duration of his call so she could return the receiver to the wall inside the nurse's station. She was having a conversation with a peer and didn't notice that the phone call had turned heated. Apparently the caller had hung up on the patient, infuriating him. When the nurse turned to take the handset, he struck her with it numerous times, giving her a severe concussion and broken vertebrae in her neck. After two years of rehab she was finally able to return to nursing, but would never again step foot on a psych unit.

Tony could relate; he'd had his share of patient assaults over the past couple of years. They'd ranged from the usual bites, pushes, and kicks to the more serious chokeholds and thrown objects.

He'd been flung through a glass wall by a patient who was angry he'd intervened in a grossly inappropriate conversation with one of the female techs. That one pissed him off to this day because he'd found out she had invited the attention. He didn't know which of them had been crazier.

But for the most part it was relatively easy to keep the peace on the units by managing the therapeutic milieu, or patient environment. Make sure everyone had what they needed, followed the rules, observed their boundaries, and developed a healthy respect for the process.

Maybe that's one of the reasons he was so good at being effective in this place filled with depravity and heartache; he knew, without a shadow of a doubt, that they were a team, the staff and patients. Staff made the rules, patients followed them.

It was a symbiotic relationship that relied equally on both parties to exist. If one failed, so did the other. He was determined to make sure that didn't happen. Not on his watch.

Chapter 7
Attachments

"Good morning, Craig! Your brother's coming to see you today. Isn't that exciting?" Craig stared at the elderly nurse for several moments before responding.

"My brother? Are you sure?"

"Why, yes. I spoke to him on the phone myself." Well that's odd. His brother never seemed to care about anyone but himself.

"But why?" Now it was the nurse's turn to stare. Why? What on earth did he mean, why?

Finally she blustered and sputtered some response that sounded an awful lot like, "You-should-be-happy-*someone*-cares-enough-to-visit-you,-you-ungrateful-heap-of-dog-poo." He couldn't be sure of course, but he resented her for it all the same.

His mother came to see him all the time. And Gabe had come a few times, even when he wasn't leading a meeting. Granted, some patients were surrounded by visitors every evening, but they had big families. His was small. Just his brother and his parents. He couldn't expect them to be with him all the time, could he?

Trouble was, his mother was the only one who'd ever come. His father was always too busy, she'd say. And his brother was just...well, just his brother. A selfish asshole.

Barbie would never use such language, of course – refined trophy wife that she was...but he knew that's what she was thinking.

Whenever that look of distaste flitted across her delicate, aging features, she was pretty easy to read. Poor, clueless Barbie.

His parents had insisted on being called by their names ever since the boys were old enough to dare babble 'mama' and 'dada'. His father was too distant and staid to ever be a 'dad' or 'daddy', or even 'father'. And Barbie was determined to hold on to her youth at all costs.

A bottle blonde, she looked like the elderly aunt of her namesake, complete with the artificial face. She'd had at least four plastic surgeries in the last ten years, and Craig felt like the day would come that he would no longer recognize her.

That thought scared him. She was the only one in the world who loved him for all his flaws. What would happen when he could no longer identify her as his mother? Would she still love him then? Would he still love her?

He suddenly felt like curling up under the blanket on his bed, but he couldn't get into his room. He looked around wildly, his eyes landing on a small alcove off the lounge area. It was like a mirage, and he didn't recall ever having seen it before. He staggered to one of the two chairs ensconced in the secluded space and brought his knees to his chest, folding his arms around them like a small child.

A beautiful goddess occupied the other chair, and he blinked his eyes several times in an attempt to discern if the exquisite creature was real. Maybe all of this really was a figment of his imagination, he thought to himself as she stood abruptly, glared down at him for a moment, and then charged out of the alcove angrily. He couldn't concern himself with her odd behavior, though, and he clasped his hands together to stop the violent tremors that had consumed him.

He vaguely heard the rounds tech ask him if he was okay but he was unable to answer. His brain was abuzz with various scenarios involving him being abandoned by his family. Some of them were downright petrifying – like being left alone on a plateau of rock in a sea of lava, his eyes wide and his mouth poised as if to scream.

Soon the old nurse from earlier came with a pill and cup of water. She sat in the recently abandoned chair next to his and offered him the medication.

"It's your Haldol, Craig. It'll help you feel much better." He looked into the medicine cup suspiciously and then lunged for the package, opening it deftly and popping the small pill into his mouth. "Can you tell me what's going on?" the nurse asked, but he shook his head and turned away from her, burying his head in his knees.

He heard her walk away and hoped he wasn't in trouble for not telling her about his mother. That would never do. Dr. Tacee might take away his smoking privileges. But he couldn't worry about that now. He had to get a grip on himself. His brother was coming.

Soon the thoughts stopped whirring and he was able to unfurl himself from the chair. He took several deep breaths and patted himself to ensure his body hadn't flown apart as surely as his mind had done. He was a bit surprised to find himself in one piece – he had been convinced he'd have to rummage about the unit with a paper bag (plastic ones were not allowed) picking up all the little bits of himself so that he could be put back together again.

He asked to be let into the bathroom, and spent some time gathering himself in its solitude. He splashed water on his face, jerking at the cold shock of it. His mind came fully back to itself and he uttered a trembling sigh of relief. Gotta love that Haldol.

He finally wandered back to the patient lounge, blinking at the beautiful woman from the alcove. She was real. Really real. Oh what a female. He couldn't pull his gaze from her, even when she raised her hand and flipped him off. Obviously disconcerted by his unwavering stare, she left the area, breaking the trance he'd been under.

Women like that weren't for him. He knew this on a visceral level, but it didn't stop his yearning. He amended the thought: women in general weren't for him. He wasn't worthy...had nothing to offer. Isn't that what his father and brother had warned him every time he'd told them about someone who'd caught his fancy? Damn straight it was. They'd said the pleasures of a woman were for other men. Bigger, better men. Not broken, damaged half-men, like him.

He stumbled a little as he meandered toward an empty couch in front of the TV. Gotta keep his brain straight. Couldn't think about the flame-haired devil. She'd be the death of him. Probably had already been the ruin of many a young boy, he sang softly to himself, an uncontrollable gurgle bubbling into his throat. Pill couldn't be wearing off already could it?

He changed direction when he saw Eva sitting on one of the other couches. Not Eva. Close, but no cigar. He plopped down next to her and allowed his lip to curve into a semblance of a smile. He wasn't accustomed to maintaining appropriate social interactions. Eva-not-Eva returned his smile as if she was in the same boat, and he immediately relaxed.

It was much easier to be around someone who didn't expect scintillating conversation from you. Or any communication at all, for that matter. They were both content to watch Family Feud on the TV, chuckling periodically at something they found funny that was more likely a flub or faux pas than a coordinated attempt at humor. They would fail miserably as a studio audience, in spite of the direction cards.

They glanced at each other occasionally, making a comment here and there that the other didn't understand – but that was okay; they'd become comfortable enough in each other's company that they didn't have to pretend the other made any kind of sense whatsoever. That's what friends were for, right? To accept the cuckoo in one another without judgment?

A commotion at the locked doors past the nurse's station drew Craig's attention; visiting hours had commenced. Would his brother really show? He had his doubts.

The beautiful woman with the long red hair had returned, and was watching the doors with ill-concealed anticipation. Several moments later, Eva-not-Eva moved away to greet her sister, who nodded at him discretely. He nodded back far more effusively, but stopped when he realized she'd already turned her attention back to Marin. Just a courtesy. Nothing to it.

He sat watching them for a while, awed by their identical looks that somehow differed so inexplicably. When he finally turned away he noticed that the redhead was still attuned to the entrance. He hoped whoever she was waiting for didn't let her down.

Then he heard his brother's voice, and it was quite possible he momentarily entered into a state of shock. "Big brother! So good to see you!" A thunderous clap on the back brought him out of his daze.

"You too, baby brother," Craig replied, still bewildered. "What're you doing here, Pauley?"

"Barbie sent me, of course!" Of course...of course. A horse is a horse.

***

All day Lilah waited anxiously for visiting hours so she could see Mark. All day she primped in every reflective surface she could find so she'd look her very best when he came to see her. All day she practiced what she'd say and how she'd say it so it would come out perfectly when she was sitting next to him in the cozy little alcove; the perfect spot for their reunion. All day she paced past the nurse's station in case he called for her or left her a message that he would be coming to see her after all.

And once visiting hours began she planted herself in the lounge, her eyes glued to the doors. Loved ones came and went during the two-hour time frame, and she didn't budge once, even though she really had to pee. And then the visitors were being herded off the unit and out the doors, waving goodbye until they could no longer be seen.

She continued staring at the doors, her anticipation replaced by disbelief. Visiting hours were over, and he hadn't come. Again. Really she had no reason to believe he would, but that didn't have any impact whatsoever on her conviction that he would return to her, in spite of the many signs to the contrary. But today of all days she knew...she just knew...he had to come. After all, today was their anniversary.

Slowly her disbelief turned to anger, and finally to rage. Who the fuck did that cowpoke think he was? She crossed her arms over her chest and glared at the TV, unseeing. Her countenance was so ferocious no one dared to approach her, which was probably for the best – she would likely spew venom at the first person who interrupted her thoughts.

Consumed with hatred, she flitted from one plan to the next, each one focused on bringing Mark down; ruining him. Sending him running for the hills with his tail tucked between his legs. Screaming at the top of his lungs like the little girl he was.

She narrowed her eyes as a slow smile spread across her face. She would hire the best divorce attorney in town. She would take him for everything he had. She would end up with everything and he would be left with nothing. She'd change the name of his restaurant – no, *her* restaurant – to the Bleu Cheese, just to be an asshole. She'd make him pay.

As her mind cleared of all thoughts except that one, she noticed Craig staring at her again, a weird smile parting his lips. She nearly rolled her eyes at him. What the hell did that head case want? Stupid question – he wanted what all men wanted, of course.

She started to give him the finger again, but remembered what she'd overheard from his visitor earlier. He'd looked disparagingly at Craig's laceless shoes and said, "Whatsamatter, bro? We have more money than God and you can't keep yourself in shoelaces?" Apparently he didn't know they couldn't have shoelaces here. Or drawstrings or bras or belts or ties or suspenders or cowboy boots.

Who was this goof? Clandestinely, she'd turned to view the speaker, her mouth dropping as she did. He was amazing looking, and her eyes devoured him from head to toe in mere seconds. It took her no time to identify his tailor made suit, Ferragamo necktie, and TAG Heuer watch. He wasn't kidding – not even God sported such high class gear.

At the time she'd turned back to her post near the doors to watch for Mark, but now she considered the implications. 1) She'd need a man by her side while she was going after Mark – she'd never even attempted life without one, and didn't plan on starting now. 2) She wouldn't be able to get a man while she was stuck in here at the mercy of that old biddy who called herself a doctor; unless her target was here as well. 3) Though she'd much rather cozy up to the brother, if the retard was rich too he would do just fine. So instead of giving him the bird, she gestured for him to approach.

To his credit he didn't immediately assume she was gesturing to him, and he turned in a full circle to determine who she was trying to communicate with. It was so comical she nearly laughed out loud, and had to bite her tongue to avoid offending him. Finally he pointed to himself and she nodded, producing astonishment so complete she feared he may not recover from it.

Eventually he directed himself toward her and sat down gingerly on the couch. "Hi," she offered, smiling invitingly. He looked away for a long moment, then down at the hands he'd folded on his lap.

"Hi," he told them, in case they'd forgotten who he was.

"I'm Lilah," she prompted.

"That name's...that's real...Lilah. That's...real pretty." His hands obviously held an infinite amount of interest for him, because his eyes refused to stray from his lap. Lilah placed her hand on his.

"What's yours?"

"Wh...what?" he looked at her now, partly in alarm that she had touched him.

"What's your name?" she asked gently, beginning to think this was a bad idea.

"Craig. I thought...I thought you didn't like me."

"I do. I just didn't know how to get you to notice me." He snorted once, a very normal male reaction that bolstered her decision and prompted her to add, "Do you like me, Craig?"

"Yeah, I...yeah, I sure do."

"Good. Then I think we should hang out together, don't you?"

"You mean be friends?" Are you kidding me right now?

"Yes. Really good friends."

"Okay," he nodded eagerly, as if he'd just been invited to play a board game. His eyes roved over her face as if attempting to detect some kind of treachery. He wouldn't find any. She was far too adept at lying for this novice boy-man to figure her out.

They spent the rest of the evening watching movies in the lounge, she slipping her hand into his when no one was watching. Staff had a thing about fraternization between patients – some hooha about developing unhealthy relationships among a vulnerable population.

So she kept her interest in Craig under wraps; the last thing she needed after all her effort was for one of them to be moved to a different unit. Tony briefly flashed through her mind with a burst of anger, though she'd all but convinced herself he'd asked to be moved because he knew he couldn't withstand her feminine wiles and didn't want to lose his minimum wage job. He did her a favor, really; he was too far beneath her to waste her precious time.

She glanced at Craig, winking at him when he met her gaze. With a shave and a haircut and some decent clothes, he wouldn't be half bad, she decided. Not bad at all. After she'd gone to bed that night she imagined Craig's hands on her.

Except they weren't Craig's hesitant hands, they were his brother's sure ones. She followed his movements in her mind with her own on her body. Her breath quickened as her hands roamed over her abdomen, her thighs.

They stilled though when the door opened a crack to admit the ever-intrusive flashlight that beamed into her face, momentarily blinding her. "Oh, sorry. Rounds.," the tech said by rote after seeing that she was awake.

"Get OUT!" Lilah yelled, slamming the pillow over her face in frustration. She was going to die there, she was sure of it.

The next morning the physician met with her right after breakfast. Lilah wasn't expecting her until her customary afternoon appearance, after she'd attended to her private patients in her office. As a result, she hadn't had time to build up a body full of resentment, and was far more pleasant than normal.

Apparently Dr. Tacee responded favorably to the change, because she was being discharged before she knew it. She barely had time to sneak Craig a kiss and get his cell phone number before she was being hustled into her room to pack her things.

He'd seemed like a lost puppy when she'd told him goodbye, and she almost felt sorry for him. But she had every intention of hooking back up with him after he left the hospital. She had to – he was part of the Master Plan.

***

Pauley steered his car down the long, brick-paved drive leading to his parents' sizable estate. How much room did two people really need? he asked himself for the millionth time. The Phipps spread seemed ostentatious, even from his normally grandiose point-of-view.

In spite of the opulence of the surroundings, he wasn't thrilled to be here. He'd been tasked with reporting back to Barbie, and he had a feeling she'd purposely left her phone off so he'd have to come here in person to complete the obligation she'd imposed on him.

As a grown man, her demands didn't sit well with him, but he knew he had no choice. His livelihood depended on the sizable allowance he received from his father each month, and pissing off his mother would not bode well for its eternal continuation.

He certainly couldn't live without it; other than the liberal arts bachelor's degree he'd basically been handed from a private college to which his father made substantial contributions, he had no discernable talents or skills, and his work ethic was nonexistent.

He was a playboy through and through, and Barbie, at least, seemed to be accepting, and maybe even a little proud, of that fact. He was her trophy of sorts – See my handsome self-possessed son. Isn't he fabulous? But don't you have two sons, Barbie? Well, you know, Craig's always been a little different. This one, though, he'll take the helm someday!

Someday, Pauley snorted to himself as he pulled to a stop in the immense circle drive in front of the Phipps's mansion. As if James would ever feel comfortable handing over the reins of his business to anyone, let alone someone he considered lazy and unmotivated.

Admittedly, he wasn't wrong, but that wasn't entirely Pauley's fault. He and Craig had been raised in the lap of luxury, and once it became obvious the elder brother who had originally been the heir apparent wasn't quite right in the head, all eggs had been placed in the younger's basket.

If Pauley had been doted on before as the baby, now he was treated as if he were an only child in terms of resource allocation. He was given anything and everything his heart desired, and it hadn't been obvious that he would one day be expected to work the long hours James seemed to revel in in order to earn his keep.

As a result, he had really had no choice but to become spoiled, entitled, and egocentric – he was the crown prince, and all hopes of the throne rested on him. Maybe if he'd had as much of his parents' time and attention as he had their money, things would have turned out differently.

But as it was James acted as if his responsibility to his children began and ended with his sperm donation, leaving Barbie to do her best to hold the family together – when she wasn't having hot stone massages, tanning sessions, and three-hundred-fifty-dollar blowouts that made her overprocessed hair look like the prized wig of a Brazilian drag queen.

Needless to say, most of her time was spent looking the part, leaving her little for the actual work of being a mother. Not that her role models were adequate, but hey, everyone has to rise above something.

Pauley was admitted to the huge foyer by a uniformed maid who spoke little English, but responded appropriately enough to his brusque, "Barbie." He shouldn't have to be announced, for God's sake. For all intents and purposes this was his house, too. It certainly would be one day.

She gestured toward the rarely used parlor and strode away with a shush of her black uniform nylons. Pauley refused to be ushered anywhere by anyone, instead pacing like a caged animal around the enormous round marble table in the center of the entry.

After far too long, at least from his impatient perspective, Barbie issued forth from the bowels of the enormous house, her eyes brightening as they landed on her prodigal son. "Paulson," she breathed, holding out her hands for him to grasp. He did so gently – he'd never quite gotten over the belief that she was made of porcelain, as fragile as the delicate handle of a diminutive teacup.

"Pauley," he reminded her, as he did every time she uttered his name. She ignored him as usual, and he wouldn't have expected anything different. He'd briefly considered calling her 'Mom' every time she called him by his given name, but couldn't bring himself to do it. Unlike James, Barbie meant well, and it wasn't her fault she was clueless.

He leaned forward to kiss her papery cheek, getting a whiff of her customary perfume: Chanel No. 5, of course. She would never be without it, and likely had a stash in the family safe in case a nuclear explosion eradicated the world's supply. As usual, she was fully dressed, her blue pantsuit chosen carefully for its hue that set off her eyes.

She did look beautiful, he thought to himself as he noted her upswept bun, her expertly applied makeup, and her understated but infinitely expensive pearl earrings and necklace. She was well made, well maintained, and well kept. Yes, his mother had done great for herself, and he couldn't help but be proud of her. Go on with your bad self, you fierce bitch!

"Come in, Paulson. Keep me company for a while."

"I wish I could, Barbie, but I can't stay long. I have an early morning."

Her laugh sprinkled over him like drops of water from a wayward garden hose. "What's her name?" He put a finger to his lips in a gesture of secrecy. He had never been one to kiss and tell, and she knew her question was rhetorical. "Then tell me...how is your brother?"

"He seems fine. Just like always. I don't see what the big emergency was."

"You didn't see him in the beginning, Paulson. He was a mess. Paranoid. Out of his mind. Barely even knew who I was."

"Then he's better. Are you happy now?"

"Happy that you've reconnected, yes. One day, you'll be all each other has."

"Don't talk that way, Barbie. You and James will live forever."

"Your father's been under a great deal of stress," she countered.

"Old fossils like him don't die. They just petrify." He leaned into her for a brief hug before she could respond, and then turned toward the door.

The liveried maid appeared before he'd reached it, freaking him out a little. How did she do that? He couldn't stop himself from glancing around for cameras, or maybe a motion detector or two.

"Don't be a stranger, Paulson," his mother called after him as the psychic stood in attendance by the open door.

"Pauley," he muttered absentmindedly, squeezing through the doorway as far from Damien as possible.

Back in his car he found his mind returning to his visit with Craig earlier. It had been his first time inside a psychiatric facility, and he'd been nervous, though he'd never admit it.

He didn't feel guilty that he'd never visited his brother during any of his previous hospitalizations; in fact he was quite perturbed with Barbie for suddenly insisting he become involved in Craig's treatment.

First she'd dragged him to his psychiatrist's office for an outpatient appointment, then she'd expected him to begin visiting Craig in the hospital, and now she wanted him to join her for an upcoming family meeting with the therapist. What the fuck? He was not his brother's keeper, and he refused to take on that role. He'd have to put his foot down before things got out of hand.

He was surprised to find that the Institute wasn't nearly as off-putting once he'd been there for a while, though. Most of the patients seemed pretty normal, and no one was outright crazy like he'd been expecting – he'd envisioned zombies wandering around drooling and pointing at things that weren't there and men in white converging on them with straitjackets and foot-long metal needles on the end of glass syringes filled with blue fluid.

He was infinitely more surprised, however, to find himself inexorably drawn to one of the other patients. How could this be? Did it speak to some illness within himself that he'd been previously unaware of? This couldn't be normal, could it? But there it was, and it wouldn't be pushed away.

God knows he'd tried, but the pull was just too strong, and it was obvious she'd felt it too. She had been gazing toward the doors he'd come through moments before, seeming lost in her own head. He'd glanced in her direction, and then directly at her as if drawn by a magnet. She had slowly met his gaze, and held it.

They were lost in each other for so long Craig had to actually reach out and touch him to pull his attention back to their conversation. Out of the corner of his eye he saw that she had continued to stare at him for several moments before looking back toward the doors.

When it was time for him to go they exchanged another delayed glance, each seeming to communicate a need that was met in the other's eyes. He was confused, and maybe a little scared. He'd never felt such a connection before, and he was afraid to act on it. But then again, he was more afraid not to.

***

The bedside alarm buzzed quietly at half past five in the morning for exactly nine-and-a-half seconds until it was turned off by a steady hand. Strong feet followed by muscular legs appeared beyond the satin comforter as Oleander Tacee stood to pull on her silk robe.

Slipping into her house shoes, she strode purposefully down several lengths of hallway until she arrived at the central stairs of the silent house. She trod down two flights, through another expansive hallway, and into the enormous kitchen.

The housekeeper, Trudy, would not arrive for several more hours, but her presence was everywhere from the pristine surroundings to the four-course breakfast she had prepared the previous day and placed in the refrigerator for this morning's consumption to the freshly ground gourmet coffee she had dutifully set to brew in preparation for her boss's early morning rise.

Of course, none of this was done out of the goodness of her heart. No, every special touch, every extra mile, was an expectation, and her job depended on its flawless execution day in and day out. It was not easy, as evidenced by Trudy's many predecessors. But it wasn't exactly hard, either. The monstrous house was never dirty, there was hardly any laundry, and there were no children to run around after. She only had to be perfect.

After drinking her first cup of coffee, Dr. Tacee swam laps in her heated pool for half-an-hour – she firmly believed in the benefits of exercise on both the mind and the body, and swam a full two hours each day, rain or shine. After all, she had to be fit to carry out her mission, which, at over seventy years old, was almost complete.

She then placed her breakfast in the oven to warm and returned to her bedroom to shower and dress. She had already made her bed – Trudy's existence did not negate her disciplined routine. She stepped out of the shower and toweled off quickly, then entered one of the two room-sized closets that were part of the master suite to dress.

It wasn't difficult to choose her outfit for the day: by design, each article of clothing she owned was some shade of white, black, or gray. She abhorred color, and found colorful people to be flighty and irresponsible.

She slid into a gray pantsuit with a white blouse and sensible black pumps, applied a light mist of cologne – men's, because she preferred to personify power as opposed to fragility – added pearls to her ears, and gave one final pat to her severe gray chignon before leaving the suite for the day. She would not return here until her evening swim – she did not believe in loafing about napping, or even idle lounging.

Back in the kitchen she transferred the hot contents of the tin meal container to a plate of fine china, poured herself another cup of coffee, and carried all of it to the adjacent formal dining room. Though the kitchen had a bistro set near the expansive windows, she never used it. She believed if one were sitting down to eat a meal, one should do so in the appropriate environment.

She snapped open her linen napkin and laid it across her lap, leaning forward slightly to smell the delicious aroma of her food. Trudy was an excellent cook, but it never would have occurred to Dr. Tacee to commend her for it. It was simply her job.

The main course was eggs benedict today, preceded by a fresh fruit medley and a selection of croissants with warm cinnamon butter. She ended the meal with a palette cleanser; plain yogurt with a touch of vanilla extract and peppermint flakes. She then spent several moments with the daily newspaper and her last cup of coffee prior to leaving for work at precisely five till seven.

She arrived at her office at a quarter past seven on the dot and let herself in. Her receptionist, who answered the phones and scheduled appointments, would not arrive until eight-thirty, and her office manager, who coordinated the billing and took care of the practice's accounts and paperwork, came in at nine o'clock, though she was currently – annoyingly – on leave.

Dr. Tacee used the time between her arrival and that of her first client of the morning to review her charts from the previous day and make notes respective of her upcoming appointments. She would leave the office at three o'clock to round on the patients in the hospital, ending her day at seven o'clock every evening.

She found staying busy imperative for a sharp mind, and would open her practice on the weekends if her clients weren't so adverse to coming to the office on Saturdays and Sundays. Instead, she spent that time pouring over her medical journals, writing responses to articles she found of interest and occasionally submitting her own research.

Unfortunately, her current interests in terms of treatment modalities were a bit outside of the realm of traditional medicine, but isn't that what had prompted the most efficacious of breakthroughs in the history of science? She was heartened by the firm belief that her legacy would outshine all of them and would live on forever. She just had to stay the course, and never lose sight of the ultimate goal.

She breathed deeply as she passed through the waiting room turning on lights. Her receptionist, Tanisha, a lovely black girl worth her weight in gold, had set the coffee system to finish brewing at precisely a quarter past seven in the morning so that it would be ready and fresh for Dr. Tacee's unfailing arrival. She poured herself a cup and settled herself behind her desk, turning her attention to the numerous files there.

At the top of her list today was Michael Gregory's chart – not only was Dr. Barry breathing down her neck about the circumstances of his death, there was also the potential of a chart review by the state or even the American Medical Association once his autopsy results were available. She needed to be sure everything was in order to avoid red flags – that would never do at this point in the mission.

She was still deeply involved in Michael's chart when Tanisha arrived, poking her head into the office. "Hi, Doc – need anything?" Placing her unadorned finger on a passage of documentation to hold her spot, Dr. Tacee glanced up and shook her head. "Right on, Donkey Kong. You just gimme a shout if you do!" She closed the door gently, Dr. Tacee staring after her vacuously.

No one except Tanisha dared to be so irreverent in her presence, but the receptionist was simply indispensable, so Dr. Tacee had no choice but to grit her teeth through the woman's often unprofessional commentary.

Tanisha had left once, after Dr. Tacee had had the gall to try to put her in her place. After six months of pure hell with a plethora of temporary agencies and inept incompetence, she had actually appeared on Tanisha's doorstep, begging her to come back.

A highly uncharacteristic behavior to be sure, but this was her beloved practice, and she was desperate. A hefty raise and an extra week of sick pay later, her office was running smoothly again and she would never again jeopardize Tanisha's continued employment – regardless of the situation.

"Thank you, Tanisha," she finally muttered to the closed door.

The day went smoothly in spite of being short-handed, and before she knew it she was headed to the Institute for her afternoon rounds. She started with the Psychiatric Intensive Care unit, where she had a patient that had been placed in five-point restraints earlier in the day for self-harming behaviors.

According to the nurse's charting, the patient had escalated after a disappointing phone call and began banging her head on a wooden pole in the middle of the unit. A code had been called and she had been given an intramuscular injection of a powerful anxiolytic. Now she was nearly lethargic and could barely stay awake to answer the physician's questions.

Dr. Tacee had glared at the nurse across the patient's bed. "Perhaps we have too much PRN medication on board?" she chastised. In response the nurse bowed her head and nodded, taking the blame for a decision that in actuality may not even have been hers. No matter, though, the point had been made.

Her last visit was with Craig on the General Adult Psychiatric unit. As he slid into the chair across the table from her in the meeting room down the hall from the nurse's station, she looked him over with a critical eye.

He had been under her care for many years, and she had tried numerous different medications and treatments over that time – including the last-ditch electroconvulsive therapy regimen. He could not be cured, and would continue to be a drain on the system, his family, and even himself. Yes, this was the right decision.

"I have something new for you to try, Craig," she said, as she slid a package with a red round pill toward him. He picked it up and turned it over, reading the name on the back and mispronouncing it horribly.

"Tranylcypromine? What's that?"

A wide smile spread across her face. The sight was so rare all Craig could do was stare. "The answer to our prayers."

Chapter 8
Duplicity

Lilah breezed into the mahogany offices of Wood and Associates, her impeccable appearance causing the jaded receptionist's chin to drop in amazement. She looked like an A-list celebrity, far outshining even the most polished of the firm's revered clientele.

She stopped in front of the desk, tossing a perfectly coifed curl over her shoulder. "I need a divorce," she demanded, her husky voice bringing heads poking out of rooms down the hallways radiating from the reception area – each of the firm's three attorneys commanded their own suite of offices that housed their personal secretaries, legal assistants, and paralegals.

Lilah wasn't alarmed by their stares – she barely even noticed. Her entry usually had such an effect. But it took the older woman several moments to gather her thoughts enough to close her mouth and form a logical statement, which angered her. The tone of her resulting response was therefore much harsher than she'd intended.

"None of the attorneys in this practice see potential clients without an appointment."

"I'm not concerned with the other attorneys in this practice. I'm here for Steve Wood. Word is he's the best, and that's what I need. Be a sweetheart and ask him if he'd be willing to make an exception in my case, won't you –" she glanced at the name plate displayed on the elegant desktop, "– Margie? Tell him he won't be disappointed."

Straightening her spine even further, Margie's nostrils flared as she made several ill-concealed attempts to remain professional. "Mrs...?"

"Donahue."

"Mrs. Donahue, in spite of your obvious misconception to the contrary, your 'special case' is not a sufficient reason to interrupt Mr. Wood's tightly packed schedule. Now, if you'd like to make an appointment, we would be happy to accommodate you with one of the junior partners in a couple of weeks –"

Lilah's amused laugh flowed throughout the offices like hot caramel, stopping Margie's condescending speech mid-sentence. "That's unacceptable, Margie. I'm afraid I'm going to need to speak with your supervisor."

Margie stood, her spine now in danger of snapping from the hyperextension she imposed on it. "I *am* my 'supervisor', Mrs. Donahue, and I'm afraid I'm going to have to ask you to leave."

"Excuse me?"

"I said –"

"It's okay, Margie. I'll take it from here," Steve interrupted, placing his hand at the small of Lilah's back and gesturing toward his office through the double doors to the right of the front desk.

Apparently the whispers that had been spreading since her arrival had finally made their way to the head honcho, and Lilah smiled angelically at a furious Margie before turning toward the doors.

When they reached Steve's office he introduced himself and she followed suit, placing her freshly manicured hand in his. He briefly covered their perfunctory shake with his other hand, and she noted his wedding ring; the information may come in handy at some point.

Ignoring his offer to sit in one of the two exquisite antique chairs in front of his massive executive desk, she perused the view of the city from the windows occupying two entire walls of his spacious and sumptuously appointed office.

Though the view was breathtaking, her primary goal in positioning herself there was to showcase her assets. She was rewarded when his eyes slowly travelled from the top of her head to her pearl-polished toes just visible in her peep-toed platform heels and back again. Excellent.

She turned her attention back to the view momentarily; her victory dance could wait until later. "Beautiful," she murmured, referring to the view.

"Yes," he breathed, referring to anything but.

She allowed herself a small smile before turning to the business at hand. She had been irate when she'd collected her belongings from the hospital's storage department and discovered that Mark had packed every single thing she owned into the luggage set she'd used to move in with him when they'd first met.

He'd even brought her car, leaving it in the visitor parking lot and leaving the keys with security. He had completely eradicated her from his life just that quickly. Well she wasn't having it. She would have the last laugh. Bastard.

"What can I do for you, Mrs. Donahue?"

"Lilah. Please."

"Of course. Lilah." It was a caress, as it so often was when uttered by men.

"My husband kicked me out. Left me destitute. Wrote me a check for ten grand, as if that's supposed to be enough to live on. I had to lease an apartment in a low-rent neighborhood just to make the money last." She visibly shuddered, a brief sob escaping her before she covered her mouth with her hand.

"I assume you're unable to pay my retainer?" Steve asked, unmoved by her display. She shook her head, her eyes filling rapidly. He held up a hand, a frown taking over his features. As beautiful as she was, he couldn't abide hysterical women.

She read him adroitly and quickly switched tactics. This was obviously not a man to be toyed with. Her unshed tears disappeared instantly, her voice hardening, becoming more matter-of-fact.

"My husband is Mark Donahue. He is the sole proprietor of the Bleu Goose. Almost every cent he's made has been reinvested in the business. He owns the building, the furniture, the equipment – everything – free and clear. His net worth is just shy of six million dollars." Steve nodded with satisfaction; now she was speaking his language. Bolstered, she continued. "I just want my fair share, and – "

"I'm not interested in getting your fair share. I'm interested in taking him for all he's worth. I don't take cases I'm not sure I can win, and I don't take anyone's crappy 'fair share'." A slow smile lit up Lilah's face beatifically, rendering Steve speechless.

"You're my man," she said provocatively. "Will you take me on? Do it on contingency?" She held her breath – she didn't know what she'd do if he refused. She hadn't even considered a Plan B. She needed him, and only him, and that was simply all there was to it. Thankfully her luck was holding, as he slowly nodded.

"You've got yourself a deal," he said, stretching out his hand to shake on it. He held hers longer than necessary, and waited for her to meet his eyes before he said, "But it's my way or no way." He wasn't the most handsome man she'd ever met, but something about him was undeniably compelling, and she felt her pulse quickening unbidden.

"Of course," she agreed, losing herself a bit in his persistent gaze. Before she realized it she was in the parking lot starting her car, her palms cold and sweaty on the steering wheel. What was *that*? She'd never had that kind of reaction to a man before. It was disconcerting and not wholly pleasant. He was an enigma, to be sure.

She drove around the streets of the city aimlessly for what felt like hours, though she could ill afford to waste gas – this racecar inhaled the stuff. She'd never felt so alone, even when her mother died. Oh, who was she kidding? She'd felt free when that sad, dour woman had left this world.

There'd been no fun left in her...no happiness. Her disapproving eyes had followed Lilah around relentlessly, as if condemning her for her beauty, even back then, during her gangly, awkward teenage years. As if she didn't want her daughter, her only child, to pull herself out of that shithole and build a better life for herself – no matter what it took.

Yes, her mother's death had been a relief, and she couldn't force herself to pretend differently. This aloneness, though...this was harrowing. Draining. She couldn't visit Craig, or even call him on the phone for comfort – the Institute had a strict rule that former patients couldn't contact current ones for thirty days after they'd been released.

She could pretend to be someone else, disguise her voice, but she had no idea who would be on his call list. She was truly all alone, and began hyperventilating, her heart beating so quickly she feared it would gallop out of her chest. Her symptoms worsened when she crossed the bridge to the seedy part of town where the stupid social worker at the hospital had found her a cheap walk-up.

She gulped air as she drove past garbage-strewn sidewalks and closed up shops, their doors and windows boarded and covered in graffiti, their inventory long since purged by petty thieves and looters. What was she *doing* here?

From a young age, she'd learned about men; how to manipulate them to get what she wanted...how to read them and predict their reactions. How to ensure she would never have to worry about food or clothing or shelter ever again. And yet, here she was. Struggling to figure out how to make ten thousand dollars last for the year or two Steve had said her contested divorce would take.

Her dire financial state was seriously cramping her style. If only she had some idea when Craig would be discharged, she could plan accordingly. She had no doubt she could win him over to the point he would ask her to move in with him. She'd already had him eating out of the palm of her hand within hours of turning her attention on him.

No, that wasn't the question, as far as she was concerned, she thought, as she eased her car into the garage – a welcome surprise when she'd rented the place. The question was how long could they keep him from her?

***

When Riley returned to PINA after her time off she was surprised to find Craig still there. He usually cleared quickly after being restarted on his medication, and this episode hadn't seemed to be any different.

At first she thought he'd been released and returned in the short time she'd been gone; many of their persistently mentally ill clients had had at least one incidence in which they'd return to the hospital within days, if not hours, of being released.

Mental health care just wasn't a priority, and most communities didn't have the resources to be able to maintain services for people with a mental illness outside of the inpatient hospital setting.

Whether the need was transportation to get to follow-up appointments, help with medication refills, housing, employment programs, or a combination of these, there were extensive gaps in mental health parity in every state in the country, and it was only getting worse as the problem continued to be pushed under the rug.

Certainly the stigma of mental illness was largely responsible for these disparities, but they were exacerbated by laws and policies, or the lack thereof, that allowed insurance companies and other third-party payers to limit mental health coverage in ways that would be unacceptable for comparable medical care.

Hellen, the hospital's utilization review nurse, was constantly complaining about the difficulty she had on an ongoing basis in getting patients' inpatient days covered through their carriers. It was a travesty that wouldn't change until these gross inequalities were addressed by the federal government at the national level.

Riley used to think someone really important would have to get hurt or even killed in order for politicians and lobbyists and other lawmakers to take up the cause. And yet numerous senseless deaths had occurred at the hands of individuals with a diagnosed – but untreated or undertreated – mental illness during her time as a psych nurse and nothing had changed. If the loss of kindergartners – babies! – couldn't prompt an about face in this country, what could?

Even when those in crisis actually made it into the hospital, they were usually pushed out as quickly as possible, whether they had resources to continue their treatment after discharge or not. Inpatient facilities simply couldn't afford to house them for extended periods of time, which made Craig's continued stay even more odd.

Riley poured through his chart for some indication as to the rationale for his delayed release. Maybe he was voicing suicidal or homicidal thoughts, or had had a psychotic episode in which he became violent and lashed out at a peer or staff. Those things could easily take a patient's treatment plan back to square one, though she should've heard something in report had that been the case.

But on a busy night, passing information forward that occurred on previous shifts could be inadvertently overlooked. However, such an occurrence would definitely have been documented in the chart, and she found nothing out of the norm whatsoever. Obviously she would need to go straight to the source, and there was no time like the present.

She found him sitting in the alcove with Marin, and greeted them both before asking the other woman to give them a moment of privacy. She nodded shyly and left the area quietly. Like a little dull-colored mouse. Poor thing.

Turning back to Craig, Riley sat in the chair Marin had just vacated. "How's things, Craig?"

"Okay," he said – nearly asked, in fact; suspicious even when at his baseline, which he seemed to be now. It was difficult to tell, since his mild mental retardation made him seem childlike regardless of his cognitive status.

"It's okay, Craig. We're just hanging out, right?" He visibly relaxed, melting into the chair like butter on a hot grill.

"Right, okay," he repeated her terminology, which she consciously chose to place herself on the same level as her patients, facilitating the development of a therapeutic rapport.

A big part of what a psychiatric, or behavioral health, nurse does involves maintaining the therapeutic milieu in the hospital setting. It's especially important to build therapeutic relationships with patients quickly so that they trust the nurse when interventions need to occur within the milieu. Using this technique, the nurse often changes the way he or she talks to or approaches a patient as a result.

It certainly worked with Craig, who had shifted slightly to face her and waited for her to speak with an openness that hadn't been there when she'd first sat down. "I was a little surprised to see you still here when I came in this morning. You don't usually stay so long," she said, deciding that honesty was the best policy and diving right in.

"Yup. Yup, still here."

"Did something happen this time that made your doctor decide you shouldn't go home just yet?"

"Nope, I been real good."

"I know you have, Craig. That's why I'm a little confused." Craig stared at her, bobbing his head up and down as if to music she couldn't hear. She knew he was probably sorting through the voices in his head, and quite possibly visual hallucinations as well, in an attempt to isolate what she was saying from everything else that wasn't real. It was called thought blocking.

She gave him the time he needed – adding even more to the mix would just frustrate him. Finally his creased forehead smoothed and he stopped moving his head. His reply was obviously forthcoming. "My family's coming. To a meeting. Here at the hospital."

"Your mother, you mean?" Riley had sat in on many of his family meetings in the past, and no one but his mother had ever come.

"Yup. And Pauley and James, too." She sat back in the chair, surprised. If that were really the case, Eva had outdone herself – it would certainly bode well for Craig's future if the entire family was finally on board with his treatment.

"That's awesome, Craig!" He nodded in response and didn't stop, his eyes drifting out of focus again. He was back in his own head, interacting with his internal stimuli, but she'd learned what she'd needed to.

There was no reason for him to be here. While his voices were still present, they weren't hostile and commanding like they were when he went off his medication, and a family session could just as easily be done in Eva's office as in the hospital. What was going on?

During her lunch break she texted Eva. "Feel like dancing before my tummy gets in the way?"

It didn't take long for her to respond. "Going to a movie with the hubs tonight. It's a RomCom! Means I'll be putting out later on."

"ROFL! TMI."

"Bleu Goose tomorrow?"

"If you've recovered."

"He's a pussycat. Not as spry as he used to be. I'll be good."

"Still might be verging on TMI."

"I stand corrected."

"Hey, any reason C.P. still here?"

"Wondering the same myself. Doing great on meds."

"Weird."

"Very."

"Gotta get back. Luv U."

"Luv U."

Wow. Curiouser and curiouser. Poor Hellen would have a hell of a time getting this hospitalization covered. As intimidating as Riley found Dr. Tacee, it appeared she would have to broach the subject directly with the doctor during rounds later that afternoon.

She spent an anxious couple of hours rehearsing what she would say to the arrogant psychiatrist, and ended up procrastinating when the woman finally arrived. Riley had wanted to speak to her before she'd started seeing clients, but that opportunity had come and gone. Now her last client was leaving the conference room and she was gathering her notes. She would dictate them in the physician's lounge and then be on her way. It was now or never.

Riley entered the room and closed the door just as she stood up with her things. "Are you discharging Craig today?" Riley asked, her carefully prepared speech disappearing into thin air.

"No," Dr. Tacee said curtly, staring down her royal nose at Riley as if she were a rodent.

"Because I'm not seeing any indication of why he continues to be hospitalized."

"That might be because you are not his doctor."

"No, but I'm his nurse, and my job is to advocate for my patients."

"Your job is to do what the physician tells you to do."

"I am a professional whose scope of practice is contingent on state and federal law, not the whim of the physician," Riley countered hotly, her face in flames.

"If I were you I would undergo an attitude change immediately if you don't want to find yourself advocating for your patients elsewhere, *nurse*." The last word was said with such derision Riley was rendered speechless as Dr. Tacee brushed past her and out of the room.

She stood there in the doorway of the now empty space; angry, ashamed, and appalled all at once. Her eyes stung and she blinked rapidly – she had to keep it together; she wouldn't be off work for another hour. Her phone buzzed and she grappled for it in her pocket, sure that it was Eva – her lifesaver.

"Hello?" she answered, her voice tremulous.

Steve's voice was so unexpected she froze. "Riley? Hello?"

Before she could respond, she burst into tears.

***

Eva awoke before the alarm clock, feeling rested and refreshed. She stretched luxuriously, savoring the sensation of the satin sheets against her naked body. She turned to her still slumbering husband, resting her cheek on her hands.

She stared at his beloved face for several moments before reaching out to stroke his cheek, rough with a day's worth of stubble. He sighed deeply in his sleep, a slight smile turning the corner of his lips.

She knew without a shadow of a doubt that he loved her almost as much as she loved him – though if she said it aloud he would deny it emphatically; no one has ever loved anyone more than he loved her.

Married almost ten years, they really shouldn't feel this way. They were well past the honeymoon phase, and yet they still got butterflies when they reunited after being apart for any length of time. Their arguments were never dramatic enough to elicit makeup sex, but their date nights always ended with wild couplings that would put people half their age to shame.

Eva knew she was lucky as hell, and tried never to take what she had for granted. She reluctantly drew herself away from Sleeping Beauty, her gray eyes darkening to the color of storm clouds as she turned her attention to the day ahead.

She dressed for the gym, her fuscia yoga pants and black racerback tank top flattering her slender frame. She knotted her thick sweep of hair at the top of her head, threading a couple of long hair pins through it to keep it from falling into her face during her workout.

She would be working with the bag that morning, and her muscles were already straining as if in anticipation of punching and kicking the shit out of it. She stopped in the kitchen to spoon down a tiny container of Greek yogurt and a quart of water, refilled her GO cup, grabbed her duffel bag and bounced lightly down the front steps to the street.

She relished the peace and quiet of the beautiful neighborhood before it began stirring for the day, and took a few moments to inhale the crisp morning air before throwing her things in her Jeep and heading to the gym.

After an incredibly rewarding workout during which she happily kicked Josh's ass after he unwisely offered to be a live sparring target she drove to the office, feeling exhilarated from her shower. Her gym definitely knew how to treat its clients, providing all the perks of home – hot showers, spacious dressing rooms, gourmet coffee. She could stay there forever. Alas, she had a job to do.

She arrived at her office in record time, pleased that she'd have some time to herself before her first client showed up. Her black stilettos clicked against the marble floor with each step, echoing through the building's busy lobby and drawing several appreciative stares, both male and female. Standing in front of the mirrored elevators, she evaluated herself covertly and had to agree with their positive assessment.

She looked amazing; her elegant gray pantsuit hugged her frame lovingly and complimented her light eyes, her hair was swept back into a low ponytail at the nape of her neck, her royal blue silk shell bared just a hint of cleavage and provided a pop of color to her otherwise understated ensemble.

She was a class act, and she almost felt as healthy on the inside as she appeared to be on the outside. But she wasn't – a fact she'd best remember every second of every day. She met her gaze in the reflection and quickly looked away.

When she arrived to her office on the twentieth floor she wasn't surprised to see the waiting room full. Her officemates both treated children and adolescents for ADHD, anxiety disorders, and behavioral issues, so most of their hours were arranged around school. By mid-morning, hers would be the only clients inhabiting the waiting room, and by the time she left for the afternoon it would be full of parents and their not-so-precious bundles of joy again.

She strode quickly through the cacophony, nodding at her maternal secretary before disappearing into her office and closing the door to shut out the madness. That woman had the patience of a saint.

Sighing with relief, Eva turned on the sound system, relaxing into her desk chair as its soothing sounds filled the room. She then started her coffeemaker – she couldn't face a day at the office without her morning java – and reviewed her notes.

She had a family meeting scheduled for Craig that afternoon, and was hoping James would actually show up for this one. In the meantime she had a few clients to see this morning, starting with a seventy-two-year-old female with major depressive disorder who began ECT treatments two weeks ago after several different medications failed to improve her condition.

Her seventy-five-year-old husband brought her to every single appointment, and, when she'd had to be hospitalized for the first week of treatments, he'd spent every moment of visiting hours by her side. He even stayed in the hospital waiting room for hours on end when it wasn't time to visit just to be close to her. If she died first, the man would immediately perish from grief.

Eva's phone buzzed and she opened her door to usher them in, Phoebe stooped and shuffling, led gingerly by a nearly frantic Walter, his eyes pleading with Eva to do something – anything – to help his wife. Phoebe sat finally, looking around her as if lost.

"She's doing worse, Ms. Jonas. Just look at her!" Tears glistened in his eyes as his gaze lingered on his fragile wife.

"It's the nature of the electroconvulsive therapy she's been receiving, Walter. Remember we told you she'd have some memory loss? Some disorientation?"

"She can't even dress herself no more!" he blurted, beside himself.

"All of those functions will return, and then some," Eva reassured him gently. "ECT is becoming the treatment of choice for the severely depressed elderly because it works quickly with far fewer side effects than some of those antidepressants she was taking. But it takes time. She's only had five treatments."

Walter buried his face in his hands, his shoulders shaking with his sobs. Eva walked around her desk to hand him a tissue, patting his arm consolingly. Though Phoebe was completely oblivious to her surroundings now, Eva had seen client after client miraculously recover from the majority of the symptoms of their persistent mental illness following a full series of ECT treatments.

"She will get better, Walter. She needs you to think positive. She needs you not to give up on her. She needs *you*." He nodded, and suddenly lunged forward to wrap Eva into a surprisingly strong bear hug. She was grateful his intentions weren't malicious, because he was astoundingly quick for an old man.

She thought about the sweet couple on her way to PINA later that afternoon; she understood Walter's overwhelming fear of losing Phoebe. It was her near constant prayer that whether by accident, illness, or old age, she would be the first to die in her marriage because she couldn't even begin to fathom living without her husband.

When she arrived at the locked doors of Craig's unit, Barbie and another man were already there waiting to be let in. Eva had her own Prox card, but took the opportunity to be introduced to Barbie's companion. "Eva, this is my youngest son. Paulson, this is Craig's therapist."

"Pauley," the man corrected as he turned to face Eva, his smile dazzling her. Jesus Christ, he was inhuman.

He shook the hand she mutely offered and then dropped it when she seemed disinclined to retrieve it. He looked at her strangely, but not as a result of her actions – it was as if he recognized her, though he'd never bothered to take part in Craig's treatment in any way up to this point. She wondered what had changed.

The doors were opened from the opposite side, and Tony welcomed them onto the unit. He greeted Eva warmly and she responded in kind – she really liked him, and suspected he had a serious crush on her best friend. Unfortunately, it would go unrequited; Riley was a loyal and faithful puppy, but to the wrong owner, in Eva's opinion.

Tony led the way to the conference room, passing through the patient lounge. Eva spotted her sister and gave her a slight wave before realizing Marin's rapt attention was on Pauley, just ahead of her. And his was on Marin. What the hell?

"Excuse me?" Eva interrupted brusquely, motioning toward Barbie's retreating back. Pauley caught up to his mother but not before offering Marin his own wave, which was much more exuberantly received than Eva's had been.

Her eyes narrowed on the man's back; she had the sudden feeling that things were going to get ugly.

***

The sound of his feet hitting the pavement gave Gabe an idea for his speech that afternoon at the high school across the river that was known for its rough student demographic. He'd been tossing his multitude of past speeches around in his head to no avail – none of them seemed adequate for this audience.

Granted, he may get there and discover they were all little angels, but if that wasn't the case he had to have another game plan. By the time he returned from his morning jog his alternate speech was firmed up and he felt ready to take on the day.

Energized, he made the bed, ran the sweeper over the hardwood floors on the main level, and emptied the dishwasher. His wife was so busy all he wanted was for her to be able to sit down and relax when she got home instead of worrying about cleaning. He wrote her a love note and stuck it to the fridge in case she came home in the middle of the day.

He then took a shower, shaving his face with the exception of a shadow of a goatee, and ending with a jet of cold water to sharpen his senses and put him in a fighting mood. He always spoke with more authority and conviction when in a fighting mood.

Next he dressed in a button-down chambray shirt, khakis, and chucks – a nod to his young audience. He put in contacts and traded his prescription eyeglasses for thick frames with plain lenses, selected a yellow print power tie, and shrugged into a navy blue blazer – all props to elicit a specific response.

When he was satisfied with his appearance, he settled himself into his home office; a moderate-sized room off the master bedroom. Likely designed as a sunporch, it was surrounded by windows that offered amazing views of the forests the city was slowly encroaching on, and of the river with its twin city beyond.

It sufficed as a four-season room, although during the winter months he couldn't abide spending any amount of time in it unless he was fully clothed. It was a quirky part of the house he loved as much as the rest of it.

He was able to spend a couple of hours on his latest literary creation, and was satisfied with his progress. He took a moment to proofread and edit what he'd written while it was still fresh in his mind before leaving the house for the day.

He lost himself in his speech again on the ride to the high school, and before long he was striding confidently onto the stage and up to the podium where he nodded to the principal, who had just introduced him. She walked off to the left and behind the curtain, her shoulders visibly lowering from relief once she was no longer within view of the twelve hundred students crammed noisily into the auditorium.

Tough crowd, then. Good to know – his approach always varied based on his audience. Though the pupils had not quieted down, they were watching him, probably to see how long it would take him to crack. This was not a new subject to them, and they expected to be bored to tears within seconds of hearing his voice. They were sadly mistaken.

He calmly removed his blazer, twirling it above his head by a finger for several moments before releasing it to fly into a corner of the stage, resting in a crumpled heap near the place where the fretful principal had exited just moments before. One by one conversations were abandoned, replaced by nudges and pointing fingers.

Who was this guy? Didn't he know he was supposed to retain a modicum of dignity at his highly advanced age? Nope, apparently not – his tie flung toward the back of the stage. His glasses followed, causing a slight decibel increase that immediately hushed as he walked toward the center of the dais, microphone in hand.

He had rolled up his sleeves, ran his hands through his hair, and casually placed one hand in his pocket as if he hadn't a care in the world. Almost every student watched him, mouths ajar as if expecting to be fed regurgitated food from their mama bird's beak.

He took a moment to grin victoriously – they hadn't seen anything yet. Bringing the mic to his mouth, he shouted at the top of his lungs, "Buddy you're a boy, make a big noise, playin' in the street, gonna be a big man some day!" Had they still been gossiping, or whatever it was they'd been doing while their principal was trying to get their attention, he would have out-yelled them all. As it was, his voice carried to the very last seats, high up in the full balcony.

He began stomping in rhythm, the soles of his shoes striking the platform of the stage loudly. "You got mud on your face, you big disgrace, kickin' your can all over the place!" Stomp, stomp, STOMP! Stomp, stomp, STOMP!

As he'd expected, one or two students followed suit, prompting more and more to join in. Soon the auditorium was thundering, the walls and rafters above shaking with the vibrations of hundreds of feet hitting the floor in concurrence.

"Yes!" he shouted, holding both fists in the air in victory as they chanted, "We will, we will rock you!" As distanced as this generation may be from good, honest music, Queen would forever and always bridge the gap. Thank you, Brian May.

Over the cacophony that reverberated through every bone in his body, Gabe yelled, "I want you guys to help me out here!" He kept up the rhythm with his feet to carry on what he'd started.

"I want you to pretend like your feet are a heartbeat. I know...I know; the heart goes lub-dub, right? Forget all that for now. We're taking some creative license here. How often do you get to make up your own rules, huh?" Raucous cheering.

"That's right! So you're all a living, beating heart. Beat! Live!!" The stomping grew even louder, if that was possible. "Now I'm going to give you a word, and you need to remember that word, okay?"

They shouted and clapped in affirmation. "Tree! The word is tree. Can you say it back to me so I know you know the word, guys?"

"Tree!" they shouted in unison.

"Again!"

"Tree!" What the hell was this guy getting at? Didn't matter – they were all fully engaged now.

"Okay that's our word, guys! Now what I want you to do is stop stomping. Stop. Stomping. NOW!"

It took some time but eventually everyone stopped. They seemed disappointed to no longer be making noise, but didn't appear to be disposed to picking up where they'd left off before Gabe had appeared on the stage. Good.

Very quietly, so they had to strain to hear him, to focus on his words, he instructed, "Alright. We're going to do this again, even louder and wilder than before – BUT! When I say the word 'tree' you're going to stop stomping right away. This was just the dress rehearsal...now we're going to do the real thing."

Without waiting for them to answer he started stomping again. Stomp, stomp, STOMP! Stomp, stomp, STOMP! It didn't take long for his audience to resume their pre-interruption performance as he yelled, "Living, beating heart," in rhythm to the movement of his feet.

"Your feet are the heartbeat of a healthy eighteen-year-old girl named Christina." Stomp, stomp, STOMP!

"Christina is popular, beautiful, funny, and kind." Stomp, stomp, STOMP!

"She was the princess her parents had always wanted, won Homecoming Queen three years in a row, and received a full-ride scholarship to Stanford for the upcoming fall." Stomp, stomp, STOMP!

"Her entire life is ahead of her as she gets into a 1974 Ford Mustang with a boy who's had too much to drink." Stomp, stomp, STOMP!

"She wasn't worried. She trusted him. He'd rescued kittens off the roof for her, bought her more ice cream when hers melted onto the pavement, held her hand when she was scared." Stomp, stomp, STOMP!

"She should have been worried. He was way too drunk to drive." Stomp, stomp, STOMP!

"The Mustang rounded a corner and left the road, flying down an embankment, and crashing, at almost one hundred miles per hour, into a tree..." Silence. Not one absentminded footfall. Not one laugh or sigh or whisper.

Their faces went slack as they realized the stillness of their feet – Christina's heartbeat – signified her death, this girl they didn't know. And yet, this girl they all knew. They looked around at each other; afraid...angry...ashamed.

Into the quiet, Gabe forged ahead. This is what he had come here to do. "Christina was my sister," he said, his fist striking his chest as if in an effort to stop his own heart. Now the murmurs began. Poor guy. Feel sorry for him. He lost someone he loved to the big bad drunk driver.

His speech had just turned predictable – isn't this what all adults do? Shake a finger in our face and demand from their holier-than-thou perches that we shouldn't do what all kids do? He's just like all the rest, disguised by his theatrics and his I'm-just-like-you shtick.

On the stage, Gabe heard them. He knew what they were saying. What they always said. But he had an answer for them. He started stomping his feet again; this time quietly. Reverently.

Stomp, stomp, STOMP..."Christina was my sister," he said again. "And that boy? The one who killed her?" Stomp, stomp, STOMP..."That was me."

***

Riley was out of sorts for the rest of the day as a result of her confrontation with Dr. Tacee. Perhaps sensing her anxiety, Tony waited for her to finish her charting and walked her out to her car.

"You didn't have to come all the way to the parking lot," she admonished once she'd left her own head long enough to realize she had company. "Or are you parked close by?"

He shook his head and pointed back toward the building. "My ride's chained to the bike rack," he quipped. She glanced at his wheels and nodded, barely breaking into a grin. Ordinarily she would have found him funny, but not today.

"Hey," he said quietly, bending down to peer into her averted gaze, "she's miserable and lonely and old. You're...the opposite," his mouth quirked upward in a semblance of his usual charming smile, but returned serious just as quickly.

"She's jealous and snobby, and half the time she's a bit demented. Don't give her the power to ruin your day."

Riley finally met his gaze, something she'd been avoiding because she didn't want to cry again. Crying made her angry. And puffy. But his tone, his words, were so comforting and sincere, she needed to see if his eyes were as genuine.

They were. So deep brown they were almost black, made to appear like bottomless pools by long, thick lashes, she was shocked to find such raw emotion there.

She had always thought of him as a jokester, bringing light to tense situations. He could be counted on to make everyone laugh and de-escalate the constant stress that naturally accompanied their work at the Institute.

In fact, his antics made him seem so youthful that she'd been surprised to learn he was older than she was at his birthday gathering at the Bleu Goose last year.

But now she saw maturity, life experience, and quite a bit of pain as she lost herself in his gaze. She was startled when she felt his hands on her upper arms, his grasp firm and strong as he steadied her. She hadn't even realized she'd tipped forward and gone off balance.

"Oh God, I'm so sorry. What a klutz," she sputtered, her face flushed with embarrassment.

"It's okay, Riley. You're okay." His hands loosened their hold and he stepped backward to give her some room. Come back. Hold me. She shook her head, rattling her wayward thoughts.

He'd said her name with a gentle caress, and she loved the moniker for the first time in her life. He'd made it sound so beautiful. Kind of like how he was making her feel. Like she was, indeed, okay. More than okay. Enough.

Now he stepped back further, his hands in his pockets and his eyes on the ground. Great. She'd freaked him out. She was daydreaming about him while her husband's baby was growing inside her. He must think she'd lost her damn mind.

She cleared her throat and stuck out her hand. Amusement overtook his face as he reached out to shake it. "Thanks. For..." sending shivers up my spine "...everything," she finished lamely.

"Sure," he replied warmly, and turned to bound back to the building. She watched him unchain his bicycle and bounce it off the curb on one wheel before he called out, "See ya!" and disappeared around the side of the hospital.

A boy. He was still just the boy she'd known him to be since the first day she'd met him. The man she'd glimpsed must be a cover for that devil-may-care boy inside. Or was it the other way around?

When she got home, she was surprised to find the dinner table set with her wedding china, the lights dimmed, and candles flickering everywhere. On the buffet were elegant take-out containers of all shapes and sizes arranged artfully to display a wide array of Indian food, the aroma causing her mouth to water before she'd even closed the front door.

Some romantic fool had obviously come to the wrong house, and was probably lying naked on her rose petal covered bed waiting for the subject of this ostentatious display of affection to come home. What to do?

"Hi, sweetheart." She nearly jumped out of her skin as Steve appeared in the doorway holding a glass of red wine and looking entirely too pleased with himself.

"Uh...hi." She was completely caught off guard. Who was this man, and what had he done with her decidedly nonspontaneous husband? "What's all this?" It wasn't Valentine's Day, or her birthday, or their anniversary...and who was she kidding anyway? The most she'd ever gotten from him regardless of the occasion was an impersonal Hallmark.

"You had a bad day," he said simply. Seriously? She should have those more often. And here she was being contrary when he'd been so thoughtful.

"Wow, I don't know what to say."

"You don't have to say a word, my dear. Just sit and relax. I'll do the rest."

He placed the wine glass at the setting across from hers and returned to the kitchen, leaving her to eye the wine longingly. Evidently her bad day hadn't impacted his heavy handedness. He reappeared with her customary sparkling water on ice and set it in front of her ceremoniously.

He then filled her plate, and then his, with a little bit of everything from the sideboard and set them on the table as well. Riley breathed deeply and was surprised to find that she really was able to relax after such a trying shift.

As she attacked her dinner voraciously, Steve kept up a relatively one-sided conversation, pausing occasionally to take a sip of wine or fork a delicate morsel of food into his mouth. When they'd finished their meal, Riley sat back in her chair with a sigh, smiling across the table at her husband. She didn't recall the last time she'd enjoyed his company so much.

He returned her smile as he pushed his chair away from the table and stood. "There's desert on the counter in the kitchen. Help yourself while I draw you a steaming hot bubble bath."

She watched him go, her mind racing. What had gotten into him? Maybe he was turning over a new leaf. Becoming a better husband...a better man. For the baby. She rubbed her belly tenderly and glanced across the table at his wine glass. She should cut him some slack. It wasn't wrong for him to not want her to drink while she was pregnant. Even though she knew it was perfectly fine to imbibe a bit throughout one's pregnancy, he just wanted what was best for their family.

She wandered into the kitchen and absently spooned a bite of chocolate mousse into her mouth, delighting in its creamy texture and rich flavor. She'd finished hers in no time, and ran the delicate spoon around the inside of the serving glass to get every last taste.

"Mmmm...," she groaned, jumping again when Steve's hands grasped her shoulders.

"That good?"

"That good," she agreed. He gently pushed her toward the stairs before releasing her.

"Go enjoy your bath while I clean up down here."

She did as she was told, for once not bristling at his authoritarian manner. She eased her aching body into the soothing water and leaned back against the spa pillow he'd arranged for her. She hadn't realized how much Dr. Tacee had stressed her out until she felt each of her muscles uncoil in the heat of the bath.

The everyday sounds of Steve moving around in the kitchen and cars driving by on the street beyond the bathroom window must have lulled her to sleep because she awoke to a tepid bath and her husband leaning over her menacingly.

"What –" She started to spring from the tub but he stopped her with a heavy hand to her chest. She gaped at him, too shocked to speak as fury etched itself into every crevice of his face.

"I told you this job was bad for you. For us. And it's sure as hell bad for my baby," he snarled. He pushed her further into the full tub while she thrashed about ineffectually. "If I hear about any more of these little 'incidents', you're done with that place. Do we understand each other?"

Unable to speak from gasping for air she nodded vigorously, her hands scrabbling for purchase along the smooth wall of the tub. He held her there for a few more moments before turning and slamming out of the room.

Trembling uncontrollably, she jumped out of the tub and wrapped herself in a towel, sinking to the floor before she fell onto it. The man could have happily drowned her, and she had no one but herself to blame.

Chapter 9
Awakenings

"Where's James, Barbie?" No answer. "Pauley?"

"The old man couldn't make it, Craig," Pauley said, his voice uncharacteristically compassionate. Craig stared at his brother until Eva cleared her throat, capturing his attention.

"We can still have a productive family meeting, Craig, especially since Pauley has been so good to join us this time," she reassured him, trying to keep her animosity toward Pauley to herself.

Craig thumped the table with his fist, angry that his father couldn't even be bothered with coming to this meeting. James had never been involved with him – it had always been about Pauley. He'd never once come to see him in the hospital. All he'd ever done was throw money his way. He would much rather have at least a little of his attention than all of his money.

He'd waited his whole life for his father's approval, and when he'd found out Pauley was going to become involved in his treatment plan he'd felt sure James would follow suit.

Barbie jumped at the loud noise and stared at Eva, as if ignoring Craig's outburst would make him go away. It had always been her way of dealing with things, so much so that Craig didn't even notice it anymore.

"Well, let's get started, shall we?" Eva said by way of a distraction. Barbie nodded vigorously, her gesture resembling a bobblehead. "Our concern is in successfully transitioning Craig back into the home environment."

"He'll live with us, of course," Barbie chirped, ever the good mother.

"Yes," Eva acknowledged the unnecessary interruption – Craig's physician and social worker had already discussed his discharge plan at length, and everyone was well aware he was to resume living with his parents.

Barbie pursed her lips and nodded, seeming on the verge of obstinately beating the dead horse. Eva quickly continued, circumventing her. "Craig has a treatment plan that his entire team has agreed will be the regimen he'll need to abide by at home in order to avoid an exacerbation of his illness and maintain a healthy, fulfilling life."

"Oh, yes," Barbie jumped in, eager to demonstrate her knowledge of her child's needs. "He needs to stay on his meds and stay off the alcohol." She pronounced the last word with a prolonged 'hawwwl', like the southern belle she was. Charming, really, if she weren't so damned chipper.

"That, and he needs to comply with his follow-up appointments with myself and Dr. Tacee. Also, he needs to continue his twelve steps, keep in contact with his sponsor, and attend at least three AA meetings a week."

Barbie chirruped her understanding after each of Eva's statements, causing her to clench her fists under the table to keep herself from slapping her.

"He needs to get plenty of rest, eat three well-balanced meals a day, use his coping skills when he's feeling stressed, and absolutely no drugs." Barbie jerked as if Eva actually had slapped her.

"Of course not! My boys don't use drugs," she snipped, glaring at Eva as if she was the very devil.

"These are simply rules to live by, Mrs. Phipps. There's no accusation intended." The wind taken out of her sails, Barbie snapped open her compact to ensure her face hadn't cracked as a result of her outburst. Satisfied, she returned the mirror to her purse.

"Please, call me Barbie. You know, like the dawwwl." It was a game they played. Eva always called her Mrs. Phipps and Barbie always corrected her in the same manner. Eva turned to Craig, who was staring at the wall blankly.

"Do you understand everything I've said, Craig? That you can minimize the cognitive deficits that get worse each and every time you get sick by following these recommendations?" Craig dragged his gaze away from nothingness and met Eva's direct stare. Such a beautiful angel she was.

"Yes."

"Okay. I'm glad to know we're all on the same page." She glanced at Pauley for verification, but he was distracted by the status of his cuticles. She wondered if kicking him under the table would garner a reaction, but quickly discarded the thought. She was a professional, after all.

After she dismissed the meeting Eva directed Barbie and Pauley to the doors, though it seemed apparent Pauley wanted to hang back. "It's not visiting hours. You have to go." Her voice was gruff as she unceremoniously led him by the arm off the unit.

Craig waved as the doors closed behind them, and then sat next to Marin on a couch near the television. Her gaze was fixed on the now closed doors as if waiting for them to immediately open again. She finally looked back to the TV, and the two sat in companionable silence for the remainder of the afternoon.

Pauley was the first to enter the unit for visiting hours, joining Craig and Marin at the table where they'd eaten dinner. He handed Marin a candy bar which Craig eyed hungrily before turning back to his brother. "Did you bring me one?"

"No, I brought you myself," Pauley chided, bumping Craig's shoulder with his own.

"That's not very nice, Pauley," Craig complained petulantly.

"I'll share," Marin told him, breaking the candy bar into two uneven pieces and offering him the larger one.

"Thanks." He devoured the chocolate, glaring at Pauley the entire time. Pauley roundly ignored him, focusing his attention on Marin.

"Good?" he asked when she was finished.

"Mmmm...," she responded, rolling her eyes with delight. He couldn't seem to take his eyes off her and Craig felt weird. Like he didn't belong. No, he always felt like that. More like he was in the way.

Pauley and Marin continued to stare at each other, grinning like idiots, until Eva arrived a short while later. Boy, did she look pissed as she charged past their table and jerked her head at her sister to join her on a couch as far away from them as possible. Marin must have noticed it too – she jumped up like a scolded puppy and sat obediently next to her twin.

Not long afterward Pauley took off, leaving Craig to stare into space until it was time for the evening relaxation group. He didn't feel very relaxed. He felt kind of keyed up and on edge, and his heart was beating funny. He didn't dare say anything though – they'd just put him on more meds that would make him feel even weirder.

When he met with Dr. Tacee the following day he didn't tell her about his funny heart, and he took her little red pill without complaint. She must have been happy with him because she decided to send him home. She made sure to tell him he needed to come see her every single week so he could keep taking the new pill that was going to cure him once and for all. He readily agreed – he wasn't about to make her mad.

Although he didn't understand why he couldn't just get the pill at the pharmacy and take it at home like his other medication, he kept his mouth shut. She was the doctor; she must know what she was doing. Anyway, who was he to question her?

He was ready to go when Barbie came to pick him up not long afterwards; he didn't have much to pack. He breathed deeply as they exited the front doors of the building. The fresh air felt good in his lungs. They'd been allowed to go to the enclosed courtyard several times a day weather-permitting, but the air seemed different out here. Free air.

Barbie led the way to her spotless Audi coupe and Craig folded himself into the car, immediately rolling down the window. He didn't want to feel cooped up in anything right now. They rode in complete silence; Barbie lost in her own thoughts, and Craig just lost.

After she'd parked carefully in the oversized garage she finally turned to Craig. "It's late, son. We won't be dining together tonight, but I'll have Lucretia bring you something to eat after you get settled in. We'll see you tomorrow for dinner at the usual time," her eyes travelled over his rumpled clothes, "and in the proper attire."

She leaned toward him to offer her cheek, which he slurped on indelicately. Appalled, she pulled away, fumbling in her purse for a handkerchief. "I swear, Craig, your manners leave much to be desired, and they seem to get worse with each passing day!" She swiped at the spittle covering the right side of her face and gestured for Craig to get out of the car.

"Bye bye, Barbie," he said lightly as he rounded the garage to the stone path that led to the pool. Beyond that was the pool house; a two bedroom apartment he called home. He turned on the TV and flopped onto the overstuffed white couch, digging the cell phone that was jabbing him in the thigh out of his pocket and tossing it onto the couch next to him.

It began to ring almost immediately, startling him. The only person who ever called him was Barbie, and he'd just left her back at the main house.

"Hello?" he asked with much trepidation.

"Craig?" the voice was low and sultry. "It's me. Lilah."

***

The cashier looked bored as she scanned the items in Danielle's cart, chomping on her gum with the studied effort of an old cow with its cud. Danielle waited patiently, though on the inside she felt like accosting the girl. She was on a mission – an emotional marathon.

She watched as the teenaged, acne-riddled bagger unceremoniously dumped her purchases in plastic bags; a frozen pizza, a family-sized bag of potato chips, a gallon of cookie dough ice cream, a ready-made coffee cake, three two-liter bottles of soda pop, and five king-sized candy bars.

Relieved when it was finally done, she thrust her debit card at the cow, who took another precious few moments to swipe it and return it to Danielle's eager grasp. She then grabbed the bags from the unfortunate-looking adolescent and nearly ran to her vehicle.

When she arrived home her actions became even more frenetic as she raced around the kitchen like a demon possessed, turning on the oven for the pizza, warming the coffee cake in the microwave, pouring the soda into huge glasses of ice.

Once everything was ready she dove into it compulsively, shoving bite after bite into her mouth without respect for what she was eating. She barely tasted it, her cheeks bulging from the sheer volume of food they held.

She guzzled glass after glass of carbonated liquid, reaching the point that she began drinking it straight from the bottle, no longer caring that it was warm. The ice cream was half melted, the pizza now cold and yet she continued to overindulge as if driven by something unseen.

The sounds that accompanied her binge were practically inhuman, prompting Cece to hide under the bed, as he usually did during these episodes. They were far too undignified for his feline sensibilities. Truth be told, very few of his owner's erratic tendencies scared him anymore, but he'd never quite gotten used to this kind of mayhem.

Danielle's pace gradually slowed until she could barely bring another bite to her fatigued mouth, and she finally gave up trying. Leaning back against the couch cushions, she sat there zombie-like for several moments – but her work wasn't completed; it was only half finished.

Before she could proceed, though, she needed to get rid of the evidence; not necessarily from anyone else's prying eyes, but from her own judgmental and ruthlessly shaming soul. Grabbing a large garbage bag from the kitchen she dumped everything into it – the candy wrappers, the empty plastic bottles, the pizza package, the coffee cake tin, and the chips bag with its dregs of crumbled contents gracing the bottom like orphans.

She tied the top of the trash bag into a knot and tossed it into the large bin behind the building, then carefully washed, dried, and put away the dishes. They couldn't be placed in the drain basin of the sink or even in the dishwasher as they would be a visual reminder of the devastation that had just occurred.

Finally she was ready for the last step in the ritual that had started the moment she'd dragged herself out of bed this morning, lonely, sad, and spiraling out of control. She went to the bathroom, closed the door behind her, and placed a folded towel on the floor in front of the commode. She then knelt before it and divested her stomach of its recently ingested contents.

And just like that, there it was – that feeling of control she'd been missing over the past few days. She no longer felt lost in her own life; she felt empowered...bold. She purged twice more until there was nothing left to expel, and then carefully cleaned the toilet, put away the towel, and brushed her teeth.

When she'd first began to purge her food it was quite painful, and she'd had to use her finger to gag herself. Her college roommate, who'd introduced her to binging and purging as a way to regain a sense of control, had reassured her it would get easier the more she did it. The girl had been right.

Now Danielle could puke at will, and sometimes even without trying to. Her throat used to get incredibly raw, and her stomach would cramp for days after she purged, but those things rarely bothered her anymore. Her roommate had been one smart cookie.

The only thing she'd been wrong about was the weight loss. She'd been an impossibly tiny size zero and had insisted it was because she threw up all the time. But Danielle had later discovered that most people with bulimia are of average weight – some even overweight – because the body isn't capable of evacuating all of the massive amount of calories consumed during a binge, no matter how, or how much, a person purges afterward.

Now Danielle assessed her body critically in the full-length mirror on the back of the bathroom door; at a size twelve, she knew she was considered fat by some, but voluptuous by most. She had a small waist, bodaciously curvy hips, heavily muscled thighs from her track-and-field days, and a double D chest that had yet to sag, thanks to her obsessive use of bras – the only time she went bare was in the shower and during sex, and sometimes not even then.

She'd long since given up hoping for miraculous weight loss as a result of her disorder, though she'd tried to become anorexic a couple of times. That just wasn't her thing – she didn't understand how people could go days without eating, starving themselves while their hair broke off and their skin turned colors and their nails yellowed. No, thank you – she figured she was fine just the way she was.

The next morning she woke to her alarm feeling much better, and even turned on some music to listen to while she got ready for work. While she certainly wasn't finished with the mourning process, she was anxious to return her life to some pre-tragedy consistency.

She chose a black suit which accentuated her curves – as every article of clothing she owned did – and paired it with classic black heels and a dappled silk shell. She twisted her hair into a loose chignon, allowing several tendrils to escape the bun and fall around her face. She finished her ensemble with a delicate gold watch, necklace, and earrings. Satisfied with her appearance, she fed Cece, gathered her cell phone and bag, and headed out the door.

When she arrived at the office Tanisha greeted her like a long lost relative, whispering in her ear, "Don't you ever leave me alone with this lunatic again," followed immediately by a vociferous, "I am *so* sorry for your loss! I've been praying for you, girl!" Danielle accepted her statements with gratitude – Tanisha had become a good friend since they'd begun working together.

She glanced up as her boss appeared in the doorway of her office, drawn by the commotion. While Dr. Tacee tolerated Tanisha's tomfoolery, perhaps because she was a bit afraid of her, she had no such compunction for Danielle's. The doctor seemed to know she'd never leave this dream job – it paid more than it should, the hours were great, and the surroundings were cushy. No, Danielle wasn't going anywhere, and she quickly disengaged herself from her friend to await her orders.

"You've left many things in the lurch during your absence, but the priority is the billing. I expect you to catch up on that by the end of the day." With that, Dr. Tacee turned on her heel and disappeared into her office.

"Can you believe that bitch?" Tanisha whispered to Danielle, who was too dumbstruck to respond. It didn't last long though as she squared her shoulders and followed the taciturn physician.

"I just lost my *brother*!"

"I am aware of that, but that fact does not recuse you from your responsibilities."

"He was your patient! Like, forever! Don't you care about that at all?"

"What I care about is saving my energies to help those who are still with us, and I expect you to do the same."

Danielle sputtered for several seconds while Dr. Tacee turned her attention to the documents on her desk. Impotent, her bluster draining away, Danielle returned to the front office, the look on her face so murderous even Tanisha kept her distance for the remainder of the day.

***

"You should have plenty to eat – I've stocked the shelves and fridge with everything you need, and got more paper towels, dish soap, laundry detergent, and body lotion," Eva said as she put the last of the groceries in the cabinet.

"Did you get shampoo and conditioner and a new brush like I asked?" Marin prompted, impatiently following her sister's movements with her eyes. Would she ever leave? Eva stopped, turning to stare at her twin. She couldn't recall her ever asking for grooming products. Ever.

"Yes, I put them in the bathroom," she said slowly, wondering at the sudden change. Marin looked at the floor, avoiding Eva's inquisitive gaze.

"Thanks," she murmured, barely audible. Eva shrugged and resumed her task, much to Marin's relief.

"I've filled your Mediset for the week – make sure you check it four times a day, and cross off the day on the calendar before you go to bed so you don't lose track, okay?"

"Okay." Go away. Just please go.

An interminable while later Eva made another trip around the small apartment to make sure everything was in proper order before stopping in front of the door.

"Are you sure you'll be okay here by yourself?"

"I'm sure." Oh Jesus God, just *go*!

"Okay." Another endless pause. "I love you, sis."

"I love you too, Eva." And she did. She really, really did. But would you *please just leave*!

"Okay, bye for now. Lock the door behind me."

"Yes." Because I'm an idiot.

As soon as Eva left, Marin rushed the door, threw the deadbolt, and dove for the drawer in the coffee table where she'd hidden her cell phone from her sister's prying eyes. As she'd anticipated, there were several messages, and they were all from Pauley.

She started listening to her voice mail, grinning like a maniac, when her phone chimed. Expecting Eva – it wasn't unusual for her to call from the parking lot to make sure Marin's phone was turned on – she was surprised to see Pauley's number appear on the display. She answered his call, attempting to sound nonchalant – though she was quite sure she'd failed.

"Marin? Is this you finally?" his deep sexy voice emanated through the speaker.

"It's me. I just got home a minute ago." He chuckled at what he erroneously assumed to be a reprimand.

"I don't know what it is, but I'm so taken with you, Marin," his voice caressed her face like a lover's hand, and she forgot to breathe. "I need to see you. Now."

"I don't...I don't drive."

"I'll come to you."

"Uh," she glanced around her drab apartment with something close to terror. She couldn't imagine his shining presence in such a horrifyingly dull environment. "It's kind of a mess here. I haven't been home to clean up," she began timidly.

"I don't care what it looks like, Marin. As long as I'm with you it'll be the most beautiful place on earth." No, he was lying. He'd take one look at her in this abysmal space and never want to see her again.

"Can we...can we maybe go somewhere?"

"If that's what you really want, I guess."

"Please," she implored, giving him her address after he grudgingly consented.

After they'd hung up she took a shower and washed her hair, using the fragrant shampoo and conditioner Eva had left for her. Then she brushed it until it shone, selected a flirty cocktail dress and matching slippers – Eva's doing, again – and wished for the first time in her life that she had makeup. It was probably for the best that she didn't – she'd never worn it before and would probably look like a circus clown if she started now.

At the appointed time she exited her apartment and headed toward the parking lot where Pauley waited dutifully. He appeared startled when he noticed her coming toward him, and even took a step backward until she was close enough for him to determine she wasn't her sister.

"Marin?" he asked, incredulous.

"Of course! Who else would I be?" He let out an indelicate snort; he was fairly certain that phrase had never before been uttered by an identical twin, unless in jest.

"You look amazing," he breathed.

"I clean up nice," she joked. She didn't really know what that meant, along with most other small talk, but she'd watched enough movies to pretend she did.

"Uh, yeah..." He wasn't normally so aphasic, and she found herself growing nervous under the weight of his stare.

As if sensing her discomfort, he closed his mouth and offered her his arm, leading her to his car. "Gorgeous evening, isn't it?" he asked, closing her door and rounding the vehicle to drop into the driver's seat.

"Yes, gorgeous."

It was all they said as he started the engine and pulled smoothly out of the parking lot, but this silence was comfortable, much to her surprise. Her nerves quieted as she took in his profile, strong and fine in the illumination from the dashboard.

She'd never been on a date before, and didn't quite know what was expected of her, but she instinctively felt like everything would be okay when she was with Pauley. She didn't even care where they were going, and wasn't paying attention to their route until they parked at the ferry landing.

She was delighted, and her face shone with sheer joy – it was an evening of firsts; her first real kiss came as the ferry chugged across the river and after Pauley had found a spot for them along the railing. He had cradled her body between his arms while he gripped the metal, she pointing out landmarks she recognized on the fast approaching shoreline.

Just as they were pulling to a stop he turned her in his arms and kissed her gently at first until he was sure she was amenable to his advances. He then tightened his embrace and deepened the kiss, his tongue flicking forward to tease hers in a dance she was surprisingly adept at – maybe even more so than he was.

He pulled back to look into her eyes, but all he saw there was the innocent girl he'd fallen for in the hospital. The mix was incredibly intoxicating, and he found himself hardening in response. Now he pulled away in earnest; he didn't want to scare her away.

She protested the loss of his warmth and reached out to draw him back to her, but he took both of her hands in his to prevent her from getting too close. "Let's go back to my place," he said gruffly, his voice thick with desire. She nodded, afraid he'd change his mind. Afraid she'd change hers.

Back on the road, he drove fast, his hand clenched around hers. This time she watched him openly, and he glanced at her often, flashing his dazzling smile. Please hurry. Pedal to the metal. No time to waste. She knew what they'd do at his place. She was well-versed in those activities. But she'd never wanted to do them. Not until now. She was an emotional virgin, and she was nervous as hell.

It took forever to get to his loft, yet it took no time at all. She was a study in contradictions by that point, and Pauley held on to her in the elevator as if she might bolt. She absolutely wouldn't. She was all in.

The doors opened onto the penthouse – one that would put any bachelor pad to shame. Black leather couches, projection screen, glass and stainless steel everywhere...a sunken living room surrounding a fireplace that was in and of itself a work of art. And floor-to-ceiling windows that offered an amazing view of the city skyline and beyond that, the river they'd just left.

"This is all yours?" she asked, not because she didn't think it was but because she could hardly believe it existed. She was right not to have allowed him a glimpse of her sad little world. He would've fled for sure.

"Mmm hmm...," he murmured without a touch of pride. He was too distracted by her presence in his private domain to put on airs. All he wanted was to get her in his bed, and he was sure he'd burst if he had to make small talk instead.

He guided her hand to his crotch, the fly of his pants straining from his blossoming erection. He watched her eyes grow wide as she stared into his. He held his breath, afraid he'd gone too far, too fast. He hadn't. Her eyelids fluttered closed and her tongue slipped between her lips in concentration as her hand slowly began to rub the thin, soft cloth over his penis.

He came instantly, and disappointment coursed through him. He needn't have worried; she was far from finished.

***

"If you're going to marry into *this* family, dear, you must learn to be a proper lady as opposed to –"

"A trollop?" Lilah interrupted Barbie's diatribe defensively, casting a protective glance at the gigantic diamond on her left ring finger. The one it had replaced, though far from shabby in its own right, paled in comparison.

It had been two weeks since she'd dragged Craig to the jeweler to pick out the ring, and twelve days since she'd proposed to herself on his behalf. A whirlwind romance by all accounts, and they hadn't even consummated their relationship, though she'd moved into the pool house within days of his discharge from the Institute.

"No, dear. I was going to say 'a common washwoman'," Barbie drawled, her tone one of long-suffering, though it was gentle. Lilah took pause at that, unsure if she'd just been insulted. Southern women could tell you to go jack off in your own backyard and make you feel good about doing it.

But she really liked Barbie. The woman took excellent care of herself, had spunk, and was rich beyond belief. *This* should have been her mother. Her life. So she picked out the proper fork and placed it next to the side salad, earning a delicate 'whoop' from Barbie.

She had first met the woman while lounging by the pool, Craig lumbering about in the water like an oversized walrus, occasionally pissing her off by splashing too close to her recliner.

Barbie had appeared like a golden goddess, her skin, swimsuit, and jewelry monotonal, her white-blonde hair a wild contrast to all that bronzed flawlessness. It was obvious she'd had every cosmetic procedure known to mankind; she was nipped and lifted and filled and tucked in nearly every square inch of her body.

But for all that she looked amazingly wealthy and well-preserved, and Lilah nearly drooled with envy. This was the mistress of the estate, and had it been two hundred years ago this would be a grand plantation with countless slaves running around to do her bidding. What wasn't to love about that?

Barbie had stopped in her well-heeled tracks when she'd spotted Lilah, uttering an entirely unbecoming "Oof!", as if she'd been punched in the gut. Her voice rose several octaves as she addressed her eldest. "Why, Craig! I didn't realize you had company!"

Craig appeared put upon, hesitating before awkwardly making his way to the side of the pool closest to his mother. "Barbie, this is Lilah," he uttered, with a haphazard wave of his hand in her general direction.

The older woman tittered as if embarrassed for her son, which she likely was. "I birthed this child, Lilah! And you are...what? Craig's girlfriend?"

"No," Craig blustered, suddenly beat red.

"Yes," Lilah corrected pleasantly, rolling her eyes and giving a little shake of her head. Barbie couldn't have been more thrilled. She'd prayed for some touch of normalcy for her oldest child for, well, decades now, and she'd begun despairing of it ever happening.

"Wonderful!" she squealed, clapping her hands with glee.

They were kindred spirits, Lilah and Barbie, and she couldn't have asked for a better mate for her son. The two of them chatted the afternoon away, periodically turning themselves in the sun to ensure even browning, like chicken on a rotisserie.

As Barbie stood and prepared to go back to the house, she gently squeezed Lilah's hand. "It's been so nice having another woman around who cares about how she looks. You and Craig must join us for dinner at the main house every evening. Lucretia's skills in the kitchen are legendary!"

She began to walk away, then turned before mounting the wide stone steps leading to the expansive patio off the back entry. "Oh, and you can start parking your little sports car in the garage, dear. No need to expose it to the elements behind the pool house, is there?" With that she made her final ascent, waving her fingers at them as she went.

Lilah had whipped her head around to pin Craig with her glare. "She knows I've been living here?" He shrugged his shoulders indifferently, but Lilah couldn't be so blasé. She wasn't family and didn't belong here. What if they decided to kick her out? Where would she go then?

Apparently her continued presence here wasn't up to Craig, as she'd assumed it was – it was up to his parents. It was at that moment that she'd formulated her plan to become a member of the Phipps clan – legally. Never mind that she was already married. Once her strategy bore fruit she would be divorced and no one would be the wiser.

And as the oldest child, the family business, along with its fortune, would pass to Craig when the patriarch was gone. They would be fabulously wealthy, and she would have everything she'd ever wanted. Screw Mark. She didn't need him. She'd soon have way more than he could ever have given her.

Unfortunately her social skills left much to be desired, and her first dinner with the elder Phipps's had been a disaster. It had been a seven-course meal prepared in her honor at Barbie's behest, and Lilah had never seen so many options in dinnerware. She'd used the wrong utensil at every turn, drawing disgusted grunts from an otherwise inattentive James. Craig was of no help – he used a spoon for everything, and the same one at that.

Her ignorance had been largely overlooked by the household's matriarch until she'd appeared at dinner one evening sporting her impossible to miss engagement ring. Barbie had squealed with delight, fawned over the sparkling monstrosity for all of ten seconds, and then immediately took an interest in Lilah's table manners.

After all, their engagement party would be the talk of the town, and it would 'nevah evah' do if the bride-to-be was a slovenly pig. So every day while Craig slept or watched TV or hung out by the pool Lilah was obliged to dress in her Sunday best, traipse up to the big house, and while away the hours learning how to direct a household, stand and walk and sit in a regal manner, and generally act like a lady as opposed to the dreaded common washwoman, whoever that repulsive hag might be.

Regardless, she was grateful not to be stuck in her horrible apartment in that awful neighborhood anymore. She could imagine the look on her benefactor's face if she knew the squalor Lilah had been forced to endure as a result of Mark's insensitivity. As it were, Barbie obviously could never know of her duplicitous past or her grand plans for the future would be ruined.

Her future mother-in-law had arranged a lavish party to announce the engagement, the planning of which rivaled the most ostentatious of events. From the gilded invitations to the elaborate menu to the lighting and décor, it was completely over the top, and Barbie was in her element.

With the final preparations under way and a full complement of temporary staff on hand to help Lucretia carry out her mistress's bidding, Barbie took Lilah to her favorite boutique, where they spent hours shopping for the perfect dress, shoes, handbags, and jewelry.

The exclusive shop offered only one-of-a-kind confections that were ridiculously expensive, and boasted a twenty-four-hour alteration service, which was essential since the gathering was that weekend.

The dress Barbie selected for Lilah was a simple floor-length white column of raw silk with a delicate lace overlay and scalloped neckline that skimmed her slender shoulders. Her hair was the only color the ensemble needed, her engagement ring the only adornment.

Barbie actually had tears in her eyes when Lilah stepped out of the fitting room, the attendant rushing forward with pins clamped between pursed lips, gathering the material here and there to showcase the younger woman's outlandish figure.

The afternoon of the gala Barbie's beauty team arrived in force, fawning and fluffing and oohing and ahhing their way around the women for a couple of hours before finally disappearing in a puff of face powder and a cloud of hairspray.

When they were gone, Lilah gazed at herself in the mirror for a long time. As beautiful as she'd always been, she'd never seen herself so stunning. What would Mama think of her now? Was she finally good enough for the one woman she'd always wanted to please, but had never been able to?

She was shocked to find her eyes glistening – she'd never cried over her mother before – in life or in death. So what was this?

Whatever it was, it was gone in an instant as Barbie mistook her emotion and rushed forward with a Kleenex to dab gently at the corner of her eyes.

"There, there, dear. It's not every day one gets engaged, now is it?" she asked, a bit pointedly. She then offered her arm with a smile. "Shall we?"

As they descended the stairs into the lights and cheers below, Lilah couldn't help feeling like a princess...only *her* frog would never become a prince.

***

It felt good to get back on his BMC racer, and Tony wasted no time finding his cadence once he'd turned onto the street after leaving the sprawling mansion behind. He'd worked every day of the past week because the unit had been so short-staffed, and he didn't dare ride this baby to the Institute. Chained or not, this stead was worth more than many of the cars in the parking lot, and though he was a relatively trusting soul, he wasn't stupid.

That morning he was doing his opener – he had a race tomorrow and was chasing his own record. Hunched low over his handlebars, he filled his lungs with air, reveling in the feeling of being one with his bike. Hills and curves offered little challenge for him; he was in the zone.

He started his first forty-five second sprint, pushing himself as hard as he could, timing himself on his Suunto Spartan GPS watch. He dropped back into tempo for a minute-and-a-half, returning to his sweet spot for about ten minutes before repeating the interval three more times.

It was how he prepared for each race, and by the time he road back into the courtyard of his mother's ancestral home, he felt ready for the following day. The sun was just beginning to play its hide-and-seek bedtime game, throwing the façade before him into foreboding shadow.

When Aunt Ollie died the house would be fully his, yet he had no desire to call this place home permanently. He supposed he'd have to hire a property manager or a caretaker who would live here and maintain it for the generations to come. Or maybe he could donate it to an orphanage – although that would undoubtedly turn his aunt in her newly interred grave. Ah well, plenty of time to think on it – she would likely never die.

He unclipped his cleats from the cycle and walked it to the wide terrace at the side of the house; this was his wing, and he rarely used any other entrance. He climbed the wide brick steps and entered through the double-paned French doors.

He propped his bike on the rack in the anteroom outside his suite and doffed his Diodoras and Bell Race Star helmet on the bench next to it. Then he headed down the hallway to the bathroom to turn on the shower. He was fairly dripping, and Aunt Ollie would have his head if he showed up for dinner a sweaty, smelly mess.

He'd tried it once shortly after he'd moved in, and she'd immediately set him straight. She only required his presence for the evening meal once a week, and would he please be so kind as to show her the respect she deserved by looking and smelling like the cultured gentleman he was as opposed to a street hoodlum? He'd never tried her patience again – after all, he was an amenable kind of guy.

He divested himself of his jersey, socks, and padded bike shorts prior to stepping into the steaming shower and becoming lost in his thoughts. He took much longer than usual, and by the time he'd dressed in linen slacks and a light sweater and navigated his way through the ancient manor to the dining room, dinner was already under way.

He received a glare for his efforts and waylaid an accompanying rebuke by accosting his cantankerous relative with a peck on each check. He was swatted away, but not before a smile threatened to crack her fierce countenance.

"Good evening, Aunt Ollie. It's wonderful to see you," he said, using his most charming smile, his dimples flashing mischievously.

"Good evening, Antonio. What have you been up to, you little scamp?" Her use of his given name was as much an annoyance as his misuse of hers. It was a battle neither would concede.

"Oh, you know...this and that." He placed his dinner napkin on his lap and buttered a sumptuous hot roll.

"The same, then," she demurred, forking a perfectly cooked green bean into her mouth. Dinner would progress thus until they'd both dab their lips with their linen serviette in a refined manner, push away from the table, and go their separate ways for the week.

That evening, however, they were interrupted by her cell phone, her fork clattering to her plate and her mouth drawing into a distasteful grimace as it chimed intrusively. She picked up the offending device, drawing herself up so that she was ramrod straight before answering it in a furor.

"Dr. Tacee," she snapped. Tony felt sorry for the victim on the other end of that call. By her own design, Aunt Ollie didn't have friends, so the caller was either a telemarketer or someone from the Institute. He fervently hoped it wasn't Riley – she didn't deserve to be belittled by his aunt – or by anyone else for that matter.

"You do realize your injudicious use of restraints now requires me to leave my home in the middle of the night to perform a face-to-face assessment of my client, do you not?" she responded, so much venom in her voice he was surprised she didn't turn green from the toxin.

Tony quickly finished his meal and excused himself from the table – he couldn't listen to her tear someone a new asshole without intervening, and a confrontation wouldn't get him anywhere, as he'd learned the few times he'd tried to do so in the past.

Ironically he had applied for, and gotten, the job at PINA without Aunt Ollie's involvement. Even so, she acted like he was beholden to her for his career – God forbid he could get by in the world on his own merit. Anything he did that wasn't first her idea seemed to be deserving of her scorn.

He didn't even try to talk to her about his cycling anymore. That type of activity was for those who didn't have access to a vehicle, not well-to-do folks of a professional caliber. She'd be astonished if she knew how much he'd spent on equipment and supplies and trial fees over the past several years.

And certainly she thought he was wasting his time in a full-time job that was "beneath" him. In her opinion he should have allowed her to use her considerable influence to get him back into medical school right where he'd left off instead of choosing the normal route of updating his prerequisite courses and applying for admission just like everyone else.

At the very least she felt he should double up on his courses so that he could finish in record time and move on with the important part of his life. It was bothersome to him that she considered any lower level of education insignificant, not to mention that she believed his work at the Institute was less valuable than hers.

The support staff was at the forefront of patient care, and without their good work there wouldn't be a hospital for her to send her clients to when they needed acute stabilization. They'd gotten into many heated discussions about this fact, both of them stubborn and bullheaded and unwilling to concede their stance.

They'd finally agreed to disagree, but much angst about the subject remained. Also remaining was the fact that he liked the slow pace of taking one class at a time. His first foray into post-secondary education had been a balls-to-the-wall endeavor in which he'd completed both his undergraduate degree and pre-med program in less than four years.

This time around he wanted to savor the process, as he'd found that sometimes the journey was as rewarding as reaching the destination. If he were being honest with himself he'd admit he was also afraid. What if returning to med school uncovered more hidden grief? If the familiar environment brought back the horrible depression from which he'd so narrowly escaped? He didn't think he could survive that kind of pain again, and it was quite possible his subconscious fear was more responsible for his delay in reaching his goals than anything else.

According to psychologist Erik Erikson's Stages of Psychosocial Development, Tony should be navigating the life stage of Generativity versus Stagnation, in which one is tasked with mentoring soon-to-be adult children and working toward future promotions in a well-established career.

Granted, Erikson developed his theory during a time when the average life expectancy was fifty years of age, but it was still a bit disheartening to realize he was technically nowhere near accomplishing the major tasks of even the previous life stage of Intimacy versus Isolation.

While he was far from a hermit, hiding away from everyone and everything, he hadn't exactly been fully intimate with a career, an idea, or a person to the extent Erikson had intended, either. People in the Intimacy versus Isolation stage of life were supposed to grow into social human beings who made a connection and subsequent commitment to a purpose, whether parenthood, a marriage, a cause, or a career.

He'd done none of those things, and though many of his acquaintances hadn't either, he couldn't help feeling behind in life. He hadn't even reconnected with his old friends since he'd returned from Europe, though those relationships seemed superficial and unfulfilling now. Regardless, maybe it was time to re-evaluate his priorities. Wouldn't Aunt Ollie be proud?

Chapter 10
Bad Influences

Craig watched as Lilah and Barbie gracefully made their appearance at the engagement party – *his* engagement party – and felt a swell of pride that the beautiful creature on the stairs wanted to be his wife. Though he hadn't chosen any of this, he was happy with what had transpired, and couldn't believe his good fortune.

He wasn't one of those men who made things happen, like his brother. He was one of those men things happened to. He never took the initiative; didn't even know how. Yet here he was, happy as a clam, and from the way his mother was beaming at him, had now been elevated to favorite son. Whadya think of that, Pauley?

But it didn't take long for the negative thoughts to intrude, effectively raining on his parade. They weren't the voices – those had been silenced by the medication for once. No, these were his own thoughts penetrating his brain and invading his psyche.

You know you don't deserve this. Haven't you been told a thousand times women – especially women like *that* – are not for you? That happiness is not yours for the taking? What makes you think you're suddenly worthy of the pot o' gold at the end of the rainbow? James and Pauley's words throughout the years taunted him, making him feel insignificant and invisible.

Reminders of the torments from Pauley's exclusive boarding school friends chased away the last vestiges of any confidence he'd begun to feel. What's wrong with your brother? Is he retarded? Retard! Retard! He should be locked away in the basement where retards belong!

His head pounding and his face red with shame, Craig backed away from the throng of partygoers and lurched for the doors to the patio, running on Jell-O legs past the swimming pool filled with floating lights, deserted now that the guests had been shuffled inside for the presentation of the guest-of-honor.

Finally he entered the safety of the pool house, the welcome darkness mercifully embracing him in its enshrouding arms. He didn't know how long he lay there on the couch, his arm thrown over his face as if to ward off further unpleasantness. He wasn't worried about missing the party – it had never been about him anyway.

From the moment Barbie had seen Lilah she'd taken ownership of her, and Craig had become a mere afterthought. Even his monkey suit had been a half-assed rush job, and he'd stood there in the foyer with the rest of the revelers pulling at his collar, his eyes dull and his mouth slack. He couldn't have been more out of place had he been on a penguin cliff in the middle of the ocean.

His father's expression of controlled revulsion every time he looked his way wasn't lost on him, though most such things were. Craig was surprised the man was even in attendance, though he was sure it wasn't a show of support for his oldest offspring. The fact was James had been strongly urged to attend the function by his wife, who was unwilling to take no for an answer.

Barbie's uncharacteristic forcefulness was cause for concern, and James ended up complying more to discover the reason for it than to appease her. He narrowed his eyes on Lilah, suspecting this new fixture was to blame for Barbie's insolence.

Although he acknowledged the girl kept his wife out of his hair, he'd be sure to monitor the situation closely and intervene if it became too disruptive to his freedom. With the purpose of his presence accomplished, he threw a last disparaging glance at his son and took refuge in his office suite for the remainder of the evening.

Craig dragged himself off the couch and disrobed to his undershirt and boxers before crawling into bed. He'd moved to the smaller chamber after Lilah had told him she'd be much more comfortable in the bedroom with the en suite, which also happened to be twice as large as the one he was occupying now.

He hadn't thought anything of it, even when Lucretia, who cleaned the pool house every other day, angrily stabbed a finger at his chest, proclaimed him Master, and then gestured pointedly at the suite's master bedroom. He'd pretended he didn't understand to avoid angering her further, but he got the idea she expected him to remain ensconced in his rightful place.

No matter. Lilah enjoyed it far more than he ever had, and it never occurred to him that they should in fact be sharing a bed. That he should expect some perks for giving the woman a place to live. But he'd never had a physical relationship, and hadn't the slightest clue what it might entail.

Though Pauley used to tease him relentlessly about "the birds and the bees" and had made him watch porn a few times, he'd had a hard time believing people did such things to each other, let alone liked it.

Sure, he masturbated – who didn't? – but it was a means to an end. It released a tension that nothing else could. And he certainly didn't roll around on the bed in the throes of some unseen power, his toes curling and his hands clenching the sheets as if he would take flight if not anchored.

Besides, Pauley'd told him numerous times that, just like women, sex was not for him – unless, of course, he paid a pro for it. He'd immediately discarded that unseemly notion...that was illegal! What was Pauley trying to pull anyway?

Regardless, sex was the farthest thing from his mind as the sounds of the party died down in the early hours of the morning. Shortly thereafter he heard the door of the pool house open and then close again, followed by the door to his bedroom.

What was going on? He sat up in bed, alarmed. Was it an errant party guest? An intruder? He tried to remember what he was supposed to do if someone broke into the house, but his brain was too fuzzy to think straight.

He began trembling, and held the bed covers up to his chin as if they could ward off the evil beset upon him. "Wh...who...who's there?" he stuttered, dreading the answer.

"It's me, silly," Lilah teased as she turned on the lamp and walked around the bed, dropping various articles of clothing until she stood opposite of him, naked. His eyes adjusted to the light until he was able to make out her nude form near his bed, his mouth falling open in shock.

"You left the party before I could give you your engagement present, so I brought it to you." He was confused. His present required her to have no clothes on?

In the warm glow Lilah looked like a flame nymph, and he allowed his gaze to travel her body briefly before looking away. He had the distinct impression he shouldn't be looking at her, like when he'd gotten a spanking for panting over his father's nudie magazines Pauley had found under their parents' bed.

He whipped his head back around as he felt the bed shift under Lilah's weight, his eyes widening when he realized she intended to share it with him. Was there something wrong with her room? And where was his present?

He bucked his way to the very edge of the mattress and turned away from his fiancé, pulling the covers over his head again so he wouldn't be tempted to stare. Barbie had always told him how very rude it was to stare.

When he felt Lilah's body against his he nearly jumped out of his skin, and when her hand inched toward his privates he leaped from the bed.

"Don't you want your present?" Lilah asked petulantly as he stared at her in astonishment.

"You don't have my present," he accused.

"Of course I do," she whispered, touching her lips with her fingertips. "For your present I'm going to make you feel really, really good. Down there." She gestured to his penis, which was now standing at attention in a rather embarrassing fashion.

She wiggled to the side of the bed he'd just vacated and sat at the edge, her legs spread and her hair tumbling around her nakedness like a fountain.

She reached for his boxers, jerking them down to his thighs and exposing him. She then wrapped her fingers around his swollen shaft and began to stroke him expertly, causing him to throw his head back and groan.

His fingers itched to bury themselves in the wild mass of her glorious hair, but he was afraid he might hurt her. Instead he clenched them at his sides, nearly howling as he felt her mouth close over the tip of his manhood.

He couldn't be sure, of course, but he had a feeling this might be the best present ever.

***

"You really don't have to be my taxi," Riley said to Steve as he parked his car under the huge burgundy canopy in front of PINA's main entrance.

He'd been handling her with kid gloves ever since her pregnancy had become noticeable, but some of his safety measures were a bit excessive. She hadn't driven her own car in over a month – she missed Big Bertha; not to mention her independence.

"Nonsense," he responded, taking her hand in his and bringing it to his lips.

It was the most she got from him in terms of physical intimacy these days. When she'd broached the subject with him, he'd told her he didn't want to hurt the baby, in spite of Dr. Huffman's reassurances that sex in any of its many forms would do no such thing.

After Steve had brushed his lips briefly over her fingers he placed her hand back on her stomach and patted it gently. "Besides, the two most important people in the world are in this car, and I'll go to any lengths to keep you both safe and healthy."

Riley narrowly refrained from rolling her eyes, but then immediately felt guilty; he had been the epitome of a good husband since the bathtub incident – she really shouldn't hold that over his head forever.

She didn't have time to refute him anyway – that morning State Senator Broomfeld would be holding court at the Institute in the wake of a string of heinous crimes that had been committed by André Morton, a man with a long history of mental illness.

André had recently been released from jail, where he'd been incarcerated for previous obstructions of justice. The prison psychiatrist had tried to keep the man confined because he believed him to be highly unstable, but the courts disregarded the physician's opinion. In short order André, tattooed and serpent-tongued, had committed two murders; a grandfather of five and a pregnant mother of two.

Riley had been chosen to sit on an advisory panel that would have the senator's undivided attention for an hour. It was an unprecedented opportunity to shine a light on the sorry state of mental health care not only in this city, but around the nation.

But she didn't dare disclose her involvement to her husband. He'd birth a cow. A brahma bull with a hump so big he'd need an episiotomy. No, she'd best keep that information to herself. So she kissed him goodbye, heaved her ever enlarging body out of the car, and promptly slipped and fell on a patch of ice.

"Goddammit!" Steve roared as he lunged from the driver's seat and raced around the vehicle.

She'd already picked herself up by the time he reached her, and attempted to waylay his imminent freak out with an "I'm fine! Really!" to no avail.

"I ought to sue this God forsaken place! You could've hit your head or fell on your stomach or hurt my baby!" he raged, beside himself.

"It's fine, Steve. I'll mention it to Maintenance – they just need a some more pellets out here is all."

"Yes, let's go have a word," he commanded, pulling her arm as he furiously turned toward the entrance.

Panicking, she yanked her arm from his grasp and refused to budge. "No. This is my work. You'll embarrass me and jeopardize my job." And find out the senator's here waiting to speak with me. Oh Jesus. "I would never barge into your office like that."

"It's not exactly the same thing," he scoffed, causing her to bristle.

"Isn't it?"

"Hardly," he snorted. Ass. She put up her hand as if demanding that he stay put, turned on her heel, and stalked toward the entrance. She hazarded a glance back toward him as she reached the double doors and breathed a sigh of relief as she saw him drive away.

Putting her irate husband out of her mind, she entered the welcoming warmth of the main lobby and was immediately ushered into the large conference room next to the entry by the overly enthusiastic receptionist.

"Right in here – everyone's here but the senator. Oh, look – there he is!" she squealed as she hurried back to her desk to await him as if he were a Hollywood celebrity instead of just a politician. A politician who potentially held the power to release necessary funds to the Institute if he was so inclined, Riley reminded herself.

She was surprised by how open he seemed to the needs of the mentally ill in his state, and by the time it was her turn to speak she felt at ease and bolstered by his demeanor.

"Senator Broomfeld, in the years since the regional centers for the long-term placement of the mentally ill closed, there has been more crime on the streets, more homeless gathered in hoards down by the river, more panhandlers approaching people in parking lots and at traffic lights.

The community services that were supposed to be put in place to divert those long-term residents either failed to materialize or became overrun by an underserved population.

There are many with illnesses that cannot be controlled, and they are simply unable to maintain in the community regardless of the services that may be available. For them, the closing of the 'inhumane' state hospitals in the mid-nineteen-fifties has left a gap that cannot be filled in any other way. Those facilities were their homes, and just needed revamping and oversight – not the wrecking ball.

Now the biggest mental health system in the country is the prison, and our jails are nowhere near equipped to deal with mental illness in a constructive manner – they just don't have the resources. So which is more humane?"

"I can't answer that," Senator Broomfeld declared, chagrined.

"Then let's talk about the bottom line – the almighty dollar. On paper, shutting down hospitals and merging services and cutting grant funds is beneficial to the state budget. It wins elections and satisfies constituents.

But what about the soft costs associated with sending the cops down to the bridge once a month to shoo away the unmentionables? The money lost from tourism when travelers decide not to return here after being scared by a squatter tapping on their car window? Or the emergency room bill that becomes the taxpayers' responsibility when someone's untreated psychological condition takes them outside naked in a blizzard?

You see, mental illness can't be compartmentalized. You can't lock it up in a little box and ignore it, throwing less and less money at it while hoping it will go away. It's on the medical/surgical floors and trauma units. It's in the soup kitchens and homeless shelters. It's on the streets and in the jails. And one day, sooner or later, it'll be on the doorstep right outside your home."

She sat back in her chair, satisfied to see the discomfited look that had replaced the previous easy confidence on the senator's face. He should be uncomfortable. It was a grave situation that needed to be addressed with the urgency it deserved.

The rest of the panel discussion carried on around Riley as she turned her attention to her other self-imposed task of the day. She knew in this case she may be paranoid, but she just couldn't shake the feeling that something was going on that shouldn't be.

In fact it had been nagging at her for a couple of months now, probably fed by her own personal feelings, not to mention her choice of evening television recently.

Steve had been making a point of coming home early on the days she didn't work, and they'd been watching forensic crime shows almost every night. He found them fascinating, but was able to shut them out of his mind and sleep peacefully when it was time for bed.

Riley, on the other hand, could lay awake for hours letting her imagination run wild with a host of unlikely, and some even impossible, scenarios. And try as she might to rid her mind of those scenes, they remained, taunting her with their tragic implications.

So when she arrived to the unit, she tracked Tony down, dragging him into the alcove off the patient lounge. She took a fortifying breath and said, "I think your aunt is up to something unethical. Maybe even illegal. And I need your help to stop her."

***

Marin gestured for her sister to take a seat at the small dinette in her apartment, but didn't follow suit – she was too restless by far. Why had Eva insisted on seeing her in person in spite of her assurances that she was fine?

More than fine...utterly fantastic. She held onto herself so she wouldn't float away while Eva regarded her with a critical eye for what seemed like hours. Then she sighed, her shoulders slumping uncharacteristically.

"You look great, Marin," she said finally, a note of dejection in her voice.

"And that makes you sad?" Marin questioned her twin, her high ponytail swinging with her movements. Eva glanced at her again, taking in her twinkling eyes and rosy cheeks, her white camisole just visible under her powder blue cropped sweater, her hip-hugging jeans ending at her suede ankle boots.

She'd never looked so put together, had never even bothered to make use of the many things Eva had bought for her in an attempt to make her look and feel pretty – in an attempt to assuage the guilt that threatened to overwhelm her every time she thought of her broken counterpart. Why had she survived their childhood while Marin had been destroyed by it?

"Your happiness would never make me sad, Marin."

"Well, I *am* happy," she fairly bubbled, her smile reaching every conceivable part of her being. But in spite of her words it was apparent that Eva was in fact not happy that she was happy. "What's going on, Eva?"

Her sister gazed around the apartment as if seeing it for the first time. It looked like it hadn't been lived in since she'd cleaned it last, and Marin was not a neat person by nature. "Where've you been staying, sis?"

Marin stared at her as if attempting to confabulate an alibi, but she was never able to lie with any conviction, especially not to Eva. Sighing, she flung herself into the chair across from her sister and said, "Where do you think?"

Eva closed her eyes for a long moment, and then dropped her head as if in prayer. The silence expanded between them until it became nearly unbearable. "Marin, I'm concerned about Pauley's intentions where you're concerned."

"Oh, for God's sake, Eva!" Marin exploded from the chair so forcefully it teetered on its back legs and toppled against the wall. "I feel better than I ever have!"

"Are you still taking your meds?"

"Of course I am, and Pauley even helps me remember to!"

"And what happens when things are no longer fun?"

"It's not like that. He loves me."

"He *loves* you??"

"And I love him!" Her chin lifted defiantly, challenging Eva to negate her conviction.

"Marin, it hasn't even been two months..."

"I know how I feel," she countered, folding her arms across her chest as if to ward off further attacks on her person.

"Sweetheart," Eva began gently, "I just want what's best for you. I always have, and I always will."

"And why can't you believe Pauley's what's best for me?"

"I know his type, Marin. He's a ladies man...a confirmed bachelor. He can't even commit himself to be there in support of his family – how do you expect him to be committed to you?"

"I dunno. He just is," Marin replied childishly, unwilling to even consider that Eva's concerns might be valid.

She glanced at the clock on the wall in the kitchen and subconsciously smoothed her hands over her sweater. Eva understood perfectly. Pauley was coming. Their visit was over, and Marin had no intention of heeding her advice.

Eva closed the distance between them and held her sister tightly in her arms. "I love you more than the whole wide world, Mae," she whispered, reverting to the childhood endearment. "Please don't ever forget that."

At last Marin returned her embrace. "I know, E. I've always known." Eva nodded her head and saw herself out reluctantly, Marin staring after her, conflicted.

She wanted to reassure her sister, but things were different now. She had Pauley. She felt like she could spread her own wings for once, instead of allowing Eva to do it for her.

And then she became a bit angry. Not super mad, but a tad perturbed. Hadn't her whole life been dedicated to other people? Doing what her parents wanted her to do? Their friends? The people at rehab? At the hospital? Eva? Especially Eva.

Wasn't it okay to do what she wanted for once? Couldn't she just...just...be? Without judgment or guilt or sorrow? Sure she could. Of course she could.

She winced as she righted the chair she'd mishandled; it felt like she was touching the wood through a glove. No. this couldn't be happening now. She refused to allow her disorder to rear its ugly head when her life had taken a turn for the best. There was no way she'd jeopardize what she had with Pauley over a feeling of being insensate.

She flexed her fingers and brushed them over her sweater again. She knew it was made of the softest cashmere, but she felt nothing but a one-dimensional contour. Like her senses weren't connecting to her brain.

The knock on the door jerked her back to reality, and she hurried to open it, slipping into the hallway and closing the door behind her so Pauley couldn't see into her apartment. He shook his head, but smiled, interlacing his fingers with hers as he dipped his head for a kiss.

She was distracted by the disconcerting feeling of numbness everywhere his skin touched hers, including her mouth. She nearly reached up to touch their interlocked lips to make sure they were real, but refrained – the pressure told her they were indeed still in the thrall of their kiss.

Hardly romantic, she mused to herself, to be searching for a scientific rationale of the mind-body connection as opposed to losing oneself in the moment. She had the untenable fear, though, that if she lost herself in anything at all she might never be found.

Later that night as she lay intertwined with Pauley, nothing between them but skin, she was forced to admit that her illness was not as under control as she'd hoped. When they'd made love she'd felt like marble, even inside. As if she was surrounding the hottest part of him with the most frigid part of her...like she would inadvertently turn his warm, responsive body into a cold, hard one.

Even now, as she listened to his slumberous breathing she felt like she was hovering above herself, a distant party to the miraculous coupling they'd just experienced. It was ironic that the breech in her mind that had protected her psyche as a child had now become a hindrance to the physical feelings she yearned to experience more fully.

But it didn't hamper her emotional connection to Pauley in the least. In fact, she felt overwhelmed with the depth of passion her heart could produce. She used to be afraid that she was unable to love, so deeply shattered had she been by her mother's betrayal. But now she knew better. *This* was what life was about.

She played her fingers through Pauley's hair, feeling little but the movement of the muscles and tendons under the skin of her hand, her uneasy feelings growing as she drifted to sleep beside her lover.

Her dreams that night were vivid cacophonies of vignettes depicting her escape from the throes of devil-horned men and women who chased her with open mouths that revealed gigantic black holes through which her mother's hands grabbed for her in vain.

Eva appeared just in time, a platinum princess who severed the hands with her diamond sword that she then speared through the heart of the closest chaser. Its face morphed into Pauley's and Marin threw herself next to him and covered his mouth with hers as it became a black hole again.

Through it she fell, down, down, impossibly far until she was surrounded by nothingness. No sound, no smell...nothing to touch; to feel. She sensed she was moving forward but the darkness remained complete. There was no air fanning her face, no ground beneath her feet.

She knew somehow that this was the end of the world – a physical place of foreboding from which there was no escape. And then she was shaking...shaking so hard her teeth jarred together...and she heard a name she thought might be hers but couldn't be sure because really who was she, anyway? Who were any of us, in the grand scheme of things?

And with that wholly disturbing thought she awoke in Pauley's frantic grasp.

Chapter 11
Loss

"I'm pregnant."

Pauley took the phone from his ear to look at the screen, something he'd gotten complacent about over the past several weeks. Big 'D'...great. Just great. "Congrats. Who's the lucky guy?"

"Come off it, Pauley. There hasn't been anyone else since you."

"And I'm supposed to buy that?"

"I have the paperwork to prove it."

Suddenly this mindfuck was no longer funny. He glanced at Marin, deeply asleep in his arms after their afternoon activities, and gently disengaged himself. Once locked in the massive en suite he paced the cold marble floor.

"How does that work?" he said at last.

Her words coming slow, as if explaining to a five-year-old, she said, "Well, I took some of the hair you so graciously left lying around my otherwise immaculate apartment to the lab at the hospital and had them run a comparison between your DNA and the fetus's. It was a match. One-hundred percent."

He'd stopped pacing, and stared at himself in the mirror. His face had drained of color and his eyes were wild, as if frantically searching for the escape hatch on a burning plane. Crazy bitch. Why couldn't she leave him alone?

Truth be told, she'd tried. She'd been in a funk for many weeks after Michael's funeral, binging her way to a size fourteen. But when she'd surfaced for air she was forced to assess the ravages of her life. She wanted to do right by her brother; earn the pride he'd always felt for her.

So she'd gone to see a counselor in another town an hour away so she wouldn't be recognized, intent on addressing her codependence and her eating disorder. The first couple of sessions had been productive – she'd enjoyed the undivided attention of a paid professional while she chattered endlessly about her issues, and why everyone else was to blame for them.

But when their meetings invariably began to focus on learning to take accountability for her own actions and doing the work it would require to fix herself, she'd found she was no longer interested in therapy. What was so wrong with her current coping skills, anyway?

So she'd happily resumed her binge-purge activities (more purging than binging, though – she had no intention of buying bigger clothes) and threw herself into her work.

"How the hell did they get the...the...fetus's DNA?" Pauley's distant voice brought her back to the present.

"Amniotic fluid, silly." He hadn't a clue what any of it meant, but it sounded technical and a bit like a death knell on his freedom. He began to sweat, searching his brain for a way out of this maze of terrors he suddenly found himself wending his way through.

Marin knocked timidly at the door. "Is everything okay, Pauley?" she called as if a million miles away.

"I need to see those papers," he growled into the phone.

"Sure, babe. Anytime," Danielle sang, ending the call before he could.

He opened the door to find Marin standing before it as if lost. He folded her in his arms, relishing the sensation of her naked flesh against his. "It's okay, sweetheart. I just have to take care of some things for Barbie. Be a good girl and get dressed so I can take you home."

She held him tightly as if afraid to let go. "Can't I stay here until you get back?"

"No, Mari – I'm sorry. I don't know how long it'll take, but I'll call you just as soon as I can, okay?" His voice cracked, and he struggled to regain control of his emotions. He had to get to the bottom of these lies, that's all. Then everything would go right back to normal.

Except it wouldn't, he realized later, as he sat on Danielle's couch with the official report from the hospital clutched in his trembling fingers. He glanced at her, sitting next to him and smiling benignly.

"But...I always wore a condom....," he protested weakly.

"They break." She shrugged noncommittally.

"And you were on the pill," he nearly pleaded.

"Must've forgotten that day," she responded lightly, seeming to enjoy his discomfiture.

"But...," he couldn't even formulate a complete sentence anymore.

"Truly, Pauley, I'm surprised this has never happened before as much as you screw around," she said without a hint of animosity. She seemed infuriatingly calm, and maybe even a bit triumphant.

"I'll pay for the abortion," he sighed, running his hand over his face, defeated.

"Oh, that won't be necessary. I'm keeping the baby."

"The hell you are!" he barked, bursting from the couch and turning to stare at her thunderously.

"What're you going to do, Pauley, cut it out of me in my sleep?" She laughed gaily, well aware he didn't have the balls to even contemplate such a thing.

He paced the room like it had become his cage, far too small for a magnificent beast like him. He raked his hands through his hair carelessly until it stood on end. He looked quite insane, Danielle marveled.

"I won't marry you," he finally retorted.

"I won't marry you, either," she smiled sweetly before continuing, "but you will be here for me and our baby from now on. Unless you don't care if James finds out you're shirking your responsibilities?" He distinctly heard the pounding of the nails in his coffin as he sank back onto the couch and into a despondency that threatened to swallow him whole.

Contrarily, Danielle felt nothing but elation, and the next couple of months were bliss. Pauley was back in her life more fully than ever. He treated her as though she were made of china, and had barely left her side, day or night. The sex was just as wonderful, too, though much less aerobic than it had been when they'd first met.

They'd even gone to dinner at his parents', though that fiasco was awkward at best. She already knew Barbie and Craig from Dr. Tacee's office, but meeting James was a real treat-and-a-half, and Craig's fiancé glared menacingly across the table at her the entire night.

At the end of the evening Barbie had hugged her goodbye and pronounced her the salvation of their family due to the "precious bun in her oven", and the redhead had looked as though she would thoroughly enjoy clawing her eyes out.

She didn't know what she'd done to piss off the hateful skank, but she sure as shit wasn't afraid of her bluster. In fact, she'd offered her an angelic smile as she left. "It was *so* wonderful to meet you, Lilah – I'm sure we'll be seeing a *whole* lot more of each other before the big day!" She'd rubbed her stomach pointedly and laughed when Lilah bared her teeth and very nearly hissed at her. That's right. Bring it, ho.

When they'd returned to her place Pauley had told her he was proud of her; a cherished compliment she would remember forever. In some ways it almost seemed like he *wanted* to be with her...like he was even beginning to love her. Almost.

Except that he often got that distant look in his eyes – the one that reminded her he hadn't wanted her in his life. That he was here purely out of obligation, not desire. No matter...if that was the only way she could have him, she'd take it without complaint. But when he asked her if he could tag along to her next doctor's appointment so he could hear his baby's heartbeat, she panicked.

As easy as it had been to concoct a fake laboratory report using the EMR system at the office, and as adept as she had become at manipulating her abdominal muscles to resemble a pregnant stomach, she had no way of producing a fetal heartbeat in her woefully empty womb, nor of finding a doctor corrupt enough to go along with her lie.

So she'd orchestrated her miscarriage and allowed herself to be consoled by an obviously relieved Pauley. "Will you stay with me?" she had begged pitifully with tears that, unlike the rest of her plan to win him over, didn't have to be faked.

"Of course. What kind of animal do you take me for?" he'd answered, his words brimming with sincerity.

For the next couple of weeks he was true to his word. He remained attentive; kissing her often, bringing her takeout whenever she wanted, massaging her feet every evening before bed. He watched her TV shows and laughed at her dark commentary.

But he refused to make love to her – had even started to come to bed fully clothed and sleeping on top of the covers next to her naked body. Try as she might to seduce him into another ride on the pregnancy-go-round he seemed determined to remain unencumbered of her.

And so the morning she awoke to an empty bed she knew it was over forever this time. She slowly ran her hand over the already cooled sheet and wept for what never was.

***

Riley stared at her baby boy lying so peacefully, as if asleep, in the tiny casket she'd picked out, dazed with pain, two days before.

He was so perfect, with his dark eyelashes fanned across his soft cheeks, his little button nose and sweet pursed lips, his head full of fine, curly black hair.

His little hands were balled into fists – she couldn't open them to slide her fingers into his cold grasp so she contented herself with closing her warm hand around his.

She had the crazy thought that if she could just lend him her warmth, fill his little body up with her heat, he would live again.

So she stayed like that for a long, long time, holding his fist and staring into his face, committing to memory his faultless features, panic that she wouldn't remember beginning to take a firm and insidious hold on her consciousness.

She took a shuddering breath and Eva reached out to hold her shoulders, perhaps in an attempt to keep her from falling apart from herself one limb at a time.

The funeral director, a consummate professional, hadn't allowed her to dress her son herself, no doubt because rigor mortis had to be forcibly overcome during that process – something no mother should have to experience.

But she'd brought socks with her, and now worked them onto her son's feet, his little toes forever curled into themselves in a heartwrenchingly classic newborn pose.

Riley placed the 'I love Daddy' sock on his right foot because he surely would have played competitive sports as a right-hander. The 'I love Mommy' sock went on his left foot because it was closest to his heart.

She then placed the letter that the hospital chaplain had encouraged her to write next to his small body.

Dear Kellan,

You have gone much too soon. The plans we made and the dreams we had gone with you. We had barely glimpsed the beauty of your spirit before it disappeared forever, like the most fanciful of rainbows.

You have been loved from the moment you came to be, and we loved you more and more with every heartbeat, every hiccup, and every kick until our hearts overflowed with the joy of you.

As long as we draw breath you will always be cherished, and always be remembered. You will always be our precious, perfect son. May the good Lord bless you and keep you, my sweet baby.

Love, Mommy and Daddy.

It was one of the most difficult things she'd had to do, but she was glad she'd done it. Glad he would be buried with a part of her.

Steve had flatly refused...had in fact taken part in none of the arrangements following the stillbirth of his son. Since that fateful day he had taken her to the hospital after she'd told him the baby hadn't moved in a few hours, the ultrasound confirming their worst nightmare: intrauterine fetal demise at twenty-seven-and-a-half-weeks gestation. He'd fled the exam room and she hadn't seen him since, communicating solely through text messages.

He'd been copiously absent when they'd induced her labor to deliver their baby.

He was nowhere to be found when she held their two-and-a-half pound son in her arms.

He was not there when the chaplain helped her bathe Kellan, make molds of his hands and feet, take clippings of his freshly washed hair, and dress him for his trip to the funeral home that Pastoral Services had selected for her.

And she was alone when she agonized over just the right tombstone to guard their son's grave for the rest of eternity.

She could make all the excuses in the world for his absence, but she wouldn't. She was hurting, too. So she'd done it all herself...though thankfully not all by herself. She'd had Eva and the kind chaplain and the amazing funeral director.

But when she'd finally forced herself to write the letter, it was from the both of them, unbeknownst to Steve; their final tribute to their son.

Riley turned away from the casket before the lid was closed – she couldn't bear seeing it happen, forever sealing her firstborn within its confines. She nearly fell to the floor as her knees buckled, but her mother was there on one side and her aunt on the other. Eva brought up the rear as the small ensemble exited the funeral home.

At the cemetery it was Riley's mother who needed support as the little box was lowered into the freshly dug earth, the smell of rich black soil teasing their nostrils as they listened to the funeral director inter Kellan to his forever home.

Poor Mother, Riley thought to herself as she consoled the older woman as best she could through her own pain. Her mother had experienced so much loss in her life, and now this. Riley worried about her, and made her aunt promise to take good care of her. It was an unnecessary plea – the two were as close as sisters could be.

The thought brought a fresh pang on top of her already unbearable heartache as she thought of her own sibling, as lost to her as Kellan was.

Abel had been mildly autistic, preferring his own imaginary world to the real one in which he was forced to reside. Being around people, even family, had produced near constant anguish, and he would retreat further and further into his fantasies until he was able to be alone again.

But with Riley he was almost normal. They were only a year apart in age, she the younger, and he felt he could relate to her like nobody else – she was nonthreatening to his make believe life.

They would talk for hours about everything and nothing, his face animated by the yearning in his soul to connect with another human being. He was heroic to her in those moments.

She'd been concerned about him going away to college – being around a bunch of strangers in an unfamiliar environment day in and day out – but her parents were convinced it was an opportunity to become more independent...a good start to a productive life. They'd been blinded by their unerring belief that he could be normal if he wanted it bad enough.

Though she harbored no ill will toward her parents, Riley nevertheless believed they were the cause of her brother's death more so than the noose around his neck. Her only consolation now was that her father, Abel, and Kellan would be together in heaven until she could join them again.

After the burial she arrived home to an empty house and went straight to the nursery. Sitting in the rocker she'd so enthusiastically chosen for its cheery green checkered cushions, she rocked herself to sleep, tears streaming down her cheeks.

She awoke to Steve packing fresh clothes in their bedroom, his usually fastidious appearance badly rumpled and unkempt.

"Why?" she asked, simply – she wasn't in the mood to mince words.

"I can't even look at you right now," he spat.

"So this is my fault?" she questioned, incredulous.

"Who else's?"

"No one's! It happens!"

"Who, exactly, does it happen to? Besides us, of course."

"One in every hundred-and-fifty births. Etiology unknown," she recited, the statistics ones she'd researched herself, as if arming herself with information could ward off her loss. She couldn't blame him for his anger, but it was misplaced.

"If you hadn't been working at that place –" he began, but she cut him off before he could finish.

"'That place' had nothing to do with it."

"You'll never convince me of that." He swung his suitcase off the bed and marched toward the door, obviously expecting her to move out of his way. She didn't.

"So this is it, then? You're divorcing me for my choice of employment?" She crossed her arms defensively.

"Of course not," he snapped, gnashing his teeth. "You know as well as I do that a newly divorced politician is a failed politician in this town."

She choked out a derisive laugh. "But a politician who ditches his wife the day their baby is buried is a stand-up kinda guy?"

He clenched his jaw and pushed past her, leaving her to fear for the safety of his abused teeth. "I'll be in my office." He didn't bother to look back at her as he stomped down the stairs and out the door, slamming it in his wake.

She lowered herself to the top step, staring after a man she thought she knew, left alone in a house that was never hers. She was no one now...no one except a wife who didn't really have a husband and a mother who didn't really have a child.

***

Marin ghosted through the hallways of the Institute, her wrists wrapped in bandages and her frail frame barely capable of holding her upright. Other patients passed by her but she didn't see them – she saw nothing but the color blue in all its various shades. Every scene, every vision...filled with blue upon blue under blue within blue.

She was completely out of touch with reality, even more so than during her states of catatonia when she at least had the still frame memories of her past to keep her tethered to herself. Now the rope previously connecting her mind with her body drifted in limbo, perhaps never to be reattached again.

When Eva had found her she'd been sitting on the floor of her closet amongst all the things Pauley had bought her, her cell phone gripped in her hand and her eyes staring at the wall vacantly. The slashes on her wrists had been superficial and had been made across the vein rather than along it...she was not adept at suicide.

It had been two weeks since she'd last seen Pauley, and nine days since her mind had gone blank – or rather blue – and she was lost in the netherworld of her shattered spirit. Eva was more worried than ever, of course; every day she came to sit with her for hours on end.

Side by side, saying nothing...feeling nothing. It was a welcome release compared to the abject misery she'd felt upon realizing Pauley had abandoned her. She'd been so sure of his presence in her life; so sure of their love that she hadn't even considered the possibility they could end up apart. How could they? They had melded so fully that they had become one being.

He'd taken her shopping and bought her an embarrassing amount of clothes – dresses, jeans, t-shirts and sweaters, lingerie and bras, thongs and negligees. Then there were the numerous swimsuits that rarely stayed donned during their midnight dunks in the heated pool on the roof of his building.

She had clothes to go dancing, clothes to go jogging, and several extra special outfits for their trip to Vegas he'd surprised her with the week before he'd disappeared from her life. She'd never been on a plane before, and she'd been nearly out of her mind with anticipation as she'd stood at the enormous windows watching the planes on the tarmac.

Pauley had been pleased by her excitement, which had heightened even further when their plane circled the strip, affording them an astounding view of the myriad of lights from their first-class seats. They had toasted each other with sparkling apple juice and made out shamelessly until the plane was empty and they were asked to disembark.

But the clothes and the shoes and the purses were nothing compared to the jewelry he'd showered upon her. Diamonds and pearls, rubies and emeralds, all set in white gold that shone so brilliantly they made her grey eyes look like sparkling ice.

He liked her best dressed in nothing but the wide array of precious gems he'd lace around her slender neck and delicate wrists, making love in front of the view of the cityscape through the gargantuan windows of his living room, bathed in a million twinkling lights of every color.

But now the only color was blue, the only clothes the nondescript scrubs the Institute provided to its ICU patients. No matter; she was aware of nothing. Not even the electrodes they applied to her temples or the IV they put in her arm to deliver the anesthesia and muscle relaxer directly to her bloodstream. And certainly not the joules of electricity they shot through her brain, Eva crying at her bedside during the entire procedure.

And if she experienced only blueness before, now she was relegated to a deep, dark nothingness. The rope now frayed almost beyond repair, she sat, day in and day out, in a wheelchair in front of the nurse's station being fed through a straw she sipped at instinctively, the routine broken only by the recurring ECT treatments and endless nights alone in her room.

Her twin was there more often than not, chattering incessantly, blaming herself, of course, for remaining away so long after Marin had told her to stay out of her life. She hadn't needed her anymore. She'd had Pauley. He'd take care of her from now on. So Eva had gone...but so had Pauley. He left the blue in his wake...and the blue had left the nothing in its stead.

But day by day, sometimes even hour by hour, the nothing took on a blue tint again, and gradually became brighter and more animated than anything she'd ever seen. Slowly she began to feel her heart beating inside her chest...the air filling her lungs.

She could discern the presence of her sister and taste the nutrient shake on her tongue. Not long after that she began to see shapes – blurred outlines of faces all around her. She turned to the most precious one of all, by her side through sick and sickest.

"I'm *hungry*," she complained, clearly and compellingly.

Eva jumped, shocked, letting out a bark of a laugh and then bursting into tears, hugging Marin so tightly she was in danger of choking her. "Thank God, thank God, thank you dear God –".

"Eva – I'm hungry." Surely God would understand if his disciple cut her prayer short to grab a cheeseburger for her starving sister.

It took another two weeks of ECT treatments before Marin had recovered enough from her psychotic break to be released from the Institute. Eva tried to insist that she stay with her for the time being, but Marin refused.

She wanted to go home. She wanted to be among her own things. She wanted to figure out how to live a life without Pauley in it. The longer she stayed away from her apartment, the more difficult it would be to get on with things.

So Eva finally relented, driving her home and helping her clean herself up properly – the shared bathrooms at the hospital were far from conducive to cleanliness. She stood in the shower for a long time while Eva heated up a pizza and popped in a movie. Marin was grateful for her, and enjoyed the feeling of safety she brought. But it wouldn't last forever. Eva had her own life to lead.

After she'd finished in the shower and thoroughly attended to her grooming for the first time in two months, the sisters settled down in front of the TV for a heaping dose of romantic humor – the balm for all of life's ails.

Eva kept nudging Marin's shoulder with her own in a playful manner, though Marin suspected the action was designed to convince her twin that she was real; that she actually had miraculously recovered from the abyss with no greater harm than a few marks on her wrists that were by now hardly visible. Marin couldn't blame her. She didn't feel all that real herself, and if she could have nudged her own shoulder she wouldn't have hesitated to do so.

Finally Eva left after assuring her she would stop by every single day without fail to check on her. They had hugged each other in the open doorway for an excessive amount of time, and then Marin explored her apartment as if it belonged to someone else.

Eva had put away all the things she had dragged onto the closet floor, made her bed, plugged in her cell phone, and stocked her fridge. She'd even laid out her pajamas. Classic Eva...she'd thought of everything.

Not everything – she was back again already. Marin hurried to the door and flung it open with a wide grin, which died a sudden death at the sight of Pauley standing there with his fist still raised as if to knock again. He quickly eased passed her into the apartment before she'd recovered enough to slam the door in his face.

"I've come to see you every day. You haven't been answering your door", he accused, somehow looking angry and stricken and guilty all at the same time.

"I haven't been home. I've been sick," she said pointedly. He pulled her into his arms, burying his lips in her hair. "Get out, Pauley," she demanded, pushing at his chest futilely.

"No. I'll never leave you again, Mari. I promise." And he held her until she had no choice but to believe him.

Chapter 12
Family Bonding

Eva had such difficulty being mindful of her workout that morning that she finally gave up and left the gym a mere thirty minutes after she'd arrived, causing Josh to gape after her in astonishment. She offered him an apologetic shrug, but didn't have the energy to provide an explanation.

Marin was back with Pauley. That couldn't possibly end well. And Riley had lost her baby. Where was the justice in that? She was filled with anxiety and sorrow – two triggers that were powerful enough to send her recovery over a precipice so deep it could well be never-ending.

Back at home, she attempted to wash the stink of fear from her body, the water as hot as she could tolerate and the spray as hard. It was no use, though, and she exited the stall as out of sorts as she'd entered it.

She dressed in a fitted navy suit with matching pointed-toe mules and piled her hair loosely on top of her head, slipping iridescent hair pins through it strategically to hold it in place.

Regardless of how she felt on the inside, at least she looked like she had it all together.

The office was a madhouse when she arrived, and because it was an out-of-school day for the local district, it would likely stay that way until the last client was seen that evening. She was thankful she wouldn't be around to see it – her office hours ended at two o'clock each day so that she could schedule family and individual sessions at the hospital and clinics when necessary.

She gave a bolstering nod to her receptionist, who was responsible for controlling the zoo in the waiting room. The therapists often regaled her with sweets and other goodies to express their gratitude for her steadfastness – they'd be lost without her.

"Good morning, Rosie," Eva nearly shouted to be heard over the din as she deposited a large foaming latte on the grateful woman's desk. She then retreated to her home away from home, closing the door on the craziness beyond. The silence was immediate – the offices had been fortified with an insane degree of soundproofing when she and her partners had first rented the place, and they had not been disappointed with the effect.

She uttered a relieved sigh as she turned on the fireplace and dropped into the spacious leather chair behind her desk. She opened the client file Rosie had placed in her inbox when the woman had first arrived that morning, and reviewed its contents with interest.

She had a new client today: Annabelle Jorgenson had been referred to her by PINA following an initial hospitalization for fugue. She'd been arrested for destruction of property but had gone nearly catatonic in the back of the police car, and had been taken to the Institute for treatment.

Her case had confounded her psychiatrist, who had eventually diagnosed her with dissociative identity disorder. Formerly known as multiple personality disorder, DID is a rare condition that some experts refuse to believe exists, though it's received much hype in the media.

Certainly there have been periods in which it was diagnosed more frequently, and erroneously, than in others – similar to ADHD in children who were merely being immature adults. Eva was one of the slow-to-believers, and would reserve her judgment for an undetermined point in the future.

In reviewing her knowledge of the disorder, she recalled that it's likely caused by a trauma during childhood in which the child's psyche is unable to withstand the emotional pain of the event and splits into two distinct personalities; the original weaker persona that generally remains in control of the mind, and the new stronger identity that emerges to protect the inner being during times of extreme stress or further trauma.

In Annabelle's case, three distinct alters had been documented, which means her fragile mind had been exposed to two more traumatic events that forced additional splits into other protective personas, driving her primary personality into an even weaker state of being.

Even though one's alters are intended to be a defensive mechanism for the primary personality, over time they grow stronger with use during trigger events, and eventually become parasitic to the host, attempting to take over as the primary identity.

When this happens the client spends more time under the control of a persona that is often negativistic, destructive, and violent. Because the client's true persona is unaware of the other entities living inside her mind, she is technically innocent of the actions taken by any of them. Obviously this can be a legal nightmare, but also a potential scapegoat defense if a person can convince others of their innocence.

In terms of treatment, each trauma experienced during childhood must be brought into the awareness of the original persona, usually through hypnotherapy. The client then works through the detrimental impact of the trauma using adaptive coping mechanisms and medication. Finally the alternate personalities are integrated into the primary persona one by one.

Treatment is characterized by much hard work that can be dangerous for both the therapist and the client's original identity as the alters struggle to maintain control. They may even attempt to 'kill off' each other in order to emerge as the only personality, thus changing the host forever.

The outcome would be akin to an extreme version of a chaotic personality disease such as antisocial personality disorder, which is often attributed to sociopaths. It would therefore be in Annabelle's best interest in terms of having a chance at leading a healthy, happy life to hold onto her primary personality while eradicating the others – especially the one that seemed to be inclined toward violence.

With a plan in place Eva's initial meeting with her new client went well, and the rest of her day followed suit. Before she knew it she found herself sitting in her Jeep, the melancholy from that morning threatening to reassert itself.

She knew what she needed to do, and she arrived at the small church across the river just as the AA meeting was being called to order. She slipped into a chair by the door at the back of the room, nodding to several of the other members that she recognized. Many were surprised to see her there, including Gabe, the meeting leader, who raised his hand in greeting.

This was not her normal meeting place, as she preferred locations much closer to her home or work. But she'd always felt a connection to this church, and Gabe was a phenomenal leader, so she sat back and lost herself in the proceedings. AA had saved her sanity, and her life, on more than one occasion, and she realized this may well be one of them.

After Gabe had adjourned the meeting he was surrounded by a horde of devoted members, and Eva patiently awaited her turn with the charismatic speaker. It was no wonder he was invited to speak at schools and conventions and clubs and events all over the country; his easy, self-assured style, warm tone, and persuasive banter proved incredibly endearing, and he was adored by all.

Eva was no exception, and as the room cleared out and she was left face to face with him, she found herself awestruck. "Long time no see," he quipped, a flirtatious note entering his voice as he stared at the stunning blonde. But his smile vanished when he detected an indelible sadness in her eyes. "What is it, Eva?"

The words wouldn't come, and she swayed toward him. He caught her before she fell and held her in his arms, worry etching every line of his distinguished face. He felt her shudder against him and attempted to pull away, but she had wrapped her slender arms around him and held fast.

He allowed himself a moment to enjoy the feel of her body against his before separating himself enough to look into her eyes for some hint as to what was bothering her. She shook her head slightly before moving her hands to his face, cupping his cheeks with her palms.

He glanced around the room to make sure they were alone, and then allowed himself to be pulled in for a kiss, her hands entwining around his neck and his splaying over her back, both of their wedding rings glinting in the bright fluorescent lights.

When they finally parted, they were no longer alone. The pastor who'd married them ten years ago in this very building jangled his keys impatiently, though indulgently. Time to go, kids. Get a room, for God's sake.

***

Tony walked hand in hand with Gwen, his real estate agent and current distraction, through the downtown loft he'd just purchased. He'd fallen in love with the exposed ceilings and brick walls, the gourmet kitchen and original wood floors, and the massive windows with amazing views of the river. He couldn't believe this was his new home, and could barely wait to move in.

They'd already christened the place several times that evening, even though there wasn't a stick of furniture to be found. "Happy?" she asked as she hopped onto the large granite island, swinging her legs beneath her.

"Quite. You?"

She laughed. Of course she was; she'd just made a huge commission and had enjoyed several orgasms as a bonus. Some would call her a cougar – she was nearly fifteen years older than he was – but she didn't care what others might say. Recently divorced, newly refreshed at the surgeon's office, and free to do what she wanted for once, she knew the score even if nobody else did.

Being on the prowl was the furthest thing from her mind...she was finally healthy, contented, and in control, and Tony was more than happy to be along for the ride, however long it lasted. Neither of them were looking for anything serious; he had just begun med school and she'd vowed to never again be tied to a man for anything more than an occasional dalliance.

He had to admit, though, that he'd quite enjoyed the look of horror on Aunt Ollie's face when she'd caught them kissing in the foyer after Gwen had dropped off the purchase agreement for him to sign. That she'd assumed Gwen was his new girlfriend was obvious, as was her disapproval of everything from the woman's age (forty-five) to her appearance (short skirt and high heels).

If he were being honest he'd have to acknowledge it was more likely because she was black, her skin a deep, smooth cocoa and her hair shorn to within an inch of her scalp and worn in a natural afro. Aunt Ollie was contemptuous of the exceptional.

Didn't matter...he dug everything about Gwen; her free spirit, the shape of her head, her mile-long legs – he would miss her immensely when she decided to leave him. He had no doubts she wouldn't stay long, but he was determined to enjoy her while she was willing to grace him with her presence.

When he'd next joined Aunt Ollie for their weekly dinner she had grilled him about "that black gal" until she'd infuriated him enough to cut their evening short. Though it had validated his decision to find his own place, the impetus had first come several weeks earlier when he'd told her of his choice of medical school.

Unlike his previous matriculation, he'd been admitted to the state university his father had attended as opposed to Aunt Ollie's esteemed alma mater, a private, exclusive school with a price tag to match. She had said cruel things about Luke, eventually intimating that Regina would still be alive if it weren't for him.

Tony had narrowly refrained from telling her to go to hell, instead advising her that he would no longer subject himself to her continued insults of his parents. The following week he'd shown up to dinner – to her obvious surprise – to tell her he'd decided to look for a place of his own.

He didn't want to end things on a sour note. After all, she was the only family he had left, and his mother would have wanted them to maintain some semblance of a civil relationship. She had acted hurt, but he suspected it made no difference to her whether he was in residence at the mansion or not.

And so he'd begun his house hunt with Gwen's assistance, touring everything from single family homes to duplexes, townhomes, and condominiums. Since he hadn't been planning to move anytime within the foreseeable future, he hadn't even considered where he might want to live, or in what type of abode.

Gwen had suggested he explore everything the city had to offer before narrowing his search, though he determined almost immediately that a standalone residence, or even a duplex, was not for him. He didn't need that much space, and wasn't enamored with the idea of maintaining a large yard. Aunt Ollie had a groundskeeper to keep her lawn lush and perfectly trimmed, but it didn't make sense to him to have such immaculate grounds just for show.

He saw a few townhouses he liked, but they were designed vertically as opposed to horizontally, and he had doubts he'd be able to get his bike up and down the narrow staircases without doing a great deal of damage to the walls in the process...another headache he didn't need.

The condominiums Gwen had shown him were beautiful, but were either brand new or recently renovated with the finishes and upgrades that were currently popular, lending them a sterile feeling utterly devoid of character. While he loved the amenities, the perks weren't enough to offset the luxury hotel atmosphere.

So they'd finally ended up with lofts – similar to condominiums but with a homier feel. They were generally housed in older buildings that had been refurbished to showcase their historical charm while offering all the comforts of a modern structure.

The building he'd chosen included underground parking, a large storage cage for his bike gear, an exercise room with indoor pool and hot tub, and a rooftop deck perfect for large gatherings. His loft boasted two bedrooms, two bathrooms and a den, in addition to the expansive kitchen, dining area, and living room. It also had a large wrought iron-railed balcony that offered an excellent vantage point for watching the sunset over the river.

If that weren't enough, it was close to the Institute and the university, and he found himself wondering why he'd taken so long to make this move. It was high time for him to become his own man. So he'd made an offer on the unit which was accepted in a matter of minutes, and he and Gwen had returned several times since to take measurements for window treatments and furniture.

He had nothing of his own since Aunt Ollie's estate had already been furnished with everything he needed – as a result, he'd had to spend several hours and a great deal of money at the furniture store purchasing everything he'd needed to set up his household.

He'd chosen a brown leather couch and loveseat for the living room, as well as an enormous colorful wool rug to add warmth to the bare floor. A round glass table and brown leather chairs were perfect for the dining space, and a couple of dark wood bar stools complimented the kitchen island.

He picked out a deep oak sleigh bed that weighed a ton and cost even more, changing his mind about it several times before deciding he was worth the splurge. A matching armoire and nightstands completed the set, and he finished with several lamps, artwork, and a few decorative pieces to add style and interest to the dwelling.

He spent an equal amount of time at the home store getting towels and a shower curtain, pillows and bedding, dishes and cutlery, pots and pans and glassware – and still had to return several times for things he'd forgotten. Filling a house was hard work, and by the time he'd finished he was exhausted.

As expected, Gwen had left him following the closing – she hadn't even seen the finished product, but she'd said Belize was calling her name and he'd had no choice but to let her go. Now he sat drinking a beer on his balcony, his feet crossed on the railing, toasting her memory and reliving the good old days.

He'd had his last dinner at the mansion after packing the remainder of his clothes into the trunk of his Mustang and returning his suite to the exact condition in which he'd found it. Trudy had outdone herself with lobster tails with butter sauce, scallops, asparagus spears, fingerling potatoes, and a radicchio salad, and dinner had actually been a pleasant affair until Aunt Ollie had begun haranguing him about his poor choices in women and schooling again.

"You realize, Antonio, you have a name to uphold. The Tacees are old money, and have always been cognizant of their responsibilities to uphold their ancestors' dignity and grace, even at great cost to their own whims and desires."

"You must be grateful I don't carry your last name, then, lest I besmirch your elders." She had narrowed her eyes and pursed her lips dangerously. His irreverence was not to be tolerated, but she had little, if any, control over him at this point.

"Be careful of your attitude, young man," she said anyway, simply because she was conceited enough to think he'd listen to her.

"Or what, Aunt Ollie? You'll file a Board of Mental Health petition on me? Lock me away? Overmedicate me?" Her eyes glinted malevolently, but he paid her no heed. "How did Michael Gregory's autopsy go, by the way? Any toxicology issues?" Dr. Tacee threw her napkin on the table and stood, trembling with rage.

"How dare you, you little upstart!" she spat. "You will never be half the physician I am, you ungrateful imp!"

"My only wish is to be half the physician my parents were. Where you measure up in comparison makes no difference to me," he said quietly, leaving the room, and the house, for the last time.

***

Marin discarded her fifth outfit onto the bed with a frustrated groan. "They're going to hate me," she cried.

"They won't. They'll love you as I do," Pauley reassured her indulgently.

He gently swatted her aside and selected a short plaid skirt, crisp white collared shirt, cropped cardigan, white knee-high stockings and black patent leather Mary Janes. He laid them on the bed, kissed her on the forehead, and disappeared into the shower.

When he came out, wrapped in a towel slung low around his hips, she was fully dressed, her hair held off her face with a black velvet headband. She looked fresh from the schoolroom, which was one of the things he loved most about her – her aura of innocence combined with her complete lack of decorum in bed.

In fact, she looked so appealing he dropped his towel to the floor, sat on the edge of the bed, and pulled her onto his lap, pushing aside her thong to gain entry into her sweet body. When he was done he sent her into the bathroom to fix her hair while he got dressed – they were late, but he couldn't envision a better reason.

Once they finally arrived at his parents' home they were greeted with a chilly reception from Lucretia – apparently rich people were expected to be on time for dinner. They were led to the dining room where Barbie leaped from her seat to press her cheeks to Marin's in welcome while Craig waved cordially from his spot to the left of his mother.

Next to him Lilah looked lovely in a green sink sheath and draped with emeralds, but her features were arranged into a mask of loathing. Marin was startled by the woman's apparent animosity, and was not happy to be seated across from her. She turned to James with relief when Pauley introduced them, but the feeling quickly faded upon noticing his equally hateful glare.

"Are you pregnant, too?" he asked without acknowledging the introduction, or his son's presence, in any way.

Marin was surprised into stuttering. "No...I...I...c-c-can't g-g-get pregnant..." Barbie looked crestfallen, but James appeared bored, as if he couldn't care less one way or the other. Who were these people?

Thankfully dinner was over soon and James tossed his napkin onto the table, excusing himself. Pauley squeezed Marin's hand and then followed his father out of the room, leaving her alone with the rest of his family.

Craig sat grinning at her like an imbecile, spooning raspberry tarte into his mouth as if it might race off the table at any moment.

Lilah had barely stopped glaring at her all evening, and Barbie seemed oblivious to everything except her plans for her eldest's eventual wedding.

Marin turned her attention to Barbie's endless stream of chatter and found herself wondering if the woman actually drew breath. "What do you think, dear?"

Marin jerked, alarmed to be dragged so abruptly into Barbie's soliloquy. "I didn't follow," she said apologetically, pinching herself under the table to remind herself to pay attention.

Patiently, Barbie repeated most of what she'd said over the last fifteen minutes – where had Pauley disappeared to? – ending with, "...so I've opted for live swans in the swimming pool instead of ice sculptures. Much more dramatic, don't you think?"

Marin stared at her for several seconds before realizing she was expecting an answer. "But...won't they poop in the pool?" Lilah tsk'd with disgust, but Barbie clapped her hands delightedly.

"Yes, my girl!" she crowed, causing Lilah, whose dessert Craig was now happily ingesting, to regard her as though she'd lost her mind. "Ice sculptures it is, then!" She bolted out of her chair and shouted for Lucretia as if the woman weren't standing at attention just outside the room.

Marin glanced at Craig, who was now running his finger around the inside of the empty tarte dish to ensure he hadn't missed any, and then slowly turned her gaze to Lilah. Now that Barbie had left the table, her glare had turned downright menacing, and Marin wondered if it would be rude to dismiss herself from the table.

Before she had the chance to do so, Lilah spoke, her tone cruel and vicious. "You'll have to excuse us – we're a bit confused by all of Pauley's girlfriends." Relief flooded through her – she'd been afraid this family hated her on sight when that wasn't it at all. It was Pauley's playboy past they were concerned about.

No wonder Pauley's father had barked at her and his future sister-in-law had been openly hostile all evening; they'd assumed she was just another bimbo on his long list of women. Eager to put Lilah's mind at ease, she shook her head and leaned forward, engaging.

"I know Pauley has a rather...sordid...past, but all that's over now. We've been together a long time, and I'm not going anywhere."

Lilah raised her eyebrows and rested her chin on her hand, her elbow on the table next to her now spotless tarte dish. "That's amazing," she said sweetly, earning an exuberant nod from Marin. "So the pregnant woman he brought to dinner a couple of weeks ago must've been some charity case he picked up off the street...," she mused as Marin's smile faltered.

"I don't believe you..." She felt panic creeping in, overnight bags in hand, ready to stay a nice long while.

"Why don't you just ask him yourself? I believe her name was Danielle. Good-looking blonde with enormous knockers." Lilah's gaze dropped to Marin's nearly flat chest.

"Probably just a friend," she murmured weakly, a thread of hope in her voice.

Lilah nodded helpfully. "Yeah, probably. Although I'm pretty sure Pauley introduced her as the mother of his baby – that's why James wanted to know if you were pregnant, too. Seems there's an awful lot of messing around going on," she finished innocently, her expression shifting to one of angelic servitude as Barbie came prancing back into the room.

The matriarch resumed her prattle as though she'd never left while the two women continued to stare at each other, Marin with shock and Lilah with smug satisfaction. Craig had finally become aware of the strain around him and sat slack jawed, watching them with trepidation.

Finally Marin pushed out of her chair with a tortured cry and ran from the room, leaving Barbie to stare after her in surprise. "What in the world was that all about?" she asked no one in particular as raised voices reached the foyer.

"I deserve that money! I've put up with your high-handed bullshit over thirty years!"

James's response was equally loud, but wholly unintelligible.

"You've been nothing but a sperm donor, you asshole – we practically had to raise ourselves. No wonder Craig's so fucked up!"

Pauley slammed the door to James's office, appearing in the foyer red-faced and out of breath.

"Paulson! That's not nice!" Barbie blustered, primarily for the sake of her guests. "Say you're sorry to your daddy right now..." Her demand fell on deaf ears as Pauley pointed a shaking finger toward the room that currently housed the man in question.

"I haven't had a raise in my allowance in six years. Six *years*, Barbie! I've been a dutiful son, I come to visit when you ask me to, I return your phone calls, I even babysit this doofwad when you guys leave town." His pointing finger shifted to encompass Craig in its scope of accusation. "Where's my reward, huh? I'm his only viable son, for God's sake!"

"Hey!" Lilah stood, apparently unwilling to continue to listen to the bashing of her future husband.

"Oh, shut up, toots. No one pulled your string."

"Pauley, I...," Craig started before Lilah grabbed his arm and towed him out of the house through the French doors facing the lit pool.

"I'll talk to him, son," Barbie cooed, attempting to appease the man she still thought of as her baby.

"Yes, do," he retorted, not about to soften until he saw the fruits of her labors. Right now all he had was a meager allowance and an empty promise. "Let's go, Mari," he directed as he headed for the massive front doors, Lucretia snapping her gaping mouth closed and scurrying around him to open them.

Marin hadn't budged from her position just outside the doors to the dining room, and Pauley glanced back at her in question. "Who the hell is Danielle?"

Chapter 13
Pushing Buttons

Eva struggled through her exercise regime again that morning, leaving the gym feeling frustrated and out of sorts with her body as opposed to rejuvenated and ready for the day. She felt sluggish and lethargic; two conditions to which she was not accustomed. Over the past couple of weeks, though, they had become her constant companions.

She'd always been paranoid about cancer, and had been religious about her mammograms after she'd turned thirty – though Marin teased that a lump would be evident to the naked eye on their size A cup chests.

Now Eva was consumed with fear of leukemia; she had the symptoms – she'd looked them up on WebMD. But she was too afraid to see a doctor to have her suspicions confirmed, and she didn't want to tell anyone. She felt it best to be alone on this sinking ship.

She was most worried about her sister; her husband and her best friend could go on without her, but Marin would be lost. Gabe would take care of her as best he could, of course, but without her ever present twin, Marin's remaining psyche would likely be shattered, leaving her no better off than a vegetable.

Somehow Eva got through her day with no adverse events and was eager to go home and lie down for a bit after she'd finished her notes on her last client. Beth was new to her practice, and was entering therapy for suicidal thoughts and self-harm.

Since the age of sixteen she'd been using razor blades to make delicate cuts on the skin of her upper arms, torso, and upper legs – areas where they wouldn't be readily visible. She'd said the pain and the blood were a release for the way she felt inside.

If she focused on the cuts themselves, she wouldn't be so aware of the anguish and despair in her mind. At other times she felt completely numb, using the cutting to feel something – anything. She'd said even the pain was better than nothingness.

Though she had never attempted suicide, she often had suicidal thoughts with a plan to slit her wrists or step in front of a train. As bad as a completed suicide was, it was always worse when the body was left for a loved one to find.

Eva had seen many clients who had sought her help as a result of the trauma associated with finding a child or sibling or parent after he or she had committed suicide – especially if the act had been a heinous one, like bleeding to death in the bathtub or a gunshot wound to the head.

Just as traumatized, though, is the driver of the car, bus, or train that the suicidal person chooses to walk in front of. An innocent person damaged for life because of an unavoidable collision with someone on a mission – dragged into another's misery as an unwilling participant in their last moments on earth. A selfish act, really – though Eva understood better than most the hopelessness that could lead to it.

Because her client had been able to contract for safety and had assured Eva she would call the police if that changed, she hadn't had to be hospitalized. As Eva finished her documentation of their visit, she found herself fervently hopeful that she would stay that way.

She gathered her purse and keys, waved goodbye to Rosie as she traversed the waiting room, and then crumpled to the floor as everything went black.

When she next opened her eyes she was lying in a hospital bed, an IV running a blood transfusion into the vein of one hand and Gabe holding tightly onto the other. He actually looked his age for once; deep lines of worry etching his brow.

"Is it cancer?" Eva croaked at him.

"I don't know, baby. We just got here." He brought a cup with a straw to her dry lips and she took several long sips.

"Then I haven't been out for long this time?"

Gabe's expression turned dark. "*This* time?"

"I'm sorry – I know I should've told you, but I was so scared and didn't want to worry you, too," she explained quickly, tears filling her stormy eyes.

"That's what I'm here for, Eva. We're in this together – good or bad, happy or sad...remember?" He was angry, but his voice was gentle.

"I remember," she whispered, closing her eyes. She was so tired.

"How many times?"

"What?" She struggled to recall their conversation.

"How many times have you fainted?"

"Just twice. But I was only out for a couple of minutes, if even that." He nodded and gave her more water. "What if it's cancer, Gabe?"

"It's not."

"But what if it is?"

"We kick its ass."

"And if it wins?"

"Then you quit your job and we travel the world and love each other until there's no tomorrow." His voice became gruff and he looked away from her momentarily.

"Marin?" she asked, her voice unsteady.

"We'll take her crazy ass with us."

"And after?" she insisted, refusing to take the bait. This was important. Critical.

"I'll take care of her with all the love and understanding she needs."

She nodded, her tears now falling unrestrained. "Thank you..." She held his hand as tightly as she could, willing him to feel how very much she loved him.

There was a brief knock on the door before the doctor strolled in, thumbing through his notepad. "Eva Jonas," he stated matter-of-factly, but still she nodded her head in confirmation.

The movement caused pain at the crown of her skull and she winced, reaching up to prod the lump that had formed there. "You took quite a spill, and will no doubt be quite sore over the next few days. Your concussion is mild, and I'd just suggest you take it easy for a while."

"You're releasing me?" At his curt nod, she looked to Gabe, confused.

"She thinks she has cancer," he voiced her fear aloud.

"Cancer? No...just a pretty severe case of anemia, which I'd imagine has been exacerbated by your condition. I'm leaving you with a prescription for iron supplements, folic acid, and B12 to increase your body's production of red blood cells. That should make you feel a whole lot better."

He turned to leave the room. "Wait! What condition?"

"I beg your pardon?"

"You said the anemia has been exacerbated by my condition. What condition?"

He actually looked startled, and stared from her to Gabe and back again before rechecking his notepad. She felt a cold knot of fear creep into her throat, threatening to choke her and end her happy life. She swallowed hard, attempting to dislodge it. This was it. This was when he told her she was dying – if not by cancer, then some other horrible terminal illness.

She'd dared to believe she could trick the fates into forgetting she was marked from conception for a life full of nothing but pain, loss, and heartache. As far as she'd tried to run, they'd found her at last, and they were pissed she'd wasted their precious time. She closed her eyes in defeat.

"Well, your pregnancy, of course..." The doctor's voice seemed to come from a great distance as she opened her eyes to detect the falsehood in his expression, sure that this must be someone's idea of a cruel joke.

"We're pregnant?" Gabe repeated, his worried expression replaced by one of shock.

"Yes, by several months according to the hormone levels. You didn't know?" This he addressed to Eva, obviously assuming she just hadn't told her husband yet.

"No, I...I...I've been irregular for years...and...and at my age I figured maybe I was going into menopause..." Gabe gaped at her. This was news to him – he hadn't realized she'd so fully given up on their dream of having children. She gave him an apologetic grimace and turned her attention back to the doctor.

"You're thirty-eight, Ms. Jonas. You're nowhere near menopause. We'll go ahead and perform an ultrasound before you leave today, and then you'll need to follow up with an obstetrician right away to begin prenatal care."

After he'd left the room they stared at each other for a long time. "A baby?" she asked him tentatively, trying out the word, rolling it around on her tongue to get used to the sound.

"A baby," he agreed, as if doing the same thing.

Before long the ultrasound technician arrived amid a bustle of machinery, plopping gel from the warmer onto Eva's stomach and rolling the Doppler device around in the goo to lubricate it. It felt weird, and Eva was grateful for Gabe's presence.

The tech moved the device from place to place, landmark to landmark, for a long time with no success, and Eva's fears returned with a vengeance. Could God be so cruel as to give them the wonder of a pregnancy only to yank it away just as suddenly? The answer was clear: it had happened to Riley. It could just as easily happen to her.

She gazed at her husband, his face awash with exuberant expectation, and felt a tremendous sense of loss on his behalf. He'd always talked about how full their life would be when they had kids one day – it was a dream that was fed constantly by his faith in God and his unwavering belief in positive energy.

She, on the other hand, was much more pragmatic, especially when it became apparent her biological clock had run out of batteries. Now she gasped in surprise when the Doppler finally picked up a rapid heartbeat.

"Is there something wrong with it? It doesn't sound normal...," she asked, referring to the strange echo that followed each of the fetus's heartbeats, resembling more of a thrum as opposed to individual sounds. Before she could get herself worked up again (cardiomegaly? a congenital heart defect? Tetralogy of Fallot?), the tech shook her head.

"Nope, that's just two heartbeats. You're having twins."

***

On the boardwalk overlooking the river, Gabe sat cross-legged on a blanket in front of a roaring fire, facing a large crowd of AA members who had gathered for the annual retreat. There was a crispness in the air that rendered the heat from the leaping flames welcome in their midst.

Unlike their meetings, the retreat held a sense of revelry; three of the members present had earned their one-year coin. This was no easy feat, and was indeed cause for celebration. Allowing the crowd to cajole for a while, Gabe gazed around him, nodding at those who caught his eye.

He was glad to see Craig there, but had never seen the good-looking man sitting next to him. He shook off a sense of foreboding as he made a mental note to find out more about him. Turning his attention back to the matter at hand, he called for order and waited patiently for everyone to settle down.

"I want to start with a poem by an anonymous author that I think we'll find worthy of discussion," he began, his voice compelling and clear. Murmurs of approval and anticipation reached him as he prepared to recite the familiar passages from memory:

The darkness is our enemy...our most formidable of foes.
Its depths we cannot hope to see; its secrets we can't know.
Black is the symbol of our despair, our heavy cape of fear.
It drives us to insanity, destroying everything dear.
Caught in an undertow of grief and loss and pain,
We live an existence of acts that leave an indelible stain.
That which we refuse to face becomes our burial clothes;
A wardrobe we don stealthily, ignorant of its deadly prose.
We are not without our sorrow; regret is our cross to bear.
The thread of second chances stitched into the garments we wear.
Blinded to its beckoning stance and unhindered by its glare,
We gambol and strut and saunter and dance into its ensnaring lair.
Though we ask for deliverance from its temptation, already we're far too late.
For evil has long since outwitted our souls, forever more lying in wait.
Only God can help us now, upon His almighty throne.
Surrender your madness born of lies; allow His will be done.

There were several moments of silence as Gabe's voice faded away into the night, his head bowed in prayer. When he finally looked to the crowd he was greeted with exuberant applause. He noticed Craig's friend watching him intently and experienced a chill that had nothing to do with the light breeze blowing across the river. Who was this guy?

After the clapping had died down Gabe questioned the group about specific passages in the poem. "What do the first two lines mean to you? 'The darkness is our enemy...our most formidable of foes. Its depths we cannot hope to see; its secrets we can't know.' If you think of those lines in terms of alcohol, what do you come up with?"

"Monty, alcoholic."

"Hi, Monty."

"To me it means the drink is dark, and that we can't see it for what it really is, and so it's dangerous to us. The most dangerous enemy in the world."

Gabe nodded. "Good. How about the next two lines? 'Black is the symbol of our despair, our heavy cape of fear. It drives us to insanity, destroying everything dear.'"

"Abigail, alcoholic, addict."

"Hi, Abigail."

"It's like what Monty said...if alcohol is the darkness and the blackness, it holds us down inside of it and makes us crazy...makes us lose our jobs and hurt our families in its sneaky way."

"Alright. What about 'Caught in an undertow of grief and loss and pain, we live an existence of acts that leave an indelible stain.'?"

"Andrea, alcoholic, addict."

"Hi, Andrea."

"We drown our sorrows by drinking and it turns us into ugly people who hurt everyone around us. The ill effects of the things we do stay around long after we're gone, like a stain." Gabe nodded again – there was a lot of insight there.

"How about the next lines: 'That which we refuse to face becomes our burial clothes; a wardrobe we don stealthily, ignorant of its deadly prose.'"

"John, alcoholic."

"Hi, John."

"It's like no matter what we wear or how we dress, our addiction is all that's seen, whether other people know that's what they're looking at or not. And because we're in denial, we'll die in those clothes.

"And maybe the 'prose' part is that we think we look fine, like we're fooling everybody, but really it's sucking us in with its smooth appearance and its fancy words. Like the devil."

Gabe was struck by that word as if it was a physical assault, and he glanced at Craig's friend, who was now looking bored. He reminded him of the devil. Not the spiked tail and horns devil, but the form Satan would take while walking among men. Suave. Alluring. Dangerous.

He tore his gaze away from the man and looked out over the river, trying to gather his thoughts and recall the next two lines. "'We are not without our sorrow; regret is our cross to bear. The thread of second chances stitched into the garments we wear.'"

"Lucy, alcoholic."

"Hi, Lucy."

"I think it means we're human. We feel bad for all the chaos we create but we can't help it. So we ask for forgiveness over and over again until we're out of second chances." There were murmurs of agreement while Gabe prepared to deliver the next two lines.

"'Blinded to its beckoning stance and unhindered by its glare, we gambol and strut and saunter and dance into its ensnaring lair.','" he recited by rote.

"John, alcoholic."

"Hi, John."

"Alcohol calls to us and we go willingly. Happily even, even though there's bad there. And before we know it we're drunk again and we can't stop."

"Thanks again, John. 'Though we ask for deliverance from its temptation, already we're far too late. For evil has long since outwitted our souls, forever more lying in wait.'" He gazed around the crowd expectantly, but no comment was forthcoming, so he eventually continued.

"This one's a little more difficult to interpret. I think it's like what Lucy said. As human beings we were born fallible and weak, and by its very nature evil waits for us to slip up and allow it to take over our lives." He was satisfied by the many nods of approval his interpretation earned.

"Okay, so the final passage is the most important, in my humble opinion." He grinned as his audience pshawed him. "'Only God can help us now, upon His almighty throne. Surrender your madness born of lies; allow His will be done.'"

"Megan, alcoholic."

"Hi, Megan."

"God is our only salvation from our addiction, but we have to allow Him to bring about change in our lives."

"My thoughts exactly. As all of you have pointed out – and lived – we've all experienced the darkness of alcoholism; the hopeless abyss that drowns us. We've come to realize that God is our life preserver – our only way out of sure destruction not only of our own lives, but of those we love and who we often take with us on our journey to the bad places we insist on going."

There was more applause as everyone began gathering their things, talking to each other and enjoying the special camaraderie that drew them together, if not the cause of it.

Several members approached Gabe to ask for the name of the poem and where they might be able to find it. He was ready for them – he knew it would have a deep impact and had brought several copies with him. The verses had saved his life on more than one occasion, and he was happy to share it with others.

As the crowd disbanded he made his way to Craig, shaking his hand and thanking him for coming. He then turned expectantly to the man by his side. "Gabe, this is my brother, Pauley."

Of course. The man that was causing Eva's fear – his sister-in-law's new boyfriend. His wife had been incredibly verbal about her dislike of Pauley – she didn't trust him as far as she could throw him; if she could pick him up at all it would be to toss him off the face of the earth. Now he could see why.

Pauley was smug, insincere, and conceited, and that was all without uttering a single word. Maybe he should give him the benefit of the doubt, Gabe thought, firmly shaking the man's hand. "Nice to meet you, Pauley. It's cool that you came with Craig to the retreat."

"Uh, yeah..."

"What'd you think?"

"It was kind of weird, all the 'Hi, Johns'. Isn't it a little overboard?"

"It's a way to identify members as people as opposed to a disease. We put a name to ourselves, and allow others to acknowledge us that way."

Pauley shrugged. "To each their own, I guess."

"Will you be joining us again? In support of Craig?"

"Nah, it's not really my kind of party. Besides, I don't think Craig really has a problem. He can handle his liquor just fine."

Gabe gaped at him as he turned and walked away, Craig following behind him like a stringed puppet. The man didn't know his brother at all...or worse, didn't care.

Gabe's feelings of foreboding from earlier returned stronger than ever. No good could come from associating with that man, and he was suddenly very afraid for Marin.

***

Pauley pulled to a stop next to the pool house and turned to Craig expectantly, engine idling softly.

"Uh...you want to come in?" Craig asked hesitantly. His brother hadn't been around much after he'd moved out of the estate when he'd graduated from college, and Craig wasn't used to him anymore.

"I'm not a big fan of your fiancée," Pauley replied with a snide laugh.

"Oh, she's not here."

"Well, who knows when she'll be back."

"She won't. Barbie took her to Los Angeles to find a dress for the wedding." He said it as if it were just a homecoming dance.

Pauley was sure the 'dress' would be a gown worth tens and thousands of dollars of his inheritance. It made him hate Lilah even more – as if she hadn't caused enough problems for him as a result of her loose tongue.

If only he could figure out how to get Craig away from that hustling bitch..."Hey, buddy," Pauley suddenly exclaimed, causing Craig to jump in his seat. "Why don't you come stay with us while Barbie and Lilah are away. I'm sure you're lonely here all by yourself."

"James is here."

"Like I said...," Pauley began before changing tactics. "Do it for me. It'll be like old times. Whaddya say?"

"I guess," Craig muttered, though his memories of the 'old times' weren't exactly good ones.

To his recollection Pauley had had two games he'd played at his brother's expense: making fun of him or ignoring him. In many ways it had been like Craig was the little brother, running after Pauley wherever he went, begging to be included in whatever he was doing, and trying to get his attention any way he could.

But maybe things would be different now. Maybe Pauley wanted to rectify their relationship. He'd come to see him at the Institute, hadn't he? And he'd hung out with him at the retreat. He'd give him the benefit of the doubt. Like old times.

Pauley helped him pack some of his things and encouraged him to leave a note as to his whereabouts so Barbie wouldn't call the police. Then they were heading back downtown. During the ride Pauley kept up an easy monologue, putting him at ease.

He was grateful that a response wasn't required of him, unlike when he was with Lilah. She flew off into a rage constantly over his vague answers and missed social cues. She put him in a persistent state of anxiety, and he wasn't sad she was gone.

Once they'd arrived at the apartment Pauley greeted Marin like he hadn't seen her in days as opposed to a couple of hours, and then showed Craig around the place, stowing his overnight bag in the guest bedroom. Craig turned in almost immediately, and slept well into the following day – he'd been exhausted.

The next evening Pauley brought home several movies and two twelve-packs of beer. Marin looked puzzled as he stocked the fridge with alcohol. "Why'd you get so much? The only one who can drink all that is you."

"Craig, too," he said, as he slid a beer across the counter to his brother. Craig accepted it happily, taking a huge swig and wiping his mouth with his sleeve as he emitted a wet belch.

"Sorry," he murmured, mistaking the stricken look on Marin's face as a reaction to his poor manners. Pauley read her correctly, though, and drew her into his arms.

"Relax, babe. Beer's not his problem. As long as he stays away from the hard stuff he'll be just fine. Isn't that right, bro?"

"Yup. Yup," Craig responded after polishing off the first can and reaching for another. It was questionable whether he'd actually been following the conversation and Marin remained unconvinced, but Pauley easily distracted her with a satisfying tryst in the bedroom.

When they emerged the following morning, Craig was passed out on the couch in the living room, twenty-three empty beer cans scattered around him.

"It's not right, Pauley," Marin protested, giving him the cold shoulder until he apologized for his lapse in judgment.

"I'll take him to a meeting tonight, okay?"

"Fine."

"Please don't be mad at me, Mari. I love you." He was his most charming self, nuzzling her neck and kissing her hands until she forgave him.

But that evening he did not take Craig to AA. Instead they made the rounds to all of Pauley's old haunts, flirting and drinking their way to oblivion. Night after night they partied, graduating from beer to mixed drinks to fifths of the strongest stuff they could find.

And every night Marin waited by the door, fuming and promising to leave Pauley or call the cops to have Craig taken back to the Institute. They were empty threats, though. She would never walk out on him, and it would take much more than a string of drunk nights to get admitted to the hospital. So she yelled and screamed, but in the end allowed herself to be cajoled back into Pauley's bed where she belonged.

Everything was going according to plan until Pauley received a phone call from his mother. Thank you so much for looking after Craig. He's so lucky to have you in his life. Now be a good boy and bring him home.

But Pauley wasn't ready to relinquish his hold on his brother. Not until he was sure he'd broken the spell Lilah had over him. Two days later Barbie called again. He told her Craig wasn't ready to come home, but she wasn't having it.

"Paulson, Craig's wife-to-be is here all alone. You must impress upon him that he has a duty to her in her time of need. She misses him terribly."

"What can I say? Maybe he finally sees through the fake bitch."

"Paulson! I will not tolerate such language from you! Put your brother on the phone, son."

"He can't come to the phone right now. I'll have him call you when he's available. Ciao, Barbie." Pauley disconnected the call and glanced over at Craig, who was still sleeping off last night's bender. He met Marin's glare and shrugged his shoulders.

"What? I didn't lie – he's obviously in no condition to hold a conversation with my mother," he said, gesturing to his brother's slumped frame.

"You'll be in big trouble when she gets around to calling him on his phone," she retorted, obviously pissed at him again. Women.

"Well then I guess we should consider ourselves lucky he left his phone on his bed back at the pool house, shouldn't we?"

With an enraged grunt she flung herself back into the master suite and slammed the door behind her. Grinning, Pauley tossed his phone on the coffee table and followed her; the sex was even more amazing when she was angry.

Barbie called several more times over the course of the next couple of days, her messages becoming more and more irate. Her last voice mail held a threatening tone Pauley had never heard before from his genteel mother.

"Paulson, this is Barbie speaking." No shit. "If Craig is not back in this house by five o'clock tomorrow evening, your father and I will just have to come to you. And it won't be pretty, mister. I can promise you that."

Prompted by her Clint Eastwood routine, Pauley became a flurry of activity, and by five o'clock the following evening the three of them were checking into the executive suite at the Ritz-Carlton in San Juan.

Pauley had sold the trip to the others as one last hurrah before releasing Craig into the constraints of marriage, and they'd come willingly; unwitting accessories to his crime against his parents, but mostly against Lilah.

So they ate incredible seafood and swam in the warm waters of Puerto Rico and went shopping for island wear and took day tours to the El Yunque Rainforest and the Bacardi Rum Distillery and the Arecibo Observatory and the Bioluminescent Bay.

At night after Craig fell asleep Pauley and Marin made love on the balcony and in the hot tub and under the waterfall in the swimming pool and a thousand times in the enormous bed with the heavy drapes that made them feel like they were the only two people in the entire world.

They'd walk hand in hand on the supple sand beaches and he'd pull her into a copse of palm trees to bury his hands in her hair and his manhood in her welcoming warmth. Yes, the impromptu trip had been idyllic with the exception of their first morning at the hotel.

"I found my pills but where are Craig's?" Marin had asked Pauley before they'd gone down to breakfast.

"Oh geesh, I must have forgotten them at home..."

"How could you forget something so important?"

"Because I'm an insensitive prick?"

"No, you could never be a prick. I guess a few days without his medicine won't kill him..."

Of course their vacation would have ended immediately had he told her he'd discarded Craig's meds down the toilet the day he'd come to stay with them, but what did such pesky little details matter?

They were having the time of their lives, and no one would ever be the wiser.

Chapter 14
Remorse

Eva waited for her sister at a small table inside the coffee shop across the street from Pauley's building. She'd left Marin several messages before she'd finally called her back. Eva had refused to tell her twin her news over the phone, and Marin was just as adamant about not returning to her apartment or even allowing Eva to come to Pauley's condo.

As many red flags as this set off in Eva's mind, she pushed it into its own little compartment in her brain, never to be revisited again. It wouldn't do to antagonize her sister – she needed to be able to be there for her when Pauley inevitably screwed her over.

And she had no doubt he would – it was his modus operandi, and people like him simply didn't change. Even after the short time she'd spent with the man she had him pegged. She was sure a diagnosis of narcissistic personality disorder would be an accurate description of what ailed him.

People with this disorder were dangerous because they had little, if any, empathy toward others and displayed a remarkable disregard for the havoc they left in their wake. They thought of themselves as above reproach and violated the feelings of others without the slightest remorse.

This was the last type of person Marin needed in her life as vulnerable as she was, but what could Eva do? She wasn't psychotic or suicidal, she continued to take her medication, and she had kept all of her appointments with her treatment team.

At least a couple of these accomplishments were to Pauley's credit, as much as Eva hated to admit it; he must be involved because Marin had no other way of transporting herself across town to refill her meds or get to her doctor's office. Eva had always taken care of those things in the past, and she felt a bit useless since Pauley had come into Marin's life.

The bell above the door chimed and Eva looked up as Marin stepped into the café. She looked amazing, and Eva almost felt insipid next to her for the first time since they were little girls. Marin used to shine so bright Eva had been perpetually blinded by her essence. But that was before.

Pauley had obviously been taking very good care of her sister – at least superficially. Her hair had been permed, and now fell in an abundance of loose waves around her face. Though she wore no makeup her skin looked clear and healthy, and there was a depth to her luminous eyes that Eva hadn't recalled seeing before. Her nails were manicured and polished, and her fingers and wrists were adorned with extravagant jewels that must have cost a fortune.

And her clothes! They actually fit her slender frame as opposed to putting her in danger of being swallowed whole and never surfacing again. She wore a charcoal gray blazer that skimmed her body as though it were made for her, along with leggings and black knee-high boots.

She looked like she'd just emerged from the pages of Vogue, and like she'd never been sick a day in her life. If the circumstances in which these changes had occurred had been different, Eva would be elated for her twin. As it was, though, her joy was tempered by Pauley's obvious influence in Marin's life.

Eva stood to hug her, holding on extra tight. God, how she loved this dear heart. "I've missed you so much, sis."

"Me too," Marin responded, returning her embrace in kind. As they sat, Eva noticed the look of apprehension that crossed Marin's face, and knew she must be expecting a confrontation over her relationship with Pauley.

"I'm pregnant, Mae." Marin's expression underwent a myriad of changes before settling on surprise.

"Pregnant...," she repeated, as if searching for the meaning of the word in her often overstuffed mind.

"Yes, with identical twins." Eva had had a series of ultrasounds since discovering her pregnancy, and this was a new development.

Other than Gabe, no one else knew she was pregnant, though truth be told she didn't have many people to tell. Riley would have to be informed eventually, of course, but Eva would delay that dreaded conversation as long as possible. Losing a child would be hard enough without having to deal with your best friend's happiness over her own baby.

"Twins," Marin breathed, a faraway look entering her eyes.

Eva nodded and sipped her coffee – she didn't know if she'd ever get used to decaffeinated brew – and waited for her sister to process the information. It had certainly taken her a while to do so, and she could imagine the memories she'd just evoked for Marin.

But she couldn't know that her twin was recalling what it was like to live in a womb that wasn't kind to them, and was alarmed when she began hyperventilating and looking around her wildly as if possessed.

"Marin? What is it?"

"You have to *eat*, Eva!"

"I have been eating –"

"No! Not like you usually do. I mean really eat. And drink lots of milk and take your vitamins and stop spending so much time at the gym..." Eva began to laugh, but Marin held up her hand. "I'm dead serious, E. Do it right this time."

Since Eva had never been pregnant before, she assumed her sister must be referring to their mother's poor choices, which she would never dream of repeating. She was taken aback by Marin's vehemence, but appreciated her concern.

"Sure, Mae – we'll do it right this time." Marin nodded, obviously greatly relieved. "Tell me, how're things going for you, sis?" Eva asked by way of a much needed subject change.

Color returned to Marin's face and she visibly brightened. "Really great. Craig came to stay with us last night until Barbie comes back." Eva wasn't sure if that arrangement was good for Craig, but she supposed it was better than being alone with James.

Marin didn't seem inclined to be any more forthcoming, so Eva stood to end their visit. This time it was Marin who delayed her departure as she stared at her twin's as yet nonexistent belly.

"Promise me, Eva. Take good care of those babies," she implored, her eyes delving into Eva's so fully she could likely see her soul.

"I will, Mae. I promise."

As the weeks flew by Eva's stomach expanded exponentially – the time was drawing near when she'd have to share her news with Riley, and, as she dressed for work one morning, settling on a cream sweater dress with black boots after having discarded suit after suit that had become too snug in the waist, she knew the time had come.

Her belly protruded happily in the stretchy material as she stared at herself in the full-length mirror. She pulled her hair back into a black leather clasp at the nape of her neck and added pearls to her ears. Satisfied that she'd done the best she could to maintain her elegant appearance in spite of the tiny humans residing inside her body, she headed out.

She had a full day ahead of her, and was amused to see Gabe had packed her a bulging sack lunch when she reached the kitchen. He'd included his customary love note, and suddenly she didn't feel nearly as nervous about the conversation she'd soon be having with her still grieving best friend.

She arrived at her office an hour prior to her first appointment so that she could put herself in the right frame of mind. Though she meditated each morning before seeing clients anyway, it was especially important that day because she'd be hypnotizing Annabelle for the first time. She needed to be focused and attentive at all times to avoid causing additional trauma to the woman's already delicate psyche.

When Annabelle arrived Eva made sure she was comfortable, and then explained how the hypnosis would work. "I can't hypnotize you unless you want to be hypnotized, and I can't make you do anything you don't want to do – it's not mind control; merely suggestion."

"Okay." Annabelle nodded. "I'm ready."

Often the first session is unsuccessful because the client doesn't know what to expect, and is therefore closed to the hypnotist's influence. This session was no exception.

"Sorry about that...we'll have to try again next time."

"No, I don't think there's gonna be a next time if it's all the same to you, pretty girl."

A chill inched its way up Eva's spine. "And why's that, Annabelle?"

"Oh honey, Annabelle's long gone. She couldn't handle the memories you were trying to bring up."

"So you're supposed to be…?"

"I'm Jasmine. I've been around since she was four," she flicked her head as if motioning to someone next to her. "And I must say your skepticism is darling, doc," Jasmine continued, her demeanor calm but intense, everything from the way she talked to the languorous way she moved vastly different from Annabelle's.

Eva had never seen anything like it, and found herself reconsidering her doubts about the disorder. These were two distinct people, and she tried to tamp down her fear as she realized she was dealing with an unknown entity.

"I daresay it's not your call if Annabelle chooses to continue with the hypnosis. It's her desire to get to the bottom of her erratic behaviors, and you can't stop her."

Jasmine's expression turned ferocious as she sat up in the chair, her lithe body fairly humming with negative energy. "Can't I?" she snarled as she lunged toward Eva, a wicked-looking switchblade clutched in her hand.

Eva screamed and dove for the phone to call security but Jasmine was too fast for her newly sluggish frame, swiping the phone off the desk and swinging around to jab at her again. Eva blocked her arm and grabbed for the knife, but Jasmine's rage made her much stronger and more agile.

A thin red line appeared across the top of Eva's hand and she backed away from the other woman, her mind searching for an escape. She bumped into the lamp on the credenza behind her and turned to seize it just as Jasmine lunged again.

Eva felt the blade enter her side and a piercing pain radiated through her stomach and down toward her pelvis. She cried out in alarm and collapsed against the wall, but not before she'd swung the lamp at the other woman, connecting with a sickening crunch.

She pulled herself along the wall into a sitting position, gasping in agony and holding her side as blood flowed freely over her hand and onto the pristine white carpet. She stared down at the stain spreading across her stomach as she struggled to keep her eyes open. It was getting harder and harder to breathe, and as she lost consciousness she heard Annabelle's terrified voice like it was coming through a long tunnel.

"Eva! Oh God! What have I done?"

***

Lilah was furious when she returned home to discover Craig's absence, and became angrier by the day the longer he stayed away. It wasn't that she missed him; she just couldn't stand losing, and right now Pauley had emerged as the clear winner.

He'd swooped in and stolen Craig from her and she couldn't get him back. She'd called him nonstop when she'd discovered he was gone, livid he wasn't answering his phone until she'd realized he'd left it behind.

And when she'd gotten Pauley's number from Barbie and couldn't get him to answer her calls either, she'd damn near lost her mind. Didn't they know she was the Head Bitch in Charge of this whole deal? It was enough to ruin her entire trip, which, up until she arrived back home, had been idyllic.

They'd flown first-class, enjoying mimosas in the nearly empty luxurious cabin. They were picked up from the airport by a limousine, in which they'd continued to drink champagne in delicate flutes filled with chilled strawberries.

Barbie had reserved the penthouse suite at the Beverly Hills Sky Hill, a swanky establishment overlooking L.A. and the bay beyond. They each had their own bedroom with attached bathroom, both of which sported a Jacuzzi tub and walk-in shower.

Their balcony spanned the entire unit, and when they weren't otherwise occupied, Lilah spent all of her time gazing out over the water. She'd never felt more free than in those moments – maybe in her past life she'd been a fish.

Even though she hadn't set a date for her wedding – how could she? She was still married! – they'd visited numerous gown designers and were given private showings while feasting on hors d'oeuvres and Cosmopolitans.

By the end of their first day Lilah had chosen a designer and was excited to return to view his creations for her in a few months. It didn't hurt that he was gorgeous and all man, not that that had anything to do with her selection.

They spent the remainder of their trip at the beach, punctuated by decadent meals in overpriced restaurants that boasted impeccable service and diligently aged wine. Lilah was in heaven – she was the center of attention, had no competition for Barbie's time, and thoroughly enjoyed the lavishness that was being bestowed upon her.

As a result of all of that wonderfulness coming to an end, she was already in a foul mood when she walked into the pool house after Barbie had driven them home from the airport. She'd dropped her packages on the floor for Lucretia to put away and had immediately gone back to the main house, surprising Barbie, who no doubt hadn't anticipated seeing her again so soon.

"What is it, dear?"

"I need to let Craig know I'm home."

"He's not at the pool house?"

Lilah shook her head. No, dumbass. Why would I be asking for him if he was?

"Well, he's not here either," she cried, her voice alarmed. "Lucretia!" she yelled behind her, highly unladylike. The maid appeared almost immediately, unnerving the hell out of Lilah.

"Jess, ma'am?"

"Have you seen Craig?"

"He leff a letter. I put it in you office." Barbie huffed at her before wending her way through the hall behind the large kitchen, Lilah in hot pursuit.

She'd never been to Barbie's office before – didn't even know she had one. How would she? The woman had never worked a day in her life. But apparently the management of a household and several charitable organizations required one – it was filled with calendars, event notices, and post-it reminders.

There was also an elegant half-circle desk topped by a computer and phone system, a desk chair with embroidered cushion, a file credenza, and several bookcases. An authentic Persian rug warmed the hardwood floor, a lively fire roared in the ornate corner fireplace, and the lace curtains were opened to reveal an expansive view of the park-like front lawn.

With a feinting couch in front of the windows and its own powder room, the suite was a home away from home, and Lilah imagined her future mother-in-law spent much of her time here. It made her wonder what James's office looked like; a gentleman's apartment at a Polo club immediately coming to mind.

She crowded over Barbie's shoulder as the woman plucked the folded sheet of paper from her desk and plopped into her chair with a grunt. Evidently her refined mannerisms were not ingrained as Lilah had first presumed because they deserted her entirely when she was under stress.

I'll be at Pauley's. Craig. Barbie had immediately phoned Pauley but had to leave a message and, after thirty minutes of Lilah pacing the floor and periodically emitting outrageously annoying sighs of frustration, Barbie sent her on her way.

"I'll let you know just as soon as he returns my call, dear." That had been a week ago and Lilah was now nothing short of enraged.

Adding to her disgruntlement was the fact that she hadn't heard from Steve since well before her trip, and while she understood he couldn't be expected to communicate with her on a daily basis, she felt frequent updates should be in order. After all, he stood to gain a lucrative fee out of the deal, and she should be treated with the respect she deserved as a result.

So she dressed in a pinstripe skirt that ended half-a-foot above her knees, a low-cut white silk blouse and a flirty pair of strappy heels. She styled her hair sleek and smooth, and wore it pulled over one shoulder. With minimal jewelry and her new Hermés handbag, she felt ready to face Margie.

When she arrived at the office, though, Steve happened to be malingering at the receptionist's desk, picking through the assortment of complimentary candies she kept there like a starving man foraging for a morsel of food.

He'd jerked his head toward his office when he saw Lilah, circumventing any commentary between her and Margie – the younger woman feeling a bit let down now that she had prepared herself for a battle with the pompous employee.

Once ensconced in his office, she turned to him irritably, determined to vent her pent-up frustrations on someone – anyone. "You haven't called."

"I've been busy."

"With your paying clients."

"Yes, and your case as well. Your husband's new attorney is quite a handful."

She narrowed her eyes. She'd envisioned Mark prostrated, taking what was coming to him like the backwards cowpoke he was. Instead it seemed he was going on the defensive; an uncharacteristic move that served to darken her mood even further.

"So now you're worried?"

"Not at all. The man doesn't scare me, but his involvement has vastly increased the amount of time and effort we're forced to expend on a pro bono case."

"For which you'll be paid handsomely in the end – if you do your job right," she countered, bristling from his implication that she was a charity job.

"Of course," he replied, unwilling to appease her.

He spent the next couple of hours showing her the correspondence that had occurred between the two firms, and detailing the plan moving forward. A knock on the door was followed by Margie's head as she interrupted their scheming to advise Steve that she was leaving and that everyone else was already gone for the day.

"Would you like me to walk Mrs. Donahue out?"

"That won't be necessary, Margie, but I appreciate the offer." She stood there indecisively for several moments, her gaze shifting between the two of them as if she were mechanized.

"I suppose I could stay a bit longer and –"

"That'll be all, Margie. I'll see you tomorrow," he cut in dismissively before turning back to the documents spread out before him.

Margie hesitated in the doorway, scowling at Lilah's smug smile. Finally she backed out of the office, closing the door softly behind her. After she'd gone he ordered Chinese takeout for their dinner, moving to the deep couches set at right angles to the fully stocked wet bar on the far side of the office.

They sat turned toward each other, Lilah's leg bent at the knee so she could sit sideways on the plush cushion. She smiled provocatively after noticing Steve's gaze assiduously returning to the dark place between her spread thighs that was almost visible beneath her hitched skirt.

When his eyes eventually returned to her face he became mesmerized by the way she surrounded the chopsticks with her lips, slowly drawing each bite into her mouth in a manner that was so seductive he nearly groaned aloud, his penis straining mightily to break free of his pants.

Suddenly he stood, striding to the bar and busying himself with the wide array of alcohol there. "Want anything?" he asked gruffly as she stood too.

"Vodka sour. And the bathroom." He pressed a switch on the wall and a panel shifted to the side to reveal a short hallway flanked by closets and a fully equipped bathroom. Impressive, she thought, fingering the costly suits as she passed.

When she returned she was wearing nothing but her Manolo Blahniks, and Steve took her ferociously on each of the couches as well as the immense desk recently divested of her thick divorce file.

When she left that evening she was satisfied that he would be giving her case the attention it deserved from now on. Winner.

***

Gabe stared at his wife, worry clouding his face. He couldn't lose this woman, and his relief was palpable when she opened her eyes, gazing around the hospital room before turning to look at him.

"We have to stop meeting like this," she told him, her intact humor warming his heart.

"Agreed," he said with a shaky laugh.

"Our babies?"

"The girls are fine."

Her eyebrows shot up and she gasped. "Girls?"

He nodded. "They did an ultrasound – the wound missed your uterus by less than an inch."

"An inch," she breathed, feeling incapable of any form of communication other than repeating his statements.

Things could have ended so badly, reminding her that life hung in the balance at every moment, and that God's grace could be given or taken away at will. Gabe embraced her gently, afraid to cause her any more pain. They stayed that way for a very long time, separating only when a knock sounded at the door.

Eva's eyes widened as Riley stepped into the room. "I called her," Gabe said, answering the question in her eyes when she swung her head toward him. "She deserves to know."

Riley approached the bed, looking down at her best friend with nothing but concern. "I'm glad you're okay, Eva," she said, as she clutched Eva's hand in her own.

"I'm so sorry, Riley." Her guilt nearly choked off her words. "I wanted to tell you. I just..." She broke off, gesturing to Riley's stomach before looking away.

"Hey...," Riley began, waiting until Eva met her gaze again. "I understand. I would've done the same thing. I would," she affirmed as Eva raised her eyebrows in surprise. "You didn't want to hurt me. I get it. But please know your happiness could never increase my pain." She gently placed her hand on Eva's stomach, and Eva covered it with her own.

Thankful that it appeared he'd done the right thing by Eva, Gabe stepped out of the room to give the woman some privacy. He also needed some time to process. His world seemed to be unraveling, and there wasn't much he could do about it.

He went to the chapel and sat in a pew, gazing at the cross hanging on the front wall, backlit by a warm yellow light that made it appear to float. He felt some of his tension leave him immediately, and wondered why hospital chapels were always empty.

Wasn't this the one place, with all its sickness and pain and despair, where God's salvation was most needed? Then again, maybe in these days of advanced technology and modern medicine people relied on doctors and their scalpels much more readily than on the miraculous workings of the Almighty.

Gabe preferred a healthy dose of both. He relaxed against the back of the pew and sighed, allowing the peace to wash over him...to soothe him as nothing else could. And he definitely needed to be soothed as he thought back to his phone call with Marin.

She'd told him she couldn't come to the hospital to see her sister because she was out of town with Pauley and Craig. She'd refused to tell him where they were or when they'd be home. She'd sent Eva her love and then hung up, leaving him holding an unresponsive phone to his ear like an imbecile.

Her voice had sounded odd to him – happy, sure, but in a peculiarly manic way. A false brightness that was itself the root cause of his worry for her continued well-being. And he didn't dare tell his wife. She'd already expressed her concern over Craig missing his last three appointments with her, and had asked if he'd been coming to his AA meetings – he had not.

Now it was apparent what was getting in the way of Craig's treatment regimen: Pauley...evil incarnate, as far as Gabe was concerned. He remembered his feeling of foreboding when he'd first laid eyes on the man, and it appeared he wasn't wrong.

Born a Pisces, he'd learned at a young age that he had a gift – a sixth sense that was able to detect falsehood and deceit. An intuition he believed everyone possessed but few were able or willing to tap into. It could be quite exhausting to be so keyed into the negativity and cruel intents of others.

At first he'd had great difficulty not internalizing the malevolence of those around him, so much so that he found himself walking the line between right and wrong...between good and bad. He'd even crossed the line a few times, into drugs and shoplifting...drinking and reckless driving.

But after Christina died he righted his path and never strayed toward the 'dark side' again. He learned to become immune to the travesties of others – he was now adept at being aware of malintent without being overtaken by it. His gift now allowed him to open himself to goodness while remaining closed to evil.

It was one of the things that made him so successful as an architect of new beginnings; he could easily detect the genuine nature of others' repentance and embrace them wholeheartedly in their most vulnerable moments – a time when their own friends and family had forsaken them to deal with their demons alone.

He'd finally found his voice, and he knew he was exactly where he was supposed to be to do the greatest good in his life and in the lives of those who sought his help. But Pauley's sudden presence had greatly undermined his confidence, and he found himself struggling with the same forces that had attempted to drown him when he'd lost his sister.

In fact, he was taken all the way back to his third year, when he'd curl onto his mother's lap with his head on her protruding belly so he could feel Christina's movements. At four he would race to grab her pacifier after she'd thrown it – a game to her, but a very serious responsibility to him.

At five he taught her to descend the stairs on her bottom so she wouldn't fall. When he was six he'd read her stories, changing his voice to delight her, just like his mother used to do when he'd been her age. At seven he taught her how to ride her bike with training wheels, and begged their parents to let her learn without them – it took them two years to finally agree.

When he was eight she started kindergarten, and he walked her to and from school every day. Their teachers marveled that they never fought – everyone should be so lucky to have a big brother like him. They didn't understand that he was the lucky one. She was his entire reason.

Even when they'd become teenagers he never failed her. If she was being bullied, he'd defend her honor. If a boy was coming on too strong, he would set him straight. After he got his license, he became her chauffeur, taking her to cheerleading practice, volleyball tryouts, and football games.

When she wanted to go to the mall to see her friends he would wait for her there, hanging out in the arcade until she was ready to leave. He helped her with her homework, made sure she got up for school on time, and screened her boyfriends. He was so attentive to her their parents often joked that they weren't needed, demonstrating a decidedly hands-off approach in their upbringing.

When Gabe had started to get into trouble they'd bailed him out of numerous situations without ever setting limits or applying consequences. They were the cool parents with the most popular kids in school – they figured all Gabe needed was a little time to get his head back in the game.

But even during the bad times he never let Christina down; he may not have done much of anything else right, but was somehow still able to dote on the most important person in his world. And then she was gone.

Her funeral was held in an enormous church that couldn't contain the multitude of attendees. The wails of those who loved her soared to the impossibly high ceilings, turned into raw misery, and then rained down upon them to compound their grief. Not his, of course. His could not be multiplied. It was already an infinite sorrow that was incapable of expansion – there was nothing bigger in the entire universe.

After the service he was asked to leave his parents' home, his mother locked in Christina's bedroom and his father unable to look him in the eye as he'd delivered their decree. At twenty-one, Gabe was suddenly an only child and an orphan.

Numbly, he fled the town and didn't stop running until he found AA, and God. He worked the steps while he got his life straight, trying to find meaning in his existence. He found it when he became a sponsor. This was his purpose...his family.

And now he had Eva, and soon his daughters. He'd finally arrived at the best place he'd ever been, and he would hold onto it with every fiber of his being.

Chapter 15
World Gone Bad

When Riley returned to work she was grateful to discover that her coworkers treated her the same as they always had, other than an occasional How've you been holding up? or a brief hug. She'd been dreading this day because she'd feared it would be weird and that her peers would either fawn over her incessantly or ignore her completely as a result of their own discomfort over her loss.

Thankfully they did neither, and it was business as usual at the Institute. She was relieved to be back in her element – helping people who couldn't help themselves was what she was born to do.

Tony had been particular attentive to her needs, making her laugh with his silly faces when no one else was looking. She finally built up the courage to ask about Dr. Tacee, but he shook his head as he glanced around the unit. The walls had ears.

"I'll call you later. We'll talk then." She nodded, writing her cell phone number on a sticky note and sliding it across the desk to him. "When will you be free?" he asked as he slipped it into his pocket. She choked out a derisive laugh.

"I'm never *not* free."

"I mean when do you guys have dinner and...you know...stuff." If she weren't mistaken a slight blush colored his cheeks. He was just too adorable for words.

"There is no 'us guys' at the moment," she replied, looking away quickly as her eyes filled with tears. Damn emotions. She felt herself getting angry – her standard response to her overblown feelings.

"Oh, I see...," he muttered, seemingly at a loss for words. "Then come to my place. I'll make you dinner," he said, rallying quickly.

She looked at him dubiously. "You and me and Dr. Tacee? Gosh, let me think about that for a minute. No."

He laughed and then clarified, "I've moved. I'm just around the block now." Her eyebrows rose in surprise.

"And you feed yourself with...what...ramen noodles?"

He grabbed his chest as if he'd been shot through the heart. "I guess you'll just have to find out for yourself."

The rest of her shift dragged by due to her anticipation about dinner with Tony that night. She told herself her excitement had nothing to do with him as a man; that she was just looking forward to socializing with a friend after her long and isolated recovery. That she couldn't wait to revisit her suspicions of Dr. Tacee with the only other person she'd bothered to tell about them.

But those were just excuses. If she were being honest with herself, she'd admit that the true reason she couldn't wait to spend time with Tony was that she was extremely attracted to him. She liked everything about him. And deep down inside she knew that he made her feel like a woman in ways no one else ever had.

He listened to her...he cared about what she had to say. When he looked into her eyes they connected on a level that had nothing to do with sex, and everything to do with the basic human need to feel attached to something bigger and better than oneself. When she was around him she felt larger than life itself, and it was an incredibly heady sensation that she imagined could become quite addictive.

She'd have to be careful to guard herself around a man like him – it would be entirely too easy to fall in love with him, and she was determined not to betray the sanctity of her marriage like that. Later that evening she desperately had to remind herself of that pledge as she slipped further under his spell.

He was an enormously engaging host...he also had mad knife skills. When she'd arrived he'd given her a tour, her oohs and ahs sincere as he showed her around his place – she loved his sense of style, and found herself feeling much more at home here than she ever had in her own house.

After that he began making dinner, gathering the ingredients for homemade spaghetti and impressing her with his prowess in the kitchen. She breathed deeply as the smell of garlic, basil, and oregano filled the air.

"Where did you learn to cook like that?"

"My parents were culinary whizzes. If they hadn't been doctors they would've been chefs. I spent my childhood weekends smashing garlic with the best of them."

"You miss them."

"Every single day."

"I know the feeling." She looked away, but whipped her head back toward him as an apron came sailing her way.

"You have to earn your keep in this joint. Butter the bread, will ya?" he said in character, sending a chuckle bubbling into her throat. He knew how to lighten the mood, and she appreciated his effort more than he'd ever know.

When dinner was ready they sat at the dining room table, the lights of the city twinkling through the windows. He'd said he hadn't had time to order the custom blinds he'd chosen, but she thought the place was magical as is.

The unit was high enough that no one could see inside from the street, and it was far enough away from the neighboring buildings that privacy wasn't much of an issue. She told him so, and hoped he'd seriously consider her opinion, though she couldn't explain why it was so important to her.

They feasted on spaghetti with meat sauce, warm garlic bread, and Caesar salad with freshly grated Romano cheese applied heavy-handedly over the top. The meal was delicious, and Riley was struck again by how grown up this big kid could seem.

She'd followed him home directly after their shift had ended, so the impressive dinner he'd prepared for her had been thrown together with the ingredients he already had – he obviously maintain a fully stocked kitchen and kept his home looking presentable whether he had guests or not.

It was not something she'd expected from him based on her long-standing perceptions, something that would need to be amended if she were to be fair to him. With a start, she realized that she had long since begun to think of him as a man instead of a boy, and wondered when that had changed.

After they'd finished eating and she'd helped him with the dishes at her insistence, they took their wine out to the balcony where he lit the gas fire pit. It was very cozy, and she caught herself dozing as she gazed at the lights on the distant barges making their way up the river.

She hadn't been this at peace in a long time, and she felt like she could stay like this forever. Reluctantly she turned to the business at hand before she again became caught up in the serenity that seemed to be a natural part of her host.

"Have Michael's autopsy results come back?"

"Yes, but there was no evidence of foul play." She stared at him so intensely and for so long he felt compelled to continue. "The findings showed acute heart failure secondary to pulmonary edema."

"Couldn't that be caused by something purposeful?"

"Sure, but it's more likely to be caused by a person's own poor lifestyle choices."

"Anything on toxicology?"

"Nothing."

"Dammit!"

"We're at a dead-end, kid."

"I know something's wrong here, Tony. I just can't figure out what. But I'll bet my ass Dr. Tacee's at the center of it."

He was inclined to agree with her, but speculation was getting them nowhere, and when she dozed off for the third time in as many minutes he herded her inside and gestured to the couch.

"You're in no shape to drive out to the suburbs right now. Why don't you rest for a while? I won't bite." She hesitated, but the couch with its heavy throw looked entirely too inviting to pass up.

"Okay...but just for a little while."

When she woke up the loft was bright with sunshine, the smell of freshly brewed coffee filled the room and she could vaguely hear Tony singing horrendously off-key in the shower. Good God, she'd slept all night! She hadn't done that since before Kellan was born, and if she weren't so panicked she'd realize how well-rested she felt.

But she had no time to assess her health status as she sprinted around gathering her things before letting herself out. She was mortified that Tony might have heard her snore or belch or fart in her subconscious state, and she'd be damned if she'd stick around to let him see her after a hard night's sleep – her hair in disarray, her makeup smeared, and her breath barking after last night's garlic fest.

She was nothing short of a hot mess, and she found herself sending up a prayer to thank the good Lord for the reprieve. She nearly took it back, though, when she pulled into her driveway, Steve's car parked there as if it were judgment day. What kind of sick freak was God, anyway?

Sighing, she yanked open the overhead vanity mirror and fixed herself as best she could before squaring her shoulders and marching into the house. She had nothing to be ashamed of, and she was through being intimidated by this man.

"Hello! I'm home!" she bellowed up the stairs belligerently before being startled half out of her skin by her husband, who looked like he'd been sitting in the same spot in the small sitting room off the kitchen all night long.

"I should never have left," he said, a surprising degree of self-deprecation lacing his words, "but I'm home now." Riley nodded mutely in response...though she was no longer entirely sure she wanted him to be.

***

As soon as Pauley, Marin, and Craig landed at the airport and grabbed their suitcases from the baggage claim carousel, Pauley packed his brother into a taxi, gave the driver James and Barbie's address, and sent him on his way.

Craig stared out the window at Pauley until he could no longer see him, and then turned back to stare at the man behind the wheel. He'd seen his brother whispering to the driver and handing him a hundred dollar bill. He wasn't stupid...he knew what was going on. He saw stuff like this on TV all the time.

Pauley was selling him on the black market...through a human trafficking website or some such thing. Hoodlums would pay top dollar for a healthy white guy like him. He'd be sold to the highest bidder and used as some old Asian dude's sex slave. Pauley'd get a pretty penny for him, and would have his revenge on James for not raising his allowance.

Pauley sure was smart, but he wouldn't get away with it. The cab driver must be in on it – he should just kill him right now...but no, he might get hurt when the man lost control of the car. Instead he waited until the vehicle stopped at a traffic light and then bolted from the backseat, winding his way toward the curb on the opposite side of the street.

He glanced back once to determine if he was being pursued, but the driver had turned his sign back on and soon was gone from view. Ha! Apparently his smarty pants brother hadn't paid the man enough to stick to the plan, and now Craig was free. Serves him right, the little criminal...

But now he had no idea where he was, and he was getting hungry. And cold. The people he passed on the sidewalk kept looking at him funny, and he was reminded that the FBI was probably still after him, too. Now he was worried about both sides of the law; the ingrates that ran the human trafficking ring and the government scientists who wanted to do awful experiments on his brain.

"You have to kill them all, Craig. All of them want to hurt you. You have no other choice," said a woman's voice near his ear. He whirled around, ready to slap the bitch, but no one was near enough to be the culprit. He must be hearing voices again.

It was why the feds wanted him so badly in the first place – he had special powers of the mind when he wasn't on his medication. He knew the secrets of the world, and it made the men in black want to shut him up and study him all at the same time.

People were looking at him again, closing around him and caging him in. They were staring at him like they knew what he was hiding, and then they began laughing at him as if they knew he'd be found out – discovered with the special gifts he carried inside his mind. He broke through the encircling crowd, swatting at them as if trying to rid himself of an annoying swarm of gnats. The laughter abruptly ceased and their jeering turned into astonished silence.

A woman with a baby stroller quickly veered into a nearby clothing shop, making him suspicious of her motives. He became sure that was no baby in the carrier, and he followed her into the store, intent on exposing her deception. When he caught up to her he grabbed the front of the stroller and whipped off the blanket. He was shocked to see a real live infant staring up at him, blinking rapidly against the bright overhead lights.

He looked up at the mother just as she began to scream. He stepped back, confused. He was suddenly frightened to find himself in an enclosed space, the clothes racks looming ominously all around him, like fabric sentinels waiting to take him down.

He saw the sales clerk whispering into the phone, and he stumbled backward toward the door, the mother's continued screaming assaulting his brain and scrambling his thoughts even further. At last he reached the door and fell through it onto the sidewalk, landing in a frigid puddle of water recently discarded by a window washer.

Some passersby stopped to stare at him while others continued on their way as if a man catapulting backwards from a storefront was the most normal thing in the world. Stunned, he crab walked his way out of the puddle, and then lurched to his feet and ran wildly down the street and around the corner, knocking over several gawkers in the process. He rounded a few more blocks, working his way toward a less populated area of town.

"You are so stupid. There's no one on earth dumber than you," a male voice snarled at him.

"I told you those people needed to die. But you just couldn't do it, could you? You're worthless. I hate you. I *hate* you!" The woman's voice from earlier now sounded distinctly menacing, and as he raised his hands to his ears, several more voices joined in.

They pressed down on him, ridiculing and insistent, growing louder and more frightening with each passing moment. He huddled on a park bench, his knees drawn to his chest and his arms wrapped around himself in an attempt to ward off the mean people in his head.

He must've fallen asleep because when he awoke it was quite dark and his head was silent. He left the park and wandered aimlessly for what felt like hours, though the sky was getting no lighter. He wondered what time it was, and what his mother was doing right now. Was she back from her trip? Had she missed him? Cause he sure as hell missed her.

He began whimpering as he passed dark house after dark house, recognizing nothing and feeling utterly alone. As he passed a stone path disappearing between two hedges along the side of a well-kempt Tudor, he felt compelled to follow it, ending up in a secluded backyard with a multitude of trees and surrounded by a half-wall made up of large stones.

The neighbors' houses were not visible due to the thick foliage, and he sank onto a swing hanging from a thick limb of one of the massive oaks to contemplate his dilemma. He needed to find his way home, but couldn't trust strangers – Barbie had always told him they were up to no good. He couldn't go to the cops, though he'd been assured he could count on people in uniform – but they would surely notify their brethren in the FBI.

One thing was sure; he had to get somewhere warm before he froze his ass off. He clumsily hopped off the swing and crept toward the house, staying low to the ground like he'd seen the heroes do in the movies. Those guys were always getting themselves into and out of tight spots. He bet they'd know what to do about Pauley all right.

When he reached the back of the house he noticed a crack in a window just above his head. He dragged over a chair from the patio and worked on the screen. He was finally able to tear through it and paused before continuing, listening for sounds of discovery.

Hearing none, he raised the window and pulled himself through the torn screen, racking himself on the kitchen faucet on the way in.

Grabbing his man bits, he rolled around on the floor for several moments, biting his lip to keep from crying aloud. Once he'd recovered enough to stand, he looked around with trepidation at the darkened room. There didn't seem to be any pets scampering around, and the occupants were evidently sound sleepers.

"You're one lucky son-of-a-bitch," he whispered to himself, causing an immediate rejoinder from his voices.

"You're one big dummy is what you are."

"Shit for brains."

"Who do you think you are, scuzzbucket?"

"Shhhh!" he uttered loudly, nearly crapping himself when he heard a toilet flush upstairs. He searched frantically for a hiding place, but these people were minimalists. What little furniture there was was sleek and glass, offering no amount of protection whatsoever. He was so screwed.

He heard footfalls in the upstairs hallway and the light in the stairwell came on. He backed into the space between the fridge and the pantry, attempting to make himself as small as possible.

"You should've grabbed a knife, you nincompoop. Now you can't kill anybody."

"You've really done it this time. They'll find you for sure."

"You're toast...burnt toast, with butter."

Craig kept making shushing noises as he slumped down the wall to the floor, his hands covering his ears and his eyes as wide as pie plates. He heard steps coming toward the kitchen and he squeezed his eyes shut, hoping the act might make him invisible.

After a few moments of silence he opened one eye and peered around the room, at first seeing only emptiness. But then he saw the man at the sink, obviously staring at the wide open window with its torn screen though his back was to him. Craig knew he was dead now, no doubt about it.

He glanced at the knife block next to the sink and nearly cried out when the man's hand reached for it, the sound dying in his throat when the hand closed around a glass sitting on the counter instead. The hand then poured itself a glass of water, brought it to the mouth to be drunk, and then placed it back on the counter. The man then turned around and left the room.

Craig gaped at the empty doorway through which he'd just exited, and then shrieked like a banshee when he jumped back into the kitchen, his hands wrapped tightly around a Louisville Slugger. What happened afterward Craig had no idea...he and his voices promptly fainted.

***

Lilah sat in her rental car outside of Steve's office, waiting for him to make an appearance. She'd disguised herself with sunglasses and a headscarf, and behind the heavily tinted windows of the vehicle she was nearly indistinguishable.

She'd rented the car solely for the purpose of remaining incognito – a good choice, apparently, as Steve cautiously pulled out of his building's parking garage, looking around anxiously for her sports car before continuing down the street. She waited until several cars had passed before maneuvering into traffic, following him at an acceptable tailing distance.

His attentiveness was understandable, she had to admit; she'd been a bit of a stalker lately. It was completely his fault, though. After several evenings of illicit physical activities all over his office, he had shut her off. He'd said he felt guilty for cheating on his wife, and that he was going back home. He should've thought of that before he started screwing her.

She'd continued to make advances, sure that he couldn't withstand her charms for long. But the bastard had responded by demoting her case to one of the junior lawyers and directing Margie to throw her out if she kept insisting on seeing him. The woman had been thrilled to comply, dialing 9-1-1 with flourish when Lilah had attempted to get past her into Steve's office.

He'd then filed a restraining order against her and now she couldn't even enter the building without breaking the law. The attorney now assigned to her case had to arrange to meet her elsewhere to discuss the proceedings to adhere to the order – he was quite obviously uncomfortable with the situation, and she was quite obviously pissed.

She found it hard to believe all this fuss was over the pedantic dark-haired woman in the photographs in Steve's office. She didn't look like anything special in Lilah's opinion, though she seemed familiar. Lilah didn't pay much attention to other women, though, so she didn't recognize her. She was sure the woman wasn't big news, like a local celebrity – although she looked like she could easily be a news anchor. How boring.

No matter; who she was made no difference to Lilah, and she narrowed her eyes on the back of Steve's car as he approached a yellow light. Ever the law abiding citizen, he slowed to a stop before it had turned red, and she breathed a sigh of relief as she stepped on the brake pedal three cars behind him. If she lost him now all of her planning would be for nothing.

God she hated him. He'd taken what she'd offered so self-righteously, enjoying the way she'd made him feel without a care for the ramifications of those acts. And when he was done he thought he could just discard her and return to his perfect wife...to his perfect life.

He'd broken his promises by recusing himself from her divorce, and had the nerve to pretend like she was the one with the problem. She was obsessed...a veritable psycho. She could just imagine him and Margie laughing at her expense. If she ever saw that woman again she'd love to slap the smarmy grin right off her chunky chip face, and she fervently hoped the two of them would choke on their complimentary candies.

Lilah's knuckles whitened as she gripped the steering wheel so savagely it would have dissolved had it been composed of a weaker metal. She reached into the glove compartment and brandished her pistol – a gift from Mark when they'd first married.

He'd been concerned about her being home alone during his late nights at the bar. He'd taken her to the range to teach her how to use it, and she'd become a decent shot. Bless his black heart.

Now she savored in the feel of the steel on her fingertips and the heaviness of the weapon in her hand. Mark had done her a great service after all, and she'd be sure to thank him after she kicked his ass in court.

The light turned green and she dropped the gun into her lap as she continued to follow Steve. As they drove further from the city center the roads became less populated and she had to put an even greater distance between them to avoid being spotted.

He finally pulled into a private development of newly refurbished homes, the streetlights designed to resemble old-fashioned gas lamps and the street signs set on decorative wooden posts. The lawns were immaculate, the landscaping professionally designed. How delightful.

There was no way she could follow directly behind him, so she drove past the turnoff, turning around after a mile or so. Upon entering the development she drove up and down the streets as slowly as she dared until she saw his car parked in the driveway of a gorgeous two-story colonial set back from the street.

She parked down the block and killed the engine, slouching in her seat to make herself more unobtrusive. The wife came home soon after, and Steve greeted her at the door with a kiss. Who does that? Disgusted, Lilah crossed her arms and looked away, taking in the scenery of the homes closest to her.

She waited there until after dark, when the activity in the neighborhood had died down significantly. It seemed everyone on this street had a dog, which they walked several times an evening. She felt the walls closing in on her – she couldn't wait to finish her business so she could get the hell out of suburbia.

When the time had come she put her pistol in the pocket of her coat and walked up the block nonchalantly, as if she belonged there. She'd discarded her sunglasses and scarf on the passenger seat in the car, and looked like anyone else out for a stroll in this affluent neighborhood. Only she didn't have a dog.

Once she arrived at the walkway leading up to Steve's house she took a last look around the now deserted street and trotted to the porch. She rang the doorbell and then ducked behind a bush next to the front door.

The wife answered it, coming out of the house to look up and down the street before muttering to herself and turning back to the door. Just before she'd closed it behind her Lilah sprang onto the porch, shoving the door open on the stunned woman and pulling the gun out of her coat.

"Scream and you're dead," she snarled, feeling like quite the outlaw as she motioned her into a chair at the dining room table.

"You're sick. You need help." Lilah jerked toward the woman. Oh yes...now she remembered the self-confident nurse from the Institute. My, what a small world.

"Shut up. Get your husband in here before I shoot you in the head."

"Riley? Who are you –"

"Hi, Steve," Lilah interrupted before his wife had a chance to warn him of her presence. He looked around wildly at the sound of her voice, his eyes coming to a rest on the gun now pointed at his chest.

"What...?" He apparently thought better of what he was going to say and instead sunk into the chair next to his wife. He looked between the two women as if attempting to ascertain what, if anything, had been shared.

"Why are you here? What do you want?" Riley spoke up when it became clear that Steve had forgotten he was the one with the penis.

"I thought it was important for you to know your husband fucked my brains out while he was living at his office, and –"

"Bull shit," he roared at the same time his wife said, "I don't believe you." They looked at each other in solidarity before turning back to the crazy woman holding them hostage.

"How else would I know he hadn't been staying here?" Lilah addressed Riley, though she continued to hold the gun on Steve.

"I assume you stalked us...followed me home from work and then started following my husband." She chanced a glance at him, knowing this would be one more major reason for him to eschew her career at the Institute.

"She doesn't know I sought your services for my divorce, Steve?" He closed his eyes as Riley turned to him inquisitively.

"Is that true?"

"Yes, but it doesn't mean anything happened."

"But it did, of course. A lot," Lilah interjected.

"We're not listening to any more of your lies," Steve shouted, attempting to shut out her words. As if suddenly remembering he was the man of the house, he sprang to his feet and rounded the table, intent on getting his hands around his ex-lover's slender neck.

Lilah shot his foot and he howled in pain as he fell to the floor. Riley froze for an instant before jumping up to attend to him; it was evident that she hadn't believed the gun was loaded. She stared at the other woman beseechingly as she wrapped Steve's foot tightly with a linen napkin to staunch the bleeding.

"Please," she begged, but her plea fell on deaf ears as Lilah placed a tiny recording device on the couple's dining room table, pressed 'play', and left the house amid the distant sound of sirens and the distinctive stridency of Steve's lovemaking.

Chapter 16
Angel of Mercy

Tony stood up with a broad grin on his face as Danielle walked into the Bleu Goose for their dinner date. She looked amazing in a little black dress, her recent weight loss emphasized by a narrow gold belt around her waist, which matched the bangles around both wrists and the hoops in her ears. She wore her hair loose, and it fell around her shoulders in magnificently enormous curls.

The woman knew how to make an entrance, drawing nearly every male eye her way. The two hugged as she reached the table, turning many of those stares envious. "Hey gorgeous," Tony complimented her as he held her chair. A pretty blush spread across her cheeks and she swatted his arm.

"Oh, stop it some more, you handsome lug, before you swell my head." He winked at her outlandishly before summoning their server to place their order.

He'd been looking forward to seeing her all day, and after they'd dispensed with the niceties, he rubbed his hands together with anticipation. "Gimme."

"My, my, aren't we demanding?"

"Hey, I've wined and dined you, as promised. Now it's your turn."

"Okay, okay!" she joked, pulling a stuffed manila envelope from her bag and shoving it across the table. He picked it up as if it held the crown jewels and gazed at her adoringly.

"You realize you're the best, right?"

"Of course," she responded drolly, waving away his adulation.

"Did you have any trouble?"

"None whatsoever," she answered, then leaned forward suddenly, her hand gripping his arm fiercely. "If you find something in those files – something she did to hurt my brother..."

"Then she's going down. I promise." Tears filled Danielle's big beautiful eyes as she stared at him, possibly attempting to determine if blood really could be trumped by water in his mind. It could, and he hoped his unflinching eye contact conveyed his sincerity. Besides, he was losing circulation to his arm.

He'd met Danielle when she'd first started working for his aunt, and they'd become good friends over the years. They had a mutual respect for each other, and she was well aware he'd never betray his promise to her.

He knew the moment her inner battle was settled in his favor by the look of resignation that entered her eyes – not to mention the slight lessening of the death grip she had on his arm.

They were startled out of their intense nonverbal communication by Mark, who'd had to clear his throat loudly several times to get their attention. "Sorry to interrupt, guys – just wanted to say 'hi' and ask what you thought of that new steak special we added to the menu." He looked a bit uncomfortable as his gaze settled on the hand Danielle had yet to remove from Tony's sleeve.

"Amazing, as usual," Tony reassured him as he disengaged himself from his dinner companion to shake the man's hand.

"So this is...you two are...," he began, seeming unable to express his thoughts.

"No, no – we're just friends, hanging out in your fine establishment," Tony clarified, more in tune to Mark's discomfort than Danielle, who seemed particularly clueless at the moment.

"Really?" Mark visibly brightened before turning to Danielle for verification. Tony nearly laughed at the man's enthusiasm, and was relieved when Danielle seconded his statement and put the man's mind at ease.

"Just friends," she nodded.

"Why don't you have a seat? Take a load off?"

"Don't mind if I do," he responded, immediately sliding into the booth next to Danielle. "Hi," he said softly, his voice becoming intimate.

"Hi," she responded, her tone so sweet it gave Tony a toothache. "You come here often?" she teased, earning a seductive chuckle from a smitten Mark.

"Wow! Look at the time! Gotta go! Thanks again, Dani – smooches!" he called as he dropped three twenties onto the table, grabbed the enveloped she'd given him, and dashed out of the restaurant, leaving the two to nauseate someone other than him.

When he returned home, Riley was waiting for him anxiously. She had cleared off the kitchen island to use as a workspace, and was now impatiently shifting from one foot to the other. She was wearing a loose-fitting maxi dress, had piled her hair on top of her head, and was bare-footed – she looked like a sexy gypsy, and it was all he could do not to sweep her into his arms and make love to her all night long.

He'd refrain, of course. At least until she was ready. She'd come to him as a friend, asking pitifully to rent his empty second bedroom until she was able to find her way back to the land of the living – he had no choice but to respect that.

She'd refused to move in with Eva and Gabe – their house was in shambles because of the major renovation they'd undertaken to prepare for the birth of the twins. And she couldn't stay in her own house; the soured memories and waking nightmares that had taken up residence there threatened to overwhelm her every time she set foot through the door.

And she couldn't get a place of her own – Steve had made sure her hands were tied after she'd demanded a divorce. As a result she had very little expendable income and no access to her savings. He'd gotten the last laugh after all, leaving her at the mercy of others.

It was clear the jerk had assumed she'd return to him; begging him to take her back after she'd dared to leave him over something so inconsequential as an affair with one of her former patients. But she'd knock over a bank before placing herself back under his control.

So when she'd swallowed her pride and called Tony she was beyond grateful that he'd agreed to her request. Exuberantly, in fact. She'd assured him she'd stay out of his way – that he wouldn't even know she was there...but he wasn't having it. The idea of her had been such a big part of his life for so long, he welcomed her presence, and he became more determined with each passing day to make their arrangement a permanent one.

He had set about making her as comfortable as possible in his home, taking her shopping for furniture and comfort items the day she'd arrived, refusing to allow her to spend one penny of her dwindling paycheck. He'd told her he had to furnish the room eventually anyway, and that she was just helping him do so.

Convinced, she'd selected an iron daybed, nightstands and lamps, and a vanity with matching armoire. The set was so expensive she'd refused to let him buy her anything else, but when she'd come home from work the following day she'd found the room filled with pillows, plants, prints for the walls, a huge white shag rug for the floor, and a cushy recliner placed in front of the windows so she could enjoy the view in comfort – and without curtains.

She'd been delighted, but had reprimanded him for disregarding her instructions just based on principle. But he noticed she happily spent much of her spare time in the beautiful space – a place she could call her very own at a time when her life provided far more disruption than peace. He knew she needed some time before she could even think about a new relationship, but he was fully committed to being there when that time came.

While he reheated the selection of appetizers he'd brought home from the Bleu Goose, she spread the contents of the envelope over the granite surface of the island, and they ate while walking in circles around it, searching Michael Gregory's chart for a notation or a missing page or some other indication of foul play.

But everything was in perfect order. Dr. Tacee was a fastidious record keeper, and after reading and rereading each and every page meticulously, Riley was ready to give up. Apparently her nurse's intuition had a glitch in it, because it seemed this time it was dead wrong.

The only thing left was the fax Danielle had requested from the pharmacy – it contained lists of medication that had been filled for each patient, and was just a formality as it would match the copies of the prescriptions Dr. Tacee had written in the patients' charts.

Michael had been on a multitude of medicine during his years under the physician's care, and his list was long. Nonetheless, they began the arduous task of comparing each of his prescriptions with the dispensary list.

Tony stopped short in his medicine recitation, causing Riley to glance up from the chart. "What is it?"

"This is weird..." She waited patiently as he looked back and forth among the faxed pages, correlating prescription numbers with other pertinent information. "For almost all of these meds, the pick-up was made by either Danielle Gregory or the group home manager, Trace Webster."

"Yes," she prompted; there was nothing strange about that.

"But there was one medication that was never picked up by anyone other than Aunt Ollie." Now *that* was odd – why would a physician fill her own patients' prescriptions?

"What medication was it?" she asked, flipping through the prescription copies in the chart.

"Tranylcypromine."

She looked for the matching slip, her brow becoming more furrowed as she did so. "It's not here..."

"Here's the original," he replied, holding up the sheet from the pharmacy.

"So she purposely destroyed the chart copy?"

"Or forgot to put it into the chart in the first place...or maybe she misplaced it...," he concluded, attempting to give his aunt the benefit of the doubt.

"The woman has missed not one 'and', 'the', or 'it' in this entire chart. She didn't forget or lose shit," Riley countered, not nearly as forgiving. "What is the medication for?"

He Googled it on his phone, his eyes widening as the screen loaded. He looked up at her, dazed. "It's Parnate..."

Her mouth fell open as she stared at him, perhaps waiting for a punchline that would never come. "You're telling me she knowingly gave Michael a pill that could be fatal when taken with nearly every other medication she'd prescribed for him?"

Tony nodded, unable to speak. "Oh, Jesus," she whispered, as the world once again turned itself on end.

***

Craig woke with a start, his ass hurting and his nose itching. He tried to scratch his face, but he couldn't lift his arm – it was attached to the bed with a thick leather band. He jerked his other arm with the same result, then lifted his head to look around him.

He was at the FBI testing site, and had been tied down to a highly uncomfortable bed by his wrists, his ankles, and his chest. His throat was sore and parched, his stomach rumbled uncomfortably, and he really had to pee.

He was afraid to bring further attention to himself, but if the bastards were going to slice him up and mount him on microscope slides, they were sure as hell going to feed him first.

"Hey," he mouthed, but nothing but hot air expelled from his lips with the effort. He cleared his throat and tried again, with more success. "Hey!" Soon the door was unlocked and two people stepped into the room. They looked benign enough; one carrying a blood pressure cuff and stethoscope, and the other a tray of food.

"Hi, Craig. I'm Eliza and this is Dean. We need to get a set of vitals and then do some range of motion exercises to help your circulation. If that goes okay we can start working you out of those restraints, okay?"

He nodded at her suspiciously, then turned his head to peruse the tray of food with interest. He was famished, but first had to endure being squeezed and rotated and auscultated and maneuvered. Then Eliza turned away while Dean held a urinal to his groin so he could take a leak. It was pretty embarrassing, but his sense of relief far overshadowed his shame.

Finally Dean fed him a ham sandwich and Gatorade, which felt wonderful in his aching throat, while Eliza asked him questions. "Do you know where you are, Craig?"

"FBI testing site," he replied between bites. "You're gonna cut me open and study my brain."

"Why would the United States government do that?"

"Cause I know how the world will end," he said cheerfully, guzzling the remainder of the Gatorade and looking around for more.

"You're actually in the hospital, Craig. At the Psychiatric Institute of North America." He did not respond, but gaped at her dumbly. "You caused quite a ruckus downtown, and then ended up breaking into someone's house. Do you remember that?"

"No, ma'am...no, I sure don't."

"You've been psychotic for a while, but we've got you back on your medication regimen. It's really important to stay on your meds, okay? Every time you stop you'll get sicker and sicker until you can't get well again. Do you understand?"

He nodded again. "Can I have another sandwich?"

After he'd inhaled it they released one of his arms, and every two hours after that they removed another restraint until he was free. He spent a few moments doing calisthenics next to his bed – another trick he'd seen on TV.

When the hero found himself imprisoned he wouldn't cry like a little bitch; instead he'd choose to be proactive...turning lemons to lemonade and all that jazz. "Jazz? You wouldn't know jazz if it bit you in the ass."

"Oh, shut up," he grumbled as he pitched from the room and, hopefully, away from the condemnatory voice. It wasn't like he needed those voices to feel worse about himself – James and Pauley had accomplished that feat well enough on their own.

But it seemed like the people in his head repeated the sentiments of the men in his family. As though they'd heard what had been said and then filed it away for future reference. He couldn't recall exactly when the voices had begun, but it seemed like it'd been around the time Pauley had gone away to college. They'd picked up his slack seamlessly – it was almost as if he'd still been around.

At first Craig had been afraid to tell anyone about the voices – as out of touch with reality as he'd become, he knew hearing and seeing things that weren't there was just plain crazy. But when he'd finally been hospitalized for the first time he'd had to come clean, primarily because he'd taken to talking back to them.

He was happy to find they went away completely when he was on his meds, and, unlike other patients he'd talked to, he didn't miss them at all during those times. When he wasn't on his meds, though, the only things that quieted them were alcohol and weed.

It had been one of the main reasons he'd gotten hooked, but now he used just because he liked the way it made him feel. Calm and serene, as if he hadn't a care in the world. As if he wasn't a second-class citizen in his own family. As if he wasn't nearly incapable of taking care of himself.

As he paced the short hall of the intensive care unit, his hospital scrubs so large they were in danger of falling off and leaving him disrobed, he thought about what a pickle he'd be in if his mother ever died.

She constantly assured him she wouldn't, of course, so he had no concerns about her dying of natural causes or old age. But what if she were in a car accident? Or a house fire? A plane crash? In the way of a lunatic sniper? What would he do then? How could he ever live a life without Barbie in it?

As those thoughts overwhelmed him he began mewling loudly and crouched to the floor, rocking quickly back and forth with his thumb in his mouth. They came with a shot in the butt cheek – the one that wasn't sore – and helped him back to bed, and soon he stopped feeling anything at all.

When he awoke, Barbie was sitting in a chair next to his bed, her hand covering his reassuringly. At first he thought she was a hallucination, brought upon by his fears from earlier, but she was still there after he'd rubbed his eyes and shook his head to dislodge her. He was heartened by her vibrant appearance and substantial form, now convinced that she was real.

"Hi," he said, swinging his legs off the bed and sitting at the edge of it.

"Hi, son," she replied fondly, patting his hand before releasing it. "How're you feeling today?"

"Okay, I think."

"Good. You had me worried, Craig."

"It was all Pauley's fault," he said defensively.

"Yes, I've told Paulson how incredibly disappointed he's made me."

"Is he going to jail?" Craig asked hopefully.

"Jail? Heavens no. Why on earth would he go to jail?"

He blinked at her, confused. He thought she knew. "Because he's a criminal! He tried to sell me on the black market!"

"He did no such thing. That's all part of your delusion."

He scratched his head, trying to work things out in his mind. "But...he put me in a car with a stranger and...and gave him money to take me away..."

"It was a taxi, Craig. That's what they do. You pay them to take you places." He peered at her doubtfully until she prudently changed the subject. "Your ex-fiancée is here in the hospital, as well. Isn't that ironic?" she said, her lips pursing distastefully.

"Why is she not my fiancée anymore?" he asked, stumbling over the word as he always did. Curiously, he found he didn't particularly care one way or the other about her status in his life.

"Oh, the girl is no longer suitable for us, son."

Us? "How come?"

"She's been all over the news...broke into a lawyer's house waving a gun around like a crazy person. Turns out she was already married – yes, Craig; married," she cut him off when he furrowed his brow and opened his mouth to interject.

"Anyway," she continued, barely drawing a breath, "the house belonged to her *divorce* attorney who said she was trying to threaten him into speeding up her case, no doubt so she could get her mangy claws into us," she finished, shuddering at the disaster that had nearly befallen her family.

Craig didn't know what to say – the issue seemed to be between Barbie and Lilah at this point, despite her insistent use of awkward pronouns. "What if she shows up at the pool house after they let her go?"

Barbie was shaking her head before he'd finished his question. "She won't be going anywhere for a long time, don't you worry. And even then she'll only leave here to go to a facility for the criminally insane. Besides, I just spoke to her myself."

Craig's eyes widened as he stared at her. No doubt about it – his mother was for sure a TV hero, going up against loony Lilah like that. "What'd you say?" he breathed, all besotted fan now.

"I told her she was no longer welcome in our home, and that she's not a part of our family anymore, nor will she ever be again. Then I told her all of her things had been left with security, and that she could keep the ring. She'll need it to pay her hospital bills," she concluded with a sniff.

"Well. That sure was nice of you..."

"Yes, it was. We aren't heathens, Craig."

"No," he bowed his head, properly chastened.

He spent more time at the Institute than he ever had before, and was growing restless. When he was ushered into the conference room for Dr. Tacee's rounds, she glared at him ferociously, as if angered that he was still there. It made no sense, of course; he couldn't go anywhere without her permission.

"Can I go home today?"

"Yes, I think that would be best," she nearly barked at him, pushing three packages of the little red pills across the table. "Take those while I write your discharge orders."

He didn't understand why she was so mad at him, but he did as he was told. After he'd shown her his empty mouth, wagging his tongue around like a three-year-old showing off his chewed food, she waved him off, disgusted. "Get out of my sight," she growled, causing him to bolt for the door like his tail was on fire.

Later, while he was hanging out in the lounge waiting for Barbie to pick him up, two men in suits and three uniformed police officers entered the unit, disappearing from view down the hallway he'd fled from earlier.

After a few moments and much yelling, they reappeared, surrounding a handcuffed Dr. Tacee. After they'd left the unit, Craig glanced around to see if everyone else was as shocked as he was. They were, though he wouldn't have been a bit surprised if this had been a hallucination – and not an unpleasant one at that.

***

"Hello?"

"Paulson, this is your mother."

"Yes, Barbie," Pauley sighed. Who the hell else would he think she'd be?

"Don't forget Craig's welcome home dinner tonight."

"How could I? You've reminded me every damn day for the past week."

"You're in no position to take that attitude with me, young man," she warned. He could almost see her hackles rising through the phone. She would've made a fine rooster.

"Yes, ma'am."

"I'll see you and your little friend at seven o'clock sharp." She rung off before he had a chance to respond, leaving him scowling at the phone.

He glanced at his 'little friend' as she unfurled herself from the chaise in the sun next to the windows, graceful as a feline. She came to sit on his lap, rendering him rock hard on impact.

"Dinner at Barbie's tonight?"

He nodded. "'Seven o'clock sharp'".

"I have nothing to wear."

"As much as I'd love to see you in nothing, you have plenty to wear." She pouted at him before wandering into the bedroom to spend the afternoon trying on clothes.

He found dealing with her tedious at times, like being a parent to a child who couldn't decide if she was eight or eighteen. As much as he loved her innocence, it could be trying. Sometimes he missed the easy exchanges Tiffany provided, and had thought about stopping by to dip his pen in her inkwell. But even that seemed like a hassle.

He realized he really didn't know what he wanted for once in his life, which greatly disconcerted him. While he'd never strived for success, at least he'd always known who he was and what made him tick. But that seemed to have changed recently.

He needed it back. He couldn't live in this vacuous existence indefinitely. He needed to kick start his drive before he became like normal men...boring and apathetic. Or worse, like Craig...lost and clueless.

To be fair, his feelings probably had much more to do with him than with Marin, but he'd never been one to accept blame, so he laid it squarely on her shoulders. As a result, he was unduly irritable with her on the drive to the Phipps's mansion that evening. She couldn't say anything right and was near tears by the time they reached the estate.

At dinner he roundly ignored her – though he barely said a word to anyone, sitting at the table like a sullen child who'd been denied dessert. Marin stared at her plate miserably throughout the meal while Barbie glared at her youngest son as a result of his atrocious behavior on such a celebratory occasion.

Things got lively, though, when Craig suddenly grew a set of balls and attacked James with no apparent provocation. "Why do you keep staring at me?!" he shouted at him.

James almost appeared startled as his gaze briefly flickered to Craig. "I've barely even looked at you, boy."

"You're being really mean!"

"I haven't said anything to you, either."

Pauley could argue that both of those things proved his brother's point, but he wasn't about to intervene when the evening had just gotten interesting.

"It's not my fault I'm sick."

"I'm positive that's exactly whose fault it is."

"James," Barbie butted in, but Craig held up his hand. He'd needed to say these things for a long time and didn't want to lose his nerve now.

"It's called schizophrenia. Lots of people have it, and they say it's genetic. That would make it *your* fault."

Pauley's mouth dropped open at his brother's audacity. He was so proud of him he nearly clapped him on the back. Who was this brave soul, and what had he done with Craig?

"That's assuming you're really my son; a fact I've always found rather doubtful."

Marin gasped and finally looked up from the table, her eyes wide and scared.

"James!" Barbie cried, uninterrupted this time as Craig glared at his father. "How dare you! What, I'm a cheap trollop now?" Her husband ignored her, having returned to his meal. He ate with deliberation, as if measuring each movement...each bite.

"Gee, 'Dad', I'm so sorry I have a mental illness, even though I'm not to blame."

"The only illness you have is your stupidity. You're messed up, the way you think about things, and you can't be fixed. Your mother has tried for all these years. You're broken beyond repair, and you're not worth my time."

Simultaneously Craig lurched to his feet and out the doors to the patio while Barbie reached over and slapped her husband squarely across the face. She then marched out of the room, slamming the doors behind her.

It was the most James had ever said to either of his children, and Pauley was flabbergasted. He actually felt sorry for his brother for the first time in his life. Meanwhile, his father continued eating as if nothing had happened, while Pauley and Marin gaped at each other in disbelief.

"Uh...well...I guess we best be going," he said as he grabbed her hand and dragged her out of the room. For once Lucretia wasn't there to manhandle the front doors to grant them exit – she was likely elsewhere tending to a distraught Barbie.

The couple slipped out of the house and drove home in silence. That night they made love tenderly, as if making up for everything that had been said and done. Afterward he held her in his arms, feeling at peace with her in his life once again.

They spent the following day in bed, showing each other over and over again the depth of their emotion. When they finally roused themselves from the enthusiastically rumpled bed, he took her to lunch at the barbeque joint down the street. She looked remarkably well-rested, though they'd done very little sleeping.

She wore her hair in a loose bun, errant curls falling around her face becomingly. She wore jeans with boots and a plain white t-shirt, a black blazer thrown over her shoulders for warmth. She looked young and fresh – it wouldn't be hard to believe her to be a college senior, or even a junior executive out for a bite to eat on the weekend before returning to a career that would undoubtedly skyrocket one day.

They sat next to each other at their table, he discarding her napkin every time she picked it up in favor of provocatively sucking the barbeque sauce from the tips of her fingers with his full, seductive lips.

She giggled each time he did it, likely sickening the other customers with their outrageous displays of affection, but they didn't care. This moment was theirs, and theirs alone, and no one could take that away from them.

Except Barbie, of course, Pauley thought disparagingly as he glanced at the screen of his cell phone. He let the call go to voice mail as he returned to feasting on the hands of his lover, but his phone interrupted him again...and again.

He pulled it from his pocket intending to silence the ringer, but Marin shook her head, disproving. He was lucky he had a mother who cared about him – he should treat her with the utmost respect. Sighing, he answered the phone, staring pointedly at Marin as he did so.

"Yes, Barbie," he said, waylaying her unnecessary tendency to identify herself every time she called him.

"We can't find Craig! He's gone!" she screamed into the phone, very nearly shattering his eardrum in the process.

"Chill, Barbie – I'm sure he'll turn up."

"He won't! He's been gone all night!"

"Have you called the cops?"

"I can't call them until it's been twenty-four hours...besides, I can't wait that long knowing he's out there all alone. You have to go find him, Paulson!"

"How the hell should I know where to find him, Barbie? That lunatic could be anywhere."

"Paulson, I'm not asking for your help. It's an order!" She hung up on him for the second time in as many days – an infuriating habit they'd need to discuss at some point.

"Craig's gone missing. Barbie wants me to try to find him," he said to Marin, shrugging his shoulders at her questioning look.

Together they drove back to the estate, where Barbie told them that Lucretia had found no sign that Craig had slept in the pool house the previous night, and that the entire house and grounds had been searched twice.

Pauley and Marin left from there to scour the neighborhood. It was a nearly impossible task – the beautiful homes and expansive lawns were surrounded by immense trees and deep clusters of shrubbery and brick walls. There were innumerable places to hide, and there was no way Pauley could check them all.

Soon they'd left the exclusive neighborhood and turned back toward downtown. After driving in silence for what felt like hours, Pauley almost jumped when Marin spoke. "He should never have been off his meds. It was too much for him. And the drinking made it all worse."

He dropped her hand as if it had burned him. "He was back on his meds and he was dried out at the hospital, so what does that have to do with anything?" he asked defensively.

"Maybe it was the last straw. Maybe it made him so sick this time he just couldn't get better." He glared at her as he parked his car at the riverboat launch pad. She'd just pissed him off so thoroughly he jumped out of the car and slammed the door without a word.

She stayed in the car while he walked along the boardwalk where he'd brought Craig to the AA retreat. He didn't know where else to look. He felt impotent, which filled him with a slow-burning rage. He gripped the railing as he gazed at the river, seeing nothing but a cold hard fury blurring his vision and clouding his mind.

How was any of this his fault? If anyone were to blame it was James – it was his harsh words that had sent Craig running in the first place. He'd be damned if he was going to let that fly. He got back into the car, started the engine, and then turned to Marin. "Get out," he demanded.

"What?" she asked, confused.

"I said, 'get out'".

"But Pauley, I –"

"GET OUT!!" he shouted, leaning over her to throw open her door. She scrambled out of the car and stood on the boardwalk like a statue, dazed.

Pauley gunned the engine and peeled out of the parking lot, not even bothering to glance in his rearview mirror. When he arrived back home he drained a couple of beers before he calmed down enough to think about the situation with a clear head.

But instead of going back to the river to get Marin he settled onto the couch and turned on the game. A few days apart would do them good, and when they got back together maybe she wouldn't be such a nag.

Yes, that's all that was needed to get their relationship back on track. Once she'd learned her lesson things between them would be as good as new.

Chapter 17
Goodbyes

Eva finished unpacking her last box and looked around with satisfaction. She'd made the difficult decision to move her portion of her practice to the Institute, to the third floor that was dedicated to office suites for physicians, advanced practice nurses, and therapists.

Eva leased the space to take advantage of shared services with the facility, not to mention proximity to her inpatient clientele. The surroundings weren't nearly as cushy as her previous office, and she would miss the hell out of Rosie, but the security measures here far outweighed those things.

Staff wore an alert sensor at all times; all they had to do in an emergency was push the device's alarm and a code would be called to wherever they happened to be at the time – the bathroom, the cafeteria, the parking lot, the office, the hallways. Responders would show up within seconds, well equipped to handle any possible situation.

Gabe had insisted on the change before giving her his blessing to return to work, and now she realized how wholeheartedly she agreed. She knew she would never again have felt safe elsewhere, and understood the importance of being able to be fully in the moment during therapy sessions. How would she have been able to do that if she were constantly watching her back?

After she'd finished arranging her reference books on the shelves, locked her file cabinets, and logged off her computer, she ambled through the waiting room and nodded at Jolene, the sweet secretary for the suite of offices Eva now shared. She then made her way to the elevator, trying hard not to waddle. She'd just settled herself into her Jeep when she received Marin's text. *Please come.*

She had to assume her sister meant her apartment since Eva had never been to Pauley's – which didn't bode well. He must have ended things with her again; Eva had known it was only a matter of time. At least Marin had reached out to her this time, instead of going off the deep end all by herself and being alone for who knew how long before Eva eventually found her.

She pushed the limits of both the law and her engine, arriving at her sister's place in just under a half-an-hour; a record by anyone's standards. Heaving herself out of her vehicle, she nearly ran to the building, huffed up the stairs, and knocked on Marin's door. She stretched her back while waiting for an answer – God her hips hurt.

When her twin didn't come to the door she unlocked it with her own key and entered the apartment. "Marin? I'm here!" she called, looking around the main area before moving into the bedroom. "Mae?" she questioned, the empty room unresponsive. Maybe she meant Pauley's after all, Eva thought, as she passed the bathroom.

She froze as she heard a drop of water hit the surface of the full tub. Her stomach plummeting, she flipped on the light and stifled a scream as the sight of her sister's body floating in water filled with blood slowly made its way to her brain.

"No!" she screamed as she flung herself at the bathtub, plunging her arms into the water to gather Marin to her chest. She was cold and lifeless, the deep slashes down the length of each arm long since surrendering her essence to the now tepid water.

"No, no, no, no, no!" Eva moaned, rocking her sister relentlessly, much as she'd done too many times to count during their lifetime. Chilled and soaked, she felt nothing as she sobbed, the babies kicking at the pressure of Marin's weight against Eva's stomach as she held her twin tight to her body – the only contact they would ever have with an aunt they would never know.

Eventually the police came, responding to calls from neighbors about a commotion. But they couldn't separate the two until Gabe arrived, holding his wife while the paramedics pried Marin out of her desperate grasp. The cry that emitted from deep within her was so plaintive it rocked him to his core, and caused him great concern that she might never be whole again.

The sentiment was strengthened in the days that followed. By rote she brought food to her mouth and then swallowed it automatically. She brushed her hair with instinctive strokes while staring past herself in the mirror. She went through the motions of daily living while lost deep within her own mind.

When she did glimpse her reflection it was by accident, and it sent her into a screaming fit until she was sedated. The doctor assured Gabe that the medication used to calm her was far less risky for the babies than her current mental state.

Gabe and Riley made all of the arrangements for Marin's funeral, and it was only when overhearing them talk about dressing her that Eva returned to some semblance of herself, although much less so than was typical.

"Her hair should be straight, not curly. No jewelry. None at all. And she'll need a new dress. From the store, not her closet," she said, glancing at them momentarily before returning her gaze to the fireplace, where it had remained all morning.

"Of course," Riley responded after looking at Gabe in surprise. It was the first time Eva had spoken, and Riley understood perfectly. It was imperative to Eva that her sister be committed to the earth amid none of Pauley's trappings. He had soiled her enough in life, and she should be returned to her previous state of purity prior to their final goodbyes.

So Riley found a pretty blue frock with a flounced hemline and eyelet lace around the bodice and at the bottom of the long sleeves that would effectively cover the ravaged wounds Marin had inflicted on her arms. She found slippers that matched the lace, and a headband with a ruffled overlay to push her hair back from her beautiful face.

Later, Riley spent hours at the funeral home flat-ironing Marin's hair until it was as smooth and straight as she'd ever seen it. She knew Eva would be grateful – it was an act of love for both of them.

At the funeral Eva maintained a tenuous grasp on her newly attained escape from the darkness that had insidiously overtaken her the moment she'd found her sister dead. Now she gazed at Marin's beloved face and leaned over her to press a kiss to her forehead and each cold cheek before returning to her seat for the service.

·Many of the staff from the Institute were there, and several spoke about Marin's qualities and her impact on the lives of others. Eva was thankful for every word they said, and for the reassuring presence of Gabe and Riley on either side of her.

As the attendees stood for the closing of the casket, there was a commotion at the doors of the church as a disheveled and harried Pauley entered, striding down the aisle purposefully. "Wait...please," he called, his voice breaking into a sob as he reached the front. He stared into the coffin, his face stricken. "Why?" he moaned, reaching out to touch her.

Eva surged forward, her expression outraged. "Don't you touch her!" she screamed, grabbing at Pauley to pull him away from her sister. He jerked his arm away from her and she fell back against Gabe, who tried to prevent her from approaching the man again. She wrenched out of his grasp and rushed at Pauley, looking like a wild woman in the throes of lunacy.

"Get away from her!" she screeched, her voice even higher now. "You killed her! You did this! She's dead because of you, you sick bastard!"

He turned to her, his mouth pulled into a frown, his face tormented. He looked as though he hadn't slept for days, and his expression was almost frightened, like he was being haunted by demons that no one but he could see.

Riley stepped forward and put her hand against his chest. "I can see you're hurting, but you need to go. Let Eva say goodbye in peace. Please."

In an uncharacteristic act of empathy, Pauley nodded, his gaze flickering to Eva before taking one last long look at the resting form of perhaps the only woman he'd ever really loved. He then turned and left the church, his posture hunched and his shoulders shaking.

Soon after, the casket was closed, the body was buried, and the only thing Eva had left of her twin was her letter, now lying on a satin cushion inside a heart-shaped box on Eva's nightstand.

Someday she would put it in her memory chest where it would reside alongside her wedding dress, but for now she kept it close so she could read it often, running her fingers over the script that had been penned by Marin's hand not so long ago.

Dear E,

I love you to the end of the earth and back again, and I have lived to this day only because of your will. Please don't blame yourself for my death. It is a much needed release that has been a long time coming...maybe even since the day we were born. You see, we were broken when we came into this world. Not at conception, but shortly afterward. Our mother was solely to blame for that, but she loved us, Eva. It wasn't enough, or even for very long, but she loved us for a while. Until Pauley, you and Gabe were the only ones who ever loved me since then. While your love was pure and good, Pauley's was passionate and volatile. It was so consuming I knew it would not – could not – last. But while it did there was light in my life for the very first time, and even the constant pain in my brain lessened. When he was gone, the darkness returned, blacker than ever. I can no longer live with the hurt that has spread to my heart...to my spirit...even into my very soul. I yearn for eternal peace, and this final act has become my only choice.

Yours with love forever more, Mae

***

Pauley greatly enjoyed his self-prescribed hiatus from Marin. It could be exhausting to be with her – to give her all the things she needed to stay sane. Sure, he'd been with plenty of women who'd placed high demands on his time and his body, not to mention his money.

But this was different. Every move he made could disrupt the fragile shell that encased Marin's mind, and as exhilarating as it could be to have such control over someone who seemed somehow unattainable in the true sense, it was an arduous job – and he was taking a much needed sick day.

He did all the things he couldn't do with her around, including an incredibly satisfying interlude with Tiffany. Afterward, both of them in the throes of the relaxed kind of stupor that often follows such activities, he told her they would have to curtail their trysts slightly; he wanted to be a better man for Marin.

Of course he couldn't be asked to be completely monogamous – that wasn't the Phipps family tradition. At the age of twelve Pauley had discovered that his father had been having an affair for many years. He'd confronted James, all big man defending his mother's honor.

He'd been told that this was the norm in high society. Your trophy wife gave you heirs and managed your household, and when she got around to submitting to intercourse, you'd better not disrupt her salon-fresh do. The mistress was for screwing, and if she did her job well, everyone was happy and no one was the wiser for it.

Ironically, Tiffany had similar feelings in terms of cooling off their relationship, though hers were the result of her newly discovered pregnancy. He knew her tits were bigger, but had chalked it up to a boob job. Go figure.

He was content and re-energized when he stepped out of the shower at his place less than an hour later, having successfully washed the scent of another woman off his body. Though it hadn't yet been two days since he'd left Marin at the pier, he'd decided it had been long enough. He found himself yearning for her company, and was now determined to cut their break short.

He wasn't surprised when she didn't answer his insistent knock on her door; he had no doubt she was giving him the cold shoulder as a result of his behavior. No matter – she would come around eventually and he would apologize profusely and they would have phenomenal sex.

He had a raging hard-on just thinking about it, and immediately regretted cutting Tiffany loose so spontaneously. He wasn't thinking – he should've waited until Marin was back in his bed before making such a rash decision. But he wasn't a beggar, and he refused to renege on the choice he'd made.

He considered visiting a prostitute – only the best the city had to offer, of course – but couldn't bring himself to pay for something women so freely gave him. In desperation he returned to Marin's apartment more and more frequently until a neighbor finally took pity on him and confided that she'd been taken away in a body bag a couple of days prior.

"Suicide," the elderly woman had whispered, looking around warily as if she might be smote to the ground for uttering such a word. He didn't believe her – how could he? It was a crazy story from a questionable source.

But when Barbie called him the following day with news of Marin's obituary, he was forced to face the truth: she was lost to him for good, and nothing he could do would bring her back to him. Why had she done this? Didn't she know how beautiful she was? How much he needed her? How could she do this to him?

He'd gone to the funeral to get answers. Or maybe just to see her face again, one last time. He hadn't meant to cause an uproar, though he'd considered rebuffing Eva's demands to leave. But her friend had appealed to his better judgment, and he'd realized nothing further could be gained by staying there. So he'd left, Eva's accusations ringing in his ears.

How was any of this his fault? He hadn't killed Marin with his own hands. He hadn't shoved pills down her throat or tied the noose around her neck or whatever it was she'd done to herself. If anything he had enhanced her life to a greater degree than it had ever been without him, and Eva should be grateful that her sister's last days had been spent in his company. Or most of them, anyway.

Although this knowledge gave him comfort, he found he couldn't abide being by himself, and he took up temporary residence at the now empty pool house. He spent his days following Barbie around like a bored child, which she didn't find nearly as annoying as she normally would.

She was too distracted by Craig's continued disappearance to pay Pauley much mind, spending all of her time alternating between scouring the paper for possible leads and harassing the police about their ineffectual sleuthing.

When the cops eventually came to the house to advise the family that Craig's body, covered with dried blood, had been found in a culvert just outside their neighborhood, Pauley was there to break her fall. When she had a massive stroke later that night, he was there to rush her to the hospital. And when she died of a broken heart the following day he was there to gently close her staring eyes.

Whether due to grief or guilt, it was painfully obvious that Barbie's last moments were tortured beyond reason. Now he was truly alone, and was powerless to do anything more than rale at a God he'd never believed in for the injustice of it all.

He sat alone in his spectacular home day after day, staring at the walls, which seemed intent on mocking him. There was no comfort here, but the only place he wanted to be was deep inside of nowhere, yet he had no way to get there.

Periodically he would stand at the windows, watching the city move in giant leaps all around him. He had difficulty believing life could be continuing as usual while his own was in such disarray.

James came finally, using his own key to enter. Pauley heard neither the key in the lock nor the purposeful movements the man made as he assessed the situation, ever the pragmatic businessman. With no words and little fanfare, he pushed Pauley into the shower, shoved a toothbrush and a razor into his hands, and firmly prodded him through his grooming regimen by strength of will alone.

Pauley was barely aware of being dressed in his best black suit, staring unseeingly at James as he tied his tie and combed his hair and draped his jacket over his shoulders. He didn't recall leaving his condo or getting into his father's Lincoln town car or being led blindly into the new church his mother had almost singlehandedly built from her generous contributions over the past few decades.

But he saw Barbie and Craig lying side by side in their extravagant matching coffins. He saw the huge number of spectators who had come to pay homage to a socialite and philanthropist the likes of which the city had never seen before and likely never would again. And he saw Eva, who paled in comparison to Marin in his eyes, but resembled her enough to destroy him.

His cries were at first low and guttural, growing in intensity and duration until they were alarming – one long, high-pitched moan that couldn't possibly be human. He was falling apart at the seams, and he couldn't knot the ends fast enough to avoid unraveling completely.

The suit he was wearing seemed to be stitched together more sturdily than he was, and he had the terrifying sensation that if he took it off his body would unfurl uncontrollably. How had this happened? How in the hell had he gotten here?

Lost in thought but far more lucid, he returned to the mansion with a perpetually stoic James, but couldn't tolerate being there without Barbie's enthusiastic presence or even Craig's much duller one. Yet back at his place he was assaulted by memories of Marin, and after a night of tossing and turning in his bed, he checked into a hotel.

There he had an epiphany. He just needed to start fresh. He would buy a new place and sell the old one, furnishings and all. He'd trade in his lease for the newest model that just hit the market. He'd feel like a new man, and would be able to put Marin behind him. He'd find someone else to fuck...someone who wasn't a screwed up addle-minded mess.

He couldn't push away the loss of his mother nearly so easily, but he found if he just refused to think about her and avoided the mansion altogether, he could resume his charmed life without much disruption at all.

Craig, on the other hand, was a nonentity – someone who'd always been a nuisance and incapable of providing the type of brotherly support Pauley had always envied in his friends with siblings. Admission into an exclusive club that he could never hope to achieve with his shit for brains of a lump on a log. One of the few things money couldn't buy.

Well, now he was an only child. Something he'd always dreamed of. He was the sole heir to the family fortune, and no longer had to make excuses for the dolt in the corner. He felt not one ounce of remorse for the deaths of those closest to him. Their weaknesses of mind and body were not his doing, and he refused to spend time and energy on what could have been.

They left him, not the other way around. Now he had no choice but to carry on with living, regardless of the impact those losses might have on him. This was one area in which he emulated James, who hadn't even taken time off work to mourn his wife and son.

His routine changed not at all, so adept was he at living his life to the almost total exclusion of others. It was the closest a human being could come to living in a vacuum – no one could touch him...nothing could affect him. Only his own demise would bring a stop to the machine that was James, and Pauley approved.

Chapter 18
Moving On

Tony was buzzed through the door and sat in the hard plastic chair at the chipped table where thousands of hopes and dreams had been born and then buried. The cinderblock room was small and windowless, and smelled of body odor and stale coffee.

When Aunt Ollie was led into the visitation chamber he was surprised to see how little she'd changed. Even though she was chained to an iron ring cemented to the floor and wore the orange jumpsuit and slippers that were part and parcel of incarceration, she looked as regal and stern as ever.

He didn't know what he'd expected – perhaps some sign that her heinous actions had affected her in some way...*any* way. That her resultant guilt had been eating away at her conscious, ravaging her posture and crisscrossing her face with penetrating lines. Instead she fairly glowed with inner light, and looked younger and stronger than she ever had.

"You look well, Aunt Ollie," Tony said in greeting.

"As do you, Antonio." She inclined her head as though granting him audience with someone far superior than he. Classic Ollie. "What brings you to see me finally?" she asked reproachfully, as if he were an errant child who'd failed to respond to a grandparent's birthday gift.

He nearly laughed at her audacity. Did she truly believe she was still running the show? "I needed answers. You are blood of my blood – how could we be so very different?"

"Nature versus nurture, no doubt." She shrugged, the movement rattling the chains between her wrists. "I was raised to be fiercely devoted to a cause, while you were reared to believe in nothing." She flicked her wrist at him dismissively, the jangling a fitting accompaniment to her derision.

"Are you kidding me right now? Your cause – your lifelong goal – was to commit murder?"

"I wouldn't expect you to understand, with your bleeding heart and underdog sentiments."

"Try me," he growled, gritting his teeth and fisting his hands to refrain from reaching across the table and slapping the self-satisfied smirk off her face.

At first he thought she'd refuse to talk, but after a long pause she began to speak, her voice full of purpose and righteousness. "Long ago I realized there were some conditions…some *patients*…that could not be cured. No matter what treatments were prescribed, no matter how much time or money was spent to help them. They were simply incapable of getting better.

Furthermore, they provided no value whatsoever to society, instead draining everyone around them without giving anything back, like infants do. But children grow up. These people...they remain parasitic until they die.

After years of treating them with no significant improvement – and usually great deterioration – I decided I must do something about it. Something to remove them from our presence. Specifically, something that replicated their medication regimen that would be unlikely to cause alarm on autopsy.

The fatal monoamine oxidase inhibitor interaction was the perfect plan as long as the chart didn't reflect that the patient was being given an SSRI antidepressant and an MAOI concurrently." She paused and stared at Tony as if waiting for him to commend her for her brilliance.

"How many?" he whispered instead. He couldn't process the information she'd just shared with him, even though he already knew what she'd done.

"Fifteen," she said with pride.

"Fifteen," he repeated dumbly.

"Yes. One per year with the exception of these last two."

"Michael Gregory and Craig Phipps," Tony prompted, naming her victims to remind her that they had identities. That they were *human*.

"Yes," she repeated. "It did not take Craig nearly as long to suffer the effects from the Parlodel as the rest of them."

"Hypertensive crisis."

"Their blood pressure would have increased to well above 250/150, the fluids in their vessels forcefully pushed into their lungs and other tissues, eventually causing mass hemorrhage and death," she recited, as if lecturing to an auditorium full of medical students.

She looked pleased with herself, the inner light he'd noticed previously now glimmering satanically. She was stark raving mad, he realized with a start.

"These were people, Aunt Ollie. They were loved. They had siblings, and parents, and children. They were human beings!"

"They were menaces to society. They were nuisances to their community."

"Says who?"

"Says me!"

"What right do you have to circumvent due process? To trod over their basic rights?"

"I am the expert in my field who knows there is no other way. I will be remembered as the one who had the balls to do something about the problem."

"The problem is the lack of mental health parity. The problem is the social stigma surrounding mental illness. The problem is little federal oversight of third-party payers and allocation of funds for mental health services. The problem is not your clients, who have been stricken with an illness they didn't ask for that has devastated their lives and robbed them of any hope for normalcy."

"And I have taken them out of those thankless lives. I have eased the government's burden. I have saved their loved ones from years, if not decades, of the heartache of dealing with a broken son or daughter or brother or sister. Do you not see that I am the good guy here?"

Tony stared at her for a long time before he was able to respond. How had he not seen how delusional she was? Would it have made a difference if he had? Would those fifteen people be alive right now if he hadn't been blinded to her zealousness? Could even one have been saved? Craig, he thought, sadness engulfing him.

"Did you know Craig's mother passed away the day after he was found dead in a ditch, alone and discarded like roadkill?" She gazed at him for a moment before looking away, her stature crumbling so minutely he might have missed it. But he had seen, and it was enough.

"I won't be back to visit you again, Aunt Ollie," he said, standing and signaling to the guard. "My mother wouldn't have acknowledged you as her sister had she known what you were capable of, and neither will I. You'll have access to money for whatever you need and I'll have the estate maintained in the unlikely event you're released before you die. You'll get no more from me than that.

I vow to spend my life avenging the death of your victims by crusading for humane treatment of those too sick to advocate for themselves, regardless of their 'value' to society, or lack thereof. If I can undo even a small degree of what you've done, then *my* life's mission will be realized."

Tony exited the room to the sound of chains clanking and Aunt Ollie's trembling voice echoing off the somber walls as she called after him beseechingly. "Antonio! You do not understand! I have only done what must be done! Get away, guard!! Unhand me!! Antonio!"

He refused to race back to her – to protect her from the atrocities she was sure to experience in prison. He wasn't naïve enough to believe that almost two decades of scheming and enacting her devious plans could be redacted just because he'd disowned her, or even because she'd caused the unintended death of a genteel woman; someone she could relate to far more readily than any of her victims.

No, her final pleas had more to do with self-survival than repentance, and he couldn't live with her crimes against humanity even if she could. So he kept walking, shutting her out of his head and his life.

When he arrived at the Bleu Goose the rest of his party was already there and engaged in a lively conversation he was loathe to interrupt. He sat in the empty chair Riley had been holding for him and gazed around the large table at these people who had become his closest friends, his staunchest supporters, and his most trustworthy colleagues.

Riley was sitting to his right, staring lovingly at the infant in her arms. Next to her was Mark, looking as happy as Tony had ever seen him. Across from Tony was Danielle, the reason for Mark's exuberance shining brightly on her left hand, threatening to blind them all.

Next to her was a proud Gabe, smiling around the table like the patriarch he now was. And next to him, to Tony's left, was Eva, subdued but mending. She'd probably never fully recover from the death of her sister, but she had at last returned to the land of the living, reinvesting her energies into her newborns; Marina staring avidly up at Riley and Christine fast asleep in Danielle's arms.

Tony leaned over to peer at the bundle next to him – he'd seen these babies many times since their birth; visits were a daily occurrence. But still he marveled at their exact duplication of features...their angelic expressions...their vivid blue eyes and thick curly hair the color of sunshine.

They were little gifts from heaven, and he was glad Eva had been blessed with them – she didn't deserve the pain she'd had to endure in her life. The same was true of Riley, he thought, as he rubbed her shoulder tenderly.

The two had grown very close, and had finally become intimate. Sharing in the joy of childbirth with their friends had added yet another layer to their relationship, and both had felt the time was right to take the next step. It was everything he could have dreamed of, and he couldn't imagine anyone else with whom he'd rather spend the rest of his life.

After they'd eaten dinner, Tony shared with them his disturbing conversation with his aunt, and they all agreed it would be best for society if the doctor remained imprisoned for the rest of her life. None of them would ever forget the tragedies she'd visited upon them, and they were anxious to move on to the next chapter in their lives.

At the doors to the restaurant they said their goodbyes, the future bright with promise. But before they left Riley pulled her best friend into a hug. "I'm glad you've stopped starving yourself," she whispered as she started to back away.

Eva held her tight for a moment before responding. "I'm glad you've stopped cringing around men."

Riley relaxed against her. "Honest engines from now on?"

"Honest engines."

www.ingramcontent.com/pod-product-compliance
Lightning Source LLC
Chambersburg PA
CBHW030428290526
45786CB00001B/183